Women in Nineteenth-Century Europe

Women in Nineteenth-Century Europe

RACHEL G. FUCHS
&
VICTORIA E. THOMPSON

First published 2005 by
PALGRAVE MACMILLAN
Houndmills, Basingstoke, Hampshire RG21 6XS and
175 Fifth Avenue, New York, N.Y. 10010
Companies and representatives throughout the world.

PALGRAVE MACMILLAN is the global academic imprint of the Palgrave
Macmillan division of St. Martin's Press, LLC and of Palgrave Macmillan Ltd.
Macmillan® is a registered trademark in the United States, United Kingdom
and other countries. Palgrave is a registered trademark in the European
Union and other countries.

ISBN 978-0-333-67605-9 hardback
ISBN 978-0-333-67606-6   ISBN 978-0-230-80216-2 (eBook)
DOI 10.1007/978-0-230-80216-2

This book is printed on paper suitable for recycling and made from fully
managed and sustained forest sources.

A catalogue record for this book is available from the British Library.

Library of Congress Cataloging-in-Publication Data

Fuchs, Rachel Ginnis, 1939–
    Women in nineteenth-century Europe / Rachel G. Fuchs and
Victoria E. Thompson.
        p. cm.—(Gender and history)
    Includes bibliographical references and index.
    ISBN 978-0-333-67605-9 (hardback) - ISBN 978-0-333-67606-6 (pbk.)
        1. Women – Europe – History – 19th century. I. Thompson, Victoria
Elizabeth. II. Title. III. Gender and history (Palgrave Macmillan (Firm))

HQ1587.F83 2005
305.4'094'09034—dc22   2004054938

10 9 8 7 6 5 4 3 2 1
14 13 12 11 10 09 08 07 06 05

*This book is dedicated to the women in
our lives: colleagues, teachers, and students; mothers,
daughters, and sisters; partners and friends*

Contents

Acknowledgments

Several people offered comments and encouragement as we were working on this project, and we would like to thank them for their help. Terka Acton and Sonya Barker at Palgrave Macmillan made the entire process – from formulating the book, to writing it, to final revisions, a true pleasure; many thanks to both of you. Ann Taylor Allen and an anonymous reader for Palgrave offered valuable criticism that improved the manuscript; thank you both for your time and effort. Thanks also to the members of the Women's History Reading Group at Arizona State University for reading and critiquing two of the chapters; your ideas, insights, and encouragement were most welcome. Noel Stowe, as Chair of the History Department at Arizona State University, provided a supportive environment in which to work on this book that we deeply appreciate. Robert Barnes, Jaimee Grüring, and Darby Moore-Doyle provided valuable research assistance. We are also grateful to Ute Chamberlin, Laurie Manchester, Melody Miyamoto, Laurie Arnold, and Barbara Thompson for sharing their expertise and insights with us, and to Mary Egel for preparing the index.

Introduction

During the nineteenth century, European women of all countries and social classes experienced some of the most dramatic and enduring changes in their familial, working, and political lives. This was a century of revolution – 1789, 1830, 1848, 1871 – punctuated by uprisings, rebellions, and mass demonstrations. Europeans formed new states and overseas empires, and more people gained the right to speak and write freely, to form associations, and, in the case of some men, to vote. It was also a century of repeated industrial and technological change. Mechanized printing presses, indoor plumbing, railroads, electric light, department stores, large factories, and large-scale, commercial agriculture were all introduced in the years between 1780 and 1914. Tens of thousands of people moved from countryside to city, from city to city, and from metropole to Empire. More people than ever learned how to read and write, and spent their leisure time engaged in new activities such as riding bicycles or watching motion pictures.

These changes affected women's lives in a variety of ways. Many left their homes and migrated to cities where they worked as domestic servants and as part of the growing urban labor force. Others found that their participation in family-run businesses was no longer necessary, and turned instead to caring for their homes or engaging in philanthropic work. The rise of compulsory primary education meant that more women left home to go to school, while the professionalization of medicine marginalized female midwives. Shifts in the economic structure closed off employment opportunities in one sector while opening them in another. Political upheaval brought women to the barricades and sent them into exile overseas.

As these examples indicate, the narrative of women's experiences in the nineteenth century is neither one of constant progress toward greater equality nor one of continual decline into the depths of domesticity or hard labor in industrial factories. Women's lives got better or worse depending on their own definitions of what improvement would entail, but also depending on a variety of factors that included their country of origin, their class status, and their family background. Structural and cultural factors – such as the availability of employment in a given town or attitudes toward women earning wages among a certain group of employers – also contributed in shaping the contours of any one woman's life.

This book describes the wide variety of women's experiences over the course of the century, taking into account differences based on region, class, and chronology. Inevitably, it reflects the unevenness of existing scholarship on women. While women's history continues to grow as a field, Western European countries have received far more attention than those in Central or Southern Europe, for example. In addition, in seeking to make sense of women's lives,

1

/e have found it necessary to make generalizations. In so doing, we have sought at times to reflect an experience shared by a majority of women, and at others to designate a trend that only a small number of women may have been part of, but that ultimately had a large impact on European society. An example of the first would be our discussion of reproductive and family life, while an example of the second would be our treatment of the Saint-Simonian movement.

The impact of the ideology of domesticity – and its central tenet of an ideal separation between masculine and feminine spheres – on women's legal, social, and cultural status constitutes a recurring theme of the book. The ideology of domesticity was based upon the belief that men and women were fundamentally different. During the nineteenth century, Europeans made this sexual difference a central organizing principle of social, political, and cultural life. According to the ideology of domesticity, men and women had different functions in society; they operated in separate spheres. The male, or public sphere was the realm of politics, business, and wage-earning. It was characterized by the qualities of competition, physical strength, and the exercise of reason. Men were, according to this vision, natural protectors of women; it was their job to support and safeguard their wives and daughters. The female, or private sphere was the realm of home and family. It was characterized by nurturing, morality, and virtue. Europeans believed that women were designed to bear and raise children, to teach these children to be moral citizens, and to provide a comforting and regenerative atmosphere in the home. According to this vision, both men and women, each in their separate spheres, were necessary for the proper functioning of civilization.

Of course, the ideology of domesticity was just that – an ideology. It was a set of beliefs and assumptions that contained within it a vision of how the world should work. We argue in this book that the ideology of domesticity shaped women's lives, but did not determine their course. The vision of a world divided into separate spheres did not accurately reflect the lives of women who had to work to keep food on the table. Nor did it prevent male employers from hiring these women to work in their mills, factories, and workshops. At the same time, this ideology carried weight in shaping the work women could do outside the home and how they were paid. Yet again, even women who believed in the ideology of domesticity often interpreted it in ways that allowed them to work for wages, run complex organizations, go off on safari, or run for public office. The exploration of this tension between a limited vision of men's and women's roles that could be considered the classic ideology of domesticity and the many ways in which domesticity could be recast, is one of the central themes of this book.

Women – and men – were able to interpret domesticity in a variety of ways in part because domesticity was a response to a society undergoing rapid and constant change. Although according to the rhetoric of domesticity women were relegated to the private sphere of home and family, the needs of a changing economy, growing numbers of urban poor, and advances in the technology of travel continually brought them out into the public realm. Similarly, while domesticity was a community-based vision of society, at the center of which was the conjugal family, engaging in revolutionary protest or pursuing an education could lead women to realize their capacity to act as individuals. Finally, while women were said to be guardians of tradition because their roles were rooted in nature, they were also identified as both sources and symbols of progress.

These three axes of tension – that between private and public, community and individual, and tradition and modernity – shape this book. In developing each of these themes, the book juxtaposes three elements: the experiences of women, the perceptions of women concerning their experiences and their roles in society, and the perceptions of men concerning the role of women. In exploring each aspect of these themes, we take into account class, national, and regional differences.

One of the primary themes of this work analyzes the meaning of the categories of "public" and "private" in women's lives. As many scholars have recognized, women were of central symbolic importance in creating and defining these categories, categories that became fundamental to a European culture during the nineteenth century. Yet women's lives rarely fit neatly into the discrete categories "public"/"private." This volume therefore addresses both the symbolic and actual importance of gendered notions of public and private in shaping European women's lives in the nineteenth century.

The interaction between "tradition" and "modernity" during this period of change constitutes the second major theme of the book. At different times, and for different reasons, women were associated with (and associated themselves with) both tradition and modernity. For example, many Europeans believed that peasant women symbolized the "traditional" virtues of rural life, and perceived urban women by the late nineteenth century to be dangerously "modern." Yet, peasant women faced and participated in the modernization of the countryside as it became increasingly integrated into a market economy, and the lives of urban women of all socioeconomic levels were still greatly influenced by rural values and practices. This volume thus explores the uneven and variegated modernization of women's lives during this period, a modernization that varied according to region, class, and individual experience. At the same time, it explores women's importance as a fundamental symbol of the tension between tradition and modernity.

The third major theme of the volume is the tension between community and individual. Much of the historiography on the nineteenth century focuses on the transition during this period from a society in which the group took primacy to one in which individuals became increasingly important. This volume therefore analyzes what this shift meant for women. It discusses different types of communities: those in which women played an important and active role (rural villages, working-class urban neighborhoods, certain utopian-socialist visions of community), those in which women played a largely passive and symbolic role (the nation, for example), and those in which gender was believed to be irrelevant (certain communist and progressive visions of community). The volume also examines the effects the growing emphasis on the individual had on women of different class and regional backgrounds, and explores the way in which gendered metaphors expressed the tension between community and individual.

In taking the approach that we have, we have attempted to shed new light on the long nineteenth century by looking at women's experience in different ways. While acknowledging the powerful impact of the ideology of domesticity in the real gal, social, economic, and political limitations it placed on women's lives, we also have highlighted the myriad ways in which women participated in all aspects of European life, and broke through the boundaries of the dominant ideology. Throughout the process of writing this book, we have been continually amazed and inspired by the creative ways in which women accepted, adapted, and challenged contemporary beliefs concerning women's roles in order to raise their families, earn a living, or pursue their dreams. It is our hope that students reading this book will not only learn about the lives of women in nineteenth-century Europe, but will also be prompted to reflect upon their own.

1
The Era of the French Revolution

During the last quarter of the eighteenth century private concerns played out in the public sphere and the public began to invade private space. Women became increasingly present as powerful figures in public arenas as diverse as commerce, literature, and politics. Their exercise of independent agency, however, was not always easy; the patriarchal nature and cultural prescriptions of society endeavored to place women in the private realm of hearth and home. Nevertheless, women used private space to negotiate public affairs as governments and the dominant culture tried to regulate women's private lives.

The late eighteenth century was a period of intense change. The industrial and commercial revolutions began to reshape the economies of Western Europe. New methods of manufacturing and a growing market in consumer goods changed the way in which people worked, shopped, dressed, and furnished their homes. The Enlightenment – an intellectual movement that undertook the reasoned examination of all aspects of human society – led to a questioning of traditional beliefs, especially those associated with religion. The century culminated in revolutionary movements that spanned both sides of the Atlantic, the most dramatic of which was the French Revolution of 1789. From 1789 to 1815, a series of new governments in France challenged the authority of monarchy and church, gave new power to ordinary people, and redrew the boundaries between public and private, male and female.

Many of these developments increased the tension between modernity and tradition that marked the end of the eighteenth century. The voices of enlightenment and reason and those of religion and emotion quarreled. In France, where the major Revolutionary struggles occurred, two public institutions, the Revolutionary state, representing modernity, and the Catholic Church, representing tradition, locked in combat for control of people's private lives. Within the larger contexts of the struggle between tradition and modernity, and the renegotiation of boundaries between the public and private, this chapter explores women's words and activities during the Revolutionary era, the constraints on women written into the cultural and legal codes, new notions of citizenship, and the effect of economics on women's lives and ideas.

The industrial and commercial revolutions of the eighteenth century created a thriving merchant class with increased purchasing power. In that society, women were the predominant consumers, but some were also producers. As consumers, they took a new interest in household commodities, such as silver and English china. As producers, silversmiths, such as Alice Burrows and Mary and Eliza Sumner, played a vital role in the eighteenth-century English economy. Many other women worked alongside their husbands in artisanal or commercial ventures. They were out in the public – selling, working, and shopping in greater numbers than before – as a partial result of these economic revolutions.

The Enlightenment, which laid the foundation for modern notions of state and society, extolled reason and progress. As part of Enlightenment culture, women of the middle and upper classes engaged in a variety of intellectual and social activities within the private spaces of their homes that affected the public realm of politics. They arranged salons, which some historians consider sites of female empowerment, education, and assimilation. As leaders of salons (*salonnières*), women of noble and bourgeois status organized gatherings in their luxurious and large homes, inviting leading scientists, philosophers, and men of letters. Acting as hostesses and cultural trendsetters, women excelled in the art of conversation and could influence the politics of the day through their direction of the discussions in their salons and their choice of guests. As salons became recognized arbiters of opinion, the men and women who participated gained social prestige, even as they questioned current institutions and cultural values, seeking changes and reforms. Women's crucial roles in organizing and directing these salons made them key players in the formation of a new burgeoning civil society that functioned at a level between the individual and the court and promoted social change. Such a civil society could undermine the monarchy, as the men and women of the salons often challenged the institutions of church, state, and family. Although both noble and bourgeois participated, the salons were not democratic and open to all; admission was by invitation only to the witty, clever, influential, and learned.

The salons blurred the boundaries between public and private. The private home, presided over by educated, accomplished, and well-connected women, functioned as a public space for the exchange of ideas and culture. Salons were centers of sociability, intellectual life, and power for women, before, during, and after the French Revolution and Napoleonic eras (1789–1815).

The independence and power that women gained in the salons, however, had a limited scope. Women were central to the salons, actively fostering modern cultural and political ideas based on individual rights and equality, yet the male literary and political figures who participated in the salons often excluded women from other areas of sociability. Men had other places to meet, such as coffeehouses, where they could further strengthen ties made in salons and develop habits of civil discourse in exclusively masculine spaces, thus marginalizing women from an emerging bourgeois civil society.

A *salonnière* of note, Marie-Jeanne Philpon (also known as Manon Philpon and later Manon Roland) was born in 1754 to a Parisian engraver. She was largely self-educated, favoring the writings of Plutarch and Jean-Jacques Rousseau. In 1781, she married Jean-Marie Roland de Platière, a man twenty years her senior, and a government official. She appreciated literature, politics, and writing, and reputedly wrote in her husband's name. Her salons first attracted politicians and literary figures when she and her husband lived in

Lyons (France's second largest city) and then in Paris after they moved there in 1791. Her salons in Paris were political centers for moderate Revolutionary leaders. In 1793, accused of plotting against the Revolution, she was sent to the guillotine. Upon mounting the scaffold, she purportedly uttered the now famous phrase, "O Liberty, what crimes are committed in your name." Always ambitious, with a keen involvement in politics, she was ever conscious of her life as a woman. Her own words about her salon speak of her ambivalent role:

> It was agreed that the group should meet at my house four times a week in the evening. This arrangement suited me very well. It meant I could keep in touch with public affairs, in which I was so deeply interested; it gave scope to my taste for political argument and for studying men. I knew the proper role of my sex and never exceeded it.
>
> The conferences took place in my presence but I played no part in them; I sat at a separate table, outside the men's circle, and I always had some work in my hands or wrote letters while they were talking. But however many letters I wrote … I did not miss a word of what was being said. Sometimes I had to bite my tongue to prevent myself from putting a word in.[1]

Although the Parisian salons are most well known, salons also flourished in Berlin, London, Vienna, and Warsaw. German women in several cities met in elite mixed-gender intellectual literary circles, but only in Berlin did the upper and middle classes meet in salons, engaging in an unprecedented gender, social, and religious integration. The leading *salonnières* were Jewish women, such as Rahel Levin Varnhagen, the daughter of a jeweler who gained her intellectual and secular independence, mastered several languages (as well as mathematics) and married a Christian. Another *salonnière*, Dorothea Mendelssohn, daughter of Moses Mendelssohn, had already married a man her father had chosen when she met the philosopher Friedrich Schlegel; they fell in love and she abandoned her husband and sons to be with Schlegel. These emblematic women had social prominence, whether they maintained a secular Jewish identity or converted to Christianity; their salons were vehicles of assimilation as intellectuals from Berlin as well as from other Western European cities flocked to them. As modern women, they defied the cultural separation of religion and class; nobles, commoners, and people of different religions mixed freely at these heterogeneous and secular salons. The salons gave women an entrée into the formation of public opinion in an unprecedented way.

In English cities, women joined a host of voluntary societies, such as reading clubs. In London, women and men of letters, who comprised the leading intellectual lights of the day, socialized and talked politics over tea in English women's homes. Known as the "bluestockings" (a term used to refer to English women intellectuals who gathered to discuss literary works), they paralleled the *salonnières*, but were primarily literary and educated women who participated in the debate over women's education and rights. In a traditional patriarchal society they formed a community of women, wives, and daughters of the new middle classes, which agitated for changes in women's circumstances, objecting especially to meaningless lives that often resulted from marriages arranged for social status and family economics. Bluestocking women read novels and journalistic accounts, and were active writers in a variety of genres, including advice manuals for women to improve their minds, poetry, and epistolary literary texts. Fanny Burney (1752–1840) and Hannah More (1745–1835) were two of the younger members of the bluestockings whose writings and lives remained influential into the nineteenth century.

Hannah More was also one of the earliest and best-known women who became involved with the English Evangelical movement, a reform movement within the Anglican Church. It was in the forefront of English religious life and spearheaded attempts at moral reform through its domestic and foreign missionary work. In the cities, members of this movement attempted to reform the poor and instill the ideas of thrift, sobriety, sexual virtue (abstinence), and religion among them. More did not advocate women's equality; quite the opposite, she thought that women should be in the home as keepers of the religious faith. Moreover, she did not believe in equality among the classes any more than in gender equality; she thought that the poor should know and keep their place in the social hierarchy. In one of the many paradoxes of women's lives, she did not live the life she advocated. Rather, she wrote plays, traveled around London, and sought friendship among a group of independent and intellectual men and women. Unlike other bluestockings, she developed a religious fervor that she channeled toward teaching the poor about the evils of gin and sloth. She established Sunday schools for children of the poor that provided religious instruction, and sometimes food and clothing, while also teaching them to read. This was a type of domestic missionary work typical of the Evangelicals. She also wrote didactic children's books, a genre that was popular throughout the nineteenth century. Social control of the poor, through a Christian education, was her goal. Fearing an upheaval in England similar to the French Revolution, she sought to avoid it by teaching the poor to accept their place in the social structure and to work hard.

While *salonnières* and bluestockings took on public roles in an attempt to influence opinion and morality, less than a handful of women participated in public political life as national leaders. Marie Antoinette of France (1755–93), and the enlightened despots Catherine the Great of Russia (1729–96) and Maria Theresa of Austria (1717–80) are the best known. The latter two were all-powerful, and sometimes acted as ruthless rulers attempting modernizing reforms. New ideas about proper roles for women affected the way in which both these rulers, and the women who exercised informal power, were perceived.

As men gathered in the semi-public sphere of the salons and in the public sphere of cafés to discuss political ideas, one man, Jean-Jacques Rousseau (1712–78), prescribed boundaries for women's lives in the private sphere, setting the tone for gender relations that dominated the prescriptive literature of his time and during the nineteenth century. He did this mainly through his novels, *Julie, or the New Héloise* and *Émile, or On Education*, which women eagerly read. These were romantic stories, replete with expressions of feeling and sentiment – novels to cry over. In these novels, the ideal woman was a devoted and modest wife and mother who stayed home with her babies, breast-feeding them (rather than sending them out to a mercenary wet nurse, as was the custom) nurturing them in their childhood, educating them, and giving emotional support to her husband. Rousseau argued that since women were responsible for educating their children, they themselves needed an education, preferably one carried out in the countryside, which would nurture their sensitivity to nature, away from the court intrigue of the chateaux and the salons of the cities. Women who thought more of their participation in salons and in public life than of their husbands and children were anathema to Rousseau and his legion of followers. He appealed to the idea of natural law, a glorified state of nature, and women's "natural" role as wife and mother. Rousseau's ideas contributed to the growing criticism of women's empowerment through the salons, fostering an ideology that attempted to place women in a separate private sphere, that of the home. In England, and predating Rousseau, Samuel Richardson wrote the widely read *Pamela* (1740) and *Clarissa* (1748) with dutiful daughters and wives as feminine heroines. Rousseau and Richardson postulated the eternal feminine ideal of how women should think and behave.

Women found Rousseau's writing attractive because he offered them a new type of home-based power, one limited to the family, but accessible to a greater number of women than could possibly hope to be *salonnières*. Rousseau's philosophy told them they could find happiness in a return to nature and away from the competition of men in the public sphere. They could find fulfillment in acting as moral guardians of the home, and by extension, society. In Rousseau's model, a woman's power and influence came from her ability to influence her husband to do great things and educate her children to act responsibly in society. It empowered them within the patriarchal household, making them the enforcer of family law and morality. Although Julie in *The New Héloise* marries the man her father chose for her, and not the one for whom she has a great passion, she becomes the center of her family's life. She has power within her family and community as a devoted wife and mother. Rousseau's ideology gave women a role in a changing world as the virtuous wife and devoted mother – the mainstay of the family. However, he regarded women's activities outside the home as potentially subversive to the smooth functioning of society.

Social critics may have been prone to criticize bourgeois and noble women for their activities in the public sphere, yet they were not concerned about, and even sometimes encouraged, poor and working women's public economic activities. They did not, however, encourage their political activity. From time immemorial working women had participated in public spaces through their labor and as part of their responsibility for feeding and maintaining their families. In times of scarcity, women engaged in food riots in order to obtain needed grain and bread. Women also frequently brought their goods to market where they engaged in public commerce in an open place by selling or trading their goods. Despite their presence in public, however, working women did not regularly enter the public sphere of political discussion that was becoming a cultural and political force. They were essential to society's economic functions as workers, as market women, and as feeders of their families. Although some women, such as those who sold fish in the Paris marketplace, had a traditional status as symbolic representatives of the people to the king, they were not part of the bourgeois public sphere of rational ideas and critical debate emerging at the end of the eighteenth century, and were indeed excluded from it. These women would participate in popular demonstrations that contributed to reshaping French politics during the early years of the Revolution. Over the course of the Revolution, however, their political activities were defined as inconsistent with a woman's proper role at the same time as their labor became increasingly important in support of the bourgeoisie.

Women, sexuality, patriarchy, and the law

Modern women, such as the *salonnières* and silversmiths, became more numerous within the structure of patriarchy and property. With the rise of capitalism and a commercial society, property rights became an increasingly strong buttress for the patriarchal family and society. Yet, even in pre-capitalist societies like those in areas of Eastern Europe and Russia, patriarchy prevailed. The well-ordered family was the basis of the well-ordered society, and a close philosophical relationship existed between the family structure and the social structure. Both had a strong leader as the head.

In late eighteenth-century societies from England to France to Prussia, family honor, especially that of the male head of household, was bound with his property. Marriage and family life, especially among the middle and upper classes, reflected that culture. Marriages, although increasingly love matches, were more often economic unions between two families, with the children following their fathers' wishes for a good alliance; sometimes love or affection followed. The male head of household of the rising middle classes might seek noble status and therefore dower his daughter with enough wealth to attract a titled member of the nobility. Since the daughter married into the man's family, she (and perhaps, by extension, her birth family) would obtain a title. In return, the noble family, perhaps facing relative impoverishment, would more than welcome the dowry from the untitled, but wealthy, member of the middle classes. In making a good marriage alliance, money was not the only wealth that a woman needed; she needed her virginity. A virtuous and chaste young woman was worth more on the marriage market, hence the keen interest in the morality of young women. Men, however, were encouraged to sow their wild oats. A good marriage was a mark of respectability, something men and women of the middle classes sought.

Marriage was often an economic union even for those families without landed property, since a single working person would find it very difficult to make ends meet. In rural areas, marriages were often arranged so as to unite contiguous property. Men needed someone to help with the chores and women needed someone to help provide – especially if they had a child. Marriage was a hope for security among the poor, but even those marriages did not always exclude love and romance.

Women's fidelity within marriage was a key issue. Men wanted to be sure of the paternity of their children in order for the honorable transmission of property within the family. Therefore, there were harsh sanctions against a woman's adultery throughout the nineteenth century. There was always a risk that she would have a child by a man who was not her husband and bring someone not connected by blood (semen) into the family, thus dissipating the inheritance. In numerous treatises on adultery written in the eighteenth century, the woman was always culpable. Given the importance of family property, there was widespread fear of someone unrelated to the patriarch inheriting his estate.

Themes of sexuality and seduction pervaded both the literature and the political critiques of European nobility, especially in France. According to Michel Foucault, the public took increasing interest in sex, using it as a tool to attack the aristocracy.[2] Writers and pamphleteers criticized elite women who had a variety of social and political relationships with men, referring to those women as decadent, deviant, and sexually profligate, and casting those relationships as dangerous liaisons that destroyed morals and spread political corruption. Choderlos de Laclos's novel, *Dangerous Liaisons* (1782) portrayed idle, rich, unscrupulous noble women using others as their playthings and behaving in a manner that reflected the decadence of the regime. Noble women, as well as men, engaged in sexual exploitation, to the ruin of both individuals and the state. This literature found willing readers prone to criticize the nobility, not the least because of the cult of Rousseau and the new sentiments about the sexually pure, virtuous, and naturally domestic woman, such as Sophie in *Émile*. Sophie, Émile's wife, had to be chaste so Émile could be sure of the legitimacy of his children. Mme de Tourvel of *Dangerous Liaisons* represented the decadent, licentious woman, now increasingly out of fashion.

Queens shared in the opprobrium thrown at noble women. Marie Antoinette, known as the "Austrian whore," because she was Queen Maria Theresa of Austria's daughter, was the object of pornographic diatribes. According to her critics, she had a sexual liaison with a Cardinal of the Catholic Church and engaged in sexual misconduct with her son, providing him with an education in sexual crimes. Queen Caroline of England (1768–1821) was also the object of investigations into her sexual conduct, although tales of her allegedly illicit sexual relationships did not reach the public until 1820 when her husband, George IV, tried to divorce her. It was always women's sexuality that was in question, not men's. Pornographic depictions of queens aimed to destroy the respect and power of women in the ultimate public sphere.

The question of population, which surfaced at the end of the eighteenth century, also had a bearing on women's sexual behavior. Scholars have recently noted the fear of depopulation current among certain groups of doctors and political philosophers who envisioned population and reproduction in the service of the state (as they were to do again in the nineteenth century.) In part, the increasingly secular public opinion among the political philosophers sought to liberate sexuality from the authority of the Catholic Church and put it in the service of the state. Therefore, philosophers and popular writers tended to extol the virtues of sexuality for reproduction within marriage and eschew other forms of sexuality – except for men's alleged need to be sexually active, even when not married. Along with Rousseau, they shaped the discourse of domesticity, urging marriage and reproduction for both men and women, arguing that reproduction within marriage was a natural right and duty.

These writers also wanted to legalize divorce. They supported divorce to undercut the power of the Church and to allow for new marriages that would result in more children, further increasing the birth rate. Some popular writers campaigned for divorce as early as the 1760s on the grounds that husbands should have the right to divorce adulterous wives in order to be certain of the paternity of their children and disavow children of whose paternity they were uncertain. Writers also thought that if a man could divorce his wife, the fear of divorce would make her behave. Through such debates, public discourse based on perceived state needs began to address the private lives of women as wives and mothers and make marriage and motherhood public functions. Equally important to these men, however, was the question of how to address the situation of children born out-of-wedlock while at the same time maintaining the family honor of the male genitor.

Laws reflect society, and thus eighteenth-century laws reflected assumptions concerning women and the family. Laws in both Catholic and Protestant societies relied on Roman law, but Canon law also infused Catholic societies. The law code (1750–94) of Frederick the Great of Prussia, representative of a largely Protestant state, fused Germanic customary law with enlightenment beliefs in natural rights and reason. The male middle classes were looking for bases of power and the means to assert their authority. Since the family was the linchpin of the social and political order throughout Europe, if men assured their authority over their wives and children, then they would have made a beginning in securing their position in society. England had no unified written law code, but according to the major commentaries on English laws, a married woman had no legal status; her husband was her protector, legally bound to provide for her in a situation known as coverture. In England, it took an act of Parliament to obtain a divorce and laws exercised enormous constraints on women's market activities in both England and Germany.

In France, a dominantly Catholic country, no unified system of laws existed before the Napoleonic Code (1804). Rather Canon law, Roman law, and Customary law prevailed in different parts of the country, with women's rights varying. In general, however, women were legally subservient to their fathers and then to their husbands in all areas of property and contractual law. Widows could regain some legal rights upon proof of their husband's death. Late eighteenth-century French jurisprudence, custom, and law allowed legal recourse to some women who had been victims of seduction by occasionally awarding reparations to them, or to their parents, when seduction was aggravated by fraud, violence, or kidnapping. Jurists even allowed some women to pursue the putative father of their child for child support and to redress damages to them and their honor resulting from a pregnancy. But taking a man to court for seduction and paternity was a socially differential remedy, much less accessible to the poor than to wealthy commercial families. Furthermore, if the child resulted from an adulterous relationship no legal pursuit was admissible.

During the era of the French Revolution, legislators initiated measures that affected women's private lives, considering women as passive citizens without full rights of citizenship. Family laws reflected the modern ideas of natural law mitigated by traditional customs, attitudes toward women, the right to men's sexual license, and the dominant importance of family honor. Intense legislative debates on issues of women's morality, the rights of the "natural child" and the rights of the father, eventually (1791) made it impossible for a woman legally to pursue her seducer and father of her child. Yet the sheer numbers of illegitimate children posed a problem. In one of the many paradoxes of the era, Revolutionary leaders realized that France could not provide for the children it already had, yet did not want to impose a natural child on unwilling men. Laws of 1793 stipulated that only if a father had legally recognized his "natural child" did the child have any rights to paternal care and property and the father bear any responsibility for that child. It was not a question of the mother's rights, but rather the rights of the child. However, after 1794 legislators more firmly articulated that illegitimate children did not have the right to share in the inheritance with those born within a legal marriage. Women's position was key in transmitting lineage and inheritance; therefore their role in the patriarchal family was to help protect the family property from outsiders, including illegitimate children.

Revolutionary laws on marriage and divorce resulted from women's political agitation as well as the emerging power of the Republican secular state over the Catholic Church. To reduce the power of the Catholic Church and of the clergy, marriage became a civil ceremony and a public act. In the past, marriage had been a private agreement, sanctified by the clergy. Laws also reduced the age of consent for marriage in order to free love relationships from parental restraint and to encourage legitimate births. Furthermore, if marriage were based on the mutual attraction of two individuals, then couples could separate when that attraction no longer bound them together. By the divorce law of September 1792, couples could easily divorce on several grounds: by mutual consent; when one party wanted it; in cases of spousal abandonment for two years or more; insanity; conviction for crimes entailing corporal punishment or loss of civil rights; brutality or serious injury; and dissoluteness of morals. A person could not remarry for one year, to assure the paternity of the offspring. Yet divorce was not simple; relatives became involved, and although not costly, it was time consuming.

People in the cities divorced more than those in the countryside, and they were predominantly from the artisanal, merchant, and professional classes. Women brought proceedings almost as often as men. The primary causes were long-term absence or abandonment. Abandonment had long been an informal means of divorce when divorce was illegal, but then a person could not remarry. Divorce would allow for remarriage, or property settlement, in cases in which the marriage had already broken down. But only about one-fourth remarried. Brutality and incompatibility followed as causes for divorce.

Women's writings and activities

The idea of individual rights that formed an essential part of Enlightenment and Revolutionary ideologies broke traditional molds of thought, but affected women more in their exclusion from these rights, including that of citizenship, than in their applicability. The *Declaration of the Rights of Man and Citizen*, promulgated in France in 1789, but rapidly disseminated throughout Europe, was ambivalent on the question of whether rights and citizenship were for men only. In the years that followed, debates clarified women's exclusion from full citizenship. This exclusion, however, caused writers and activists, both men and women, to take up the call for women's rights. They attempted to crack the structure of the patriarchal family and to redefine it, but they usually operated from within that very structure.

The Marquis de Condorcet (1743–94) was one of the earliest French advocates for women's rights, especially in the realm of education. Believing that the concept of natural equality included women, he reasoned that women should have the same education as men. Furthermore, he went beyond seeking equal education for women, and wanted to see them as full participants in the political public sphere, with suffrage for women of property. Unsurprisingly, Mme de Condorcet was a *salonnière*.

Probably the most well-known woman Revolutionary writer and activist was Olympe de Gouges (1748–93). Born Marie Gouze and raised in a butcher's family in the provinces of France, she came to Paris, and under her new name wrote plays, novels, and political pamphlets. She modeled her most famous and influential work, the *Declaration of the Rights of Woman* (1791), after the *Declaration of the Rights of Man* transforming it to apply to women. Embedding her argument in the Enlightenment rhetoric of equality based on the principles of natural law and natural rights, de Gouges reasoned that women should have the rights of full citizenship, within the private realm of the family and in the public realm of politics. Her position was emblematic of women's demand for rights to property, to education, and to equality with men. She did not deny women's role as mothers; rather she maintained that women could both be exemplary mothers and have equal civil rights. She further argued that men should have responsibility for paternity, at least in providing for their child's sustenance, and that all children should be declared legitimate, regardless of which side of the bed they came from.

Etta Palm d'Aelders (1743–1830), a Dutch immigrant to France in 1774 who returned to Holland in 1793, was particularly interested in the family and the poor, especially in establishing schools and training programs for poor girls. She opposed the law that stipulated that only women could be prosecuted for adultery. Furthermore, since women were responsible for feeding their families, she wanted women to be in charge of public welfare and education. Palm d'Aelders grounded her appeal in the language of republicanism and women's virtue – in what modern historians have called "Republican Motherhood."

Across the Channel, Mary Wollstonecraft (1758–97), a radical English philosopher, was the most significant woman intellectual of her time. She advocated reforms that would empower women in the public sphere and objected to male authority over women. Disagreeing with the assumptions concerning the alleged inferiority of women to men, she argued that women were not naturally inferior; society just disadvantaged and degraded them by the socializing process, by restrictive laws, and by an inferior and limited education. Wollstonecraft's *A Vindication of the Rights of Woman* is the best-known tract of the time in support of women's education. She passionately stressed women's need for education, arguing that reason should be an attribute of both women and men, and that women's situation needed reform in the interests of civic virtue. She wanted equal education and training for women so they could be equal partners with men. Paying homage to Rousseau and couching her argument in his terms, she viewed women's primary duty as that of mother; she agreed that motherhood was an avenue to virtue, but opposed Rousseau's vision that motherhood required that women limit themselves to home and family. This position, she argued, implied women's inferiority to men. Furthermore, she disagreed with Rousseau's prescription for women's education. Whereas Rousseau had argued that a woman should obtain only enough education to allow her to converse with her husband and raise her children, Wollstonecraft argued that she needed an education with rigorous academic learning so she could better raise her children, especially sons, and become independent of her husband, furthering reciprocity between them so he could further advance in the public sphere. She also advocated physical education to build strong bodies. Taking a position against coverture, she maintained that if women were free, independent, and equal, they would be better wives and mothers.

Wollstonecraft, a middle-class woman who bore a child out of wedlock, sought, but failed to achieve, the respectability that was so important to middle-class women until she married William Godwin. Acting upon her published ideas of virtue, she and William Godwin married after she became pregnant with their child. Unfortunately, Wollstonecraft died of puerperal fever at the birth of their daughter, who was named Mary. Thus, this very modern woman, in life and writings, arguing for equality and independence for women, died in the most traditional way. Mary Godwin grew up to marry the poet, Percy Bysshe Shelley, and to write *Frankenstein*. Wollstonecraft, along with Thomas Paine and William Godwin spread the ideas of the French Revolutionaries in England.

One of the most subversive *salonnières* and best-known women writers of the Revolutionary era, but writing later than Wollstonecraft, was Germaine [Necker] de Staël (1766–1817). She earned the wrath of Napoleon who exiled her from Paris in 1803 for her independent views; she went to live on her family estate in Switzerland and traveled to Italy and Germany. Born in Geneva to a family of wealth, but holding salons in Paris before her exile, she is perhaps better known for her novels than for her salons. As a romantic who adored passions and emotions, she wrote about educated women who suffered romantic tragedy. They were not weak women, but rather those who had tried to live their lives and loves outside the boundaries prescribed by Rousseau and later Napoleon. Although in her youth she was enamored of Rousseau's ideas because of his sensitivities, later in life she objected to his portrayal of meek women. Her popular novels, *Delphine* (1802) and *Corinne, or Italy* (1807), contained a not-so-veiled criticism of male-dominated society, featuring women who used their brains as well as their hearts. Her views on women's education were similar to Wollstonecraft's, but although Staël believed in, and lived, an intellectual life, affairs of the heart took priority.

Not all women wrote pamphlets or engaged in a public debate about their rights. Some just took to the streets, forming communities of revolutionaries. Poor women based their revolutionary (and counterrevolutionary) activities on their traditional behavior but added a modern purpose. They acted in the public arena to benefit their private lives. Working women often joined political clubs and formed crowds, airing their grievances and playing crucial parts in the revolutionary ferment.

A series of bad harvests in the 1780s and mounting bread prices exacerbated an already dire situation for peasant and city women, often living on the brink of poverty. As part of his effort to reform the financial system, the French monarch asked his subjects to draft petitions containing lists of grievances (*cahiers de doléance*). These petitions demonstrated the political and economic complaints of a broad segment of the population, including poor women, in all parts of the country. Many sent petitions directly to the King or Queen. Women demanded protection from economic competition, both from other women and also from men entering their trades. Many also sought education, especially vocational training for poor women, so they would not have to turn to prostitution in order to feed themselves. They also wanted some relief from taxes and protection from abusive men. These women brought their personal issues to the public sphere.

Women continued to draft petitions after the Revolution began in 1789. Pauline Léon (1768–?) a chocolate maker following the trade of her parents, organized different types of petitions; most notably she petitioned to allow women the right to bear arms (1791). Part of her argument centered on women's need to protect themselves, their homes, and families, but coded in her petition were demands for civil rights and civic participation. Théroigne de Méricourt went further than Léon and asked for a women's battalion, whom she called a company of Amazons, to fight and defend the Revolution against its enemies. Despite more than 300 signatures, Léon's petition was rejected because armed women were considered "unnatural."

In addition to petitions, women participated in public through spontaneous political activities, spurred on by economic need, which changed the course of the Revolution. For over a century, women had engaged in food riots and demonstrations with immunity and impunity. Now, they combined these public activities with modern revolutionary ideas. Many women based their political activity on the need for bread. But, they also formed clubs and sat as spectators in political assemblies.

Most significantly, they marched on the royal residence, Versailles, and brought Louis XVI and Marie Antoinette back to Paris on October 5, 1789. Angered over the steep rise in the price of bread and annoyed with the King and Queen for failing to provide the grain and bread, women gathered in Paris and decided to walk to Versailles (a distance of about 20–25 kilometers) to appeal directly to the Queen. Women always bore responsibility for feeding their families, and finding themselves unable to do so, they took to the time-honored method of procuring bread, rioting for food. This time, however, their private familial needs for food were mixed with political demands. They believed that the King and nobility were hoarding the grain that they so desperately needed. With the help of the newly formed National Guard, they seized the King and Queen and brought them to Paris. These women were not politically ignorant; they were not the apolitical Sophies idealized by Rousseau. They were typically women without young children, neither prostitutes nor "bad mothers" as some contemporaries had represented them. Those with young children did not take these risks. Thus, in attempting to resolve their private economic needs, they considered themselves to be part of the Revolution and profoundly influenced political events.

In demonstrating for food, by belonging to political clubs and by sitting at political assemblies, women behaved as part of the sovereign people, even though they did not have those legal attributes. The idea of the sovereign nation and sovereign people was revolutionary on both sides of the Atlantic.

One of the most well known and politically active revolutionary communities of women was the Society of Revolutionary Republican Women Citizens (*Citoyennes*) established in spring 1793, by ardent patriots who wanted to combat inflation and perceived hoarding. It was the first organization representing poor working women; members included tradeswomen and artisans in commerce, clothing, and crafts, and included flower sellers and washerwomen. An actress (Claire Lacombe) and a chocolate maker (Pauline Léon) founded the society. To be a member, a woman had to be of good moral standing because this group not only demonstrated and attended political meetings but also promoted virtue. Women up to age 70 were members, and most were relatively free of family responsibilities. Their estimated number ranged from 67 to 170, but their influence as leaders of a radical popular movement was greater than their numbers indicated.

As impassioned revolutionaries who supported the more radical leadership of the Revolution, they took to the streets and meeting halls demanding citizenship and a public role for women. They believed in sacrifice for the new nation, aiding the war effort, the abolition of the French monarchy, and republican ideology. Equating France with their homes, they wanted to bear arms for homeland security. As a community of radical Republicans and a leading group in the Revolutionary movement, they instigated activities in the name of the republic and the equality of all the people, including men and women, rich and poor. To them and their followers, the Republic had to include women as part of the sovereign people. They also supported other women. Viewing prostitutes as poor women with good hearts, who were not irrevocably "lost" to vice, members of this society wanted to redeem prostitutes through education and useful work. Their political interests resemble and predate the women's movement for suffrage by a century.

Many male politicians viewed these women as threatening their rule of law and their idea of public safety and accused the Society of Revolutionary Republican Women of counterrevolutionary activities. As part of a crackdown on more radical groups, in October 1793, the National Assembly, the French governing body, condemned these women for their lack of modest virtues and for appearing in the streets and in political clubs, often involved in riots and bloodshed. Referring to them as public women associated them with prostitution since the phrase "public women" usually meant prostitutes. The National Assembly banned this group, and all women's clubs, in November 1793. They asserted that women should be home, raising their children, ignoring the fact that most of these women were not mothers of young children. The closing of women's clubs drove women out of active political roles as participants in the Revolution, and women's political activity ebbed.

During the Europe-wide economic crisis of 1794, as a result of economic necessity, women returned to time-honored forms of protest. That summer yielded one of the worst harvests in Northern European history, affecting people all over the continent, especially wage workers. A terrible dearth, especially of grain and flour, was accompanied by a lack of bread and a currency collapse of 20 percent. The sick and elderly died, and crowds of women and men demonstrated demanding bread. The women were housewives concerned about feeding their families, but they were also women interested in politics. In the spring of 1795, when the meager supplies from the 1794 harvest were depleted, real famine swept over Europe. Desperate mothers cried for food for their children. To make matters worse, runaway inflation accompanied the famine. Women formed lines for food that was not available and local groups demonstrated for bread. Although some women asked only for bread, others added political demands. In France, women's demonstrations, soon joined by militant male workers, led to a major insurrection in May 1795. They marched on the government demanding "Bread and the Constitution of 1793," forcing the deputies to flee. Although never implemented, this Constitution was the most democratic, calling for universal manhood suffrage, adding a "right of subsistence" to other rights, and declaring that the government was responsible for all citizens, and that all citizens were entitled either to jobs or to adequate welfare benefits. It was likely that the women knew some of these provisions. The government attacked these demonstrators, who soon surrendered. Forbidden to attend political meetings, women again took to the streets, whereupon government officials ordered them to go back to their homes. The now dominant belief that the place of a virtuous woman was in the home combined with the fear of a mass working-class movement to produce a series of repressive decrees against women. Unlike the past tolerance of women who demanded bread because they wanted to still the cries of their hungry children, the government showed no tolerance to the women who demonstrated after 1794. The revolutionary concept of national citizenship now applied only to men – to propertied men.

Jurists and the men in legal power associated women with chaos and disorder, in part because of women's actual political activities and demonstrations, and in part because they were concerned about their property and blood lines. The idea that women would have the same rights as men terrified them because they thought it would mean the end of their model hierarchy based on gender and property. That the Society of Revolutionary Republican Women actually referred to themselves as citizens (*citoyennes*) must have galled the men in power after 1793 who maintained that politically active women contributed to sexual and social disorder. In so doing, women abandoned what was "natural" for their gender (being quiet and at home) and became, in the words of men, "unnatural" women. One revolutionary leader referred to Mme Roland as "a monster in every respect … [who] has sacrificed nature by wanting to rise above it. The desire to be learned has caused her to forget the virtues of her sex, and this forgetting, always dangerous, ends with her death on the scaffold."[3] The Republican bourgeois brotherhood tried to consolidate a revolution without their sisters who had done so much to further the Revolutionary cause.

Not all women shared republican sentiments or demonstrated in the streets for bread and citizenship. Republican ideology was secular and civil, aiming to undercut the power of religion, of the established church, and of the clergy. Whereas some women supported this secular activity, others resisted such secularization and clung to their church, priests, and religion. Still others continued to serve the church as nuns, most often as Sisters of Charity – the nursing orders. When the Revolutionary government confiscated church property, they turned many of the buildings into hospitals, but because there was no one else to staff those hospitals, they kept the nursing orders. Other nuns had to leave Paris or lose their heads. In the last years of the century, lay, rural, women led a Catholic religious revival that often took the form of religious riots in the countryside. The Concordat of 1801 between Napoleon and the Papacy led to a strengthening of women's Catholic religious orders.

The majority of the population of continental Europe was still rural. Despite the dechristianization campaign in France, rural women maintained the traditional ways of peasant religion and culture in the face of the more modern rituals of reason and the Republic. Following the most violent years of the Revolution, 1792–94, which were also years of war, some historians describe a religious revival in France as well as other countries, although the extent of this revival varied by region, by village, and by social group. To some extent the years of dearth and famine led people to find solace in religion. Some women may have felt guilty about their collaboration in the violent stage of the Revolution; others lost husbands and sons to the wars that raged from 1792 to 1815. For them, a return to religion may have been a way to assuage their guilt or comfort them in their loss. Women, deprived of most other forms of community activity, sought a social community within the church and religion. Even if they were not true believers, going to church offered them an avenue for social interaction as well as some order and purpose in their lives. Since women were guardians of the family, responsible for nourishment, they were responsible for the spiritual nourishment of their family; spiritual and bodily subsistence were linked. Women took the lead in opening churches, ringing bells, holding lay assemblies; they could get away with religious riots as they could get away with bread riots. The village bells (at least those that were not turned into war materiel) pealed for births, marriages, and deaths, as well as for daily and weekly mass. Religion and emotion contrasted with philosophy and reason. As an old rural proverb pronounced: "Men make the laws; women the traditions." Whether rural women were religious and therefore anti-Republican and counterrevolutionary is open to question. Yet, nineteenth-century Republican politicians believed this and it was one reason why they denied women the vote.

The European aftermath of the Revolution in France

The Revolution in France was the most significant event on the eve of the nineteenth century and women in other parts of Europe acted and reacted to it. Several took up the cause of women and the Revolution by adopting some of the Republican agenda and symbols. Women reacted to the widely publicized *Declaration of the Rights of Man*. An anonymous woman in Holland, basing her argument on natural law, argued that women were capable of participating in government. In Italy, at least three women (Rosa Califronia of Assisi and anonymous women in Genoa and Venice) took up their pens in 1794 and 1797 and argued for the rights of women, basing their views on the propositions that women were at least equal to men and that they had a right to take part in public forums.

In Germany, one of the leading advocates for granting civil and human rights to women equal to those of men was Theodor von Hippel who published *The Civil Advancement of Women* in 1791, and *On Improving the Status of Women*. He accused men of keeping their wives in domestic custody, comparing the status of women with that of slaves. In somewhat polemical works, he stressed equal rights and education for women and men. Although many of his bourgeois and enlightened intellectual colleagues suggested reforms giving men more rights, they drew the line at extending those rights to women. Some, such as Joachim Heinriche Campe, quite familiar with Rousseau's writings wrote in 1789 that woman's "natural" place was to be dependent on a father or husband in the home. German women writers, such as the journalist Marianne Ehrmann (1755–95) and Emilie Berlepsch (1757–1831) began to echo Revolutionary rhetoric and advocated education for women, especially to improve society and their independent positions regarding men. Ehrmann published a magazine for women, with the purpose of enlightening female friends and developing their minds. Like many of the women of the time, she centered her arguments on the need for education in order for women to better their condition. Her life and ideas were unconventional: her husband left her and she became an actress. Berlepsch also had an unconventional life, having separated from her husband. Like Ehrmann, she argued that a better education would make women more self-reliant. The current education, she complained, led to weak, melancholy, frivolous, and dependent women, seeking the applause of others.

One of the most far reaching and significant aspects of the aftermath of the Revolution and key signifier of the nineteenth century in France, Italy, Spain, portions of Germany, and even regions of the United States were the Napoleonic Civil and Penal Codes, promulgated in 1804 and 1810. Napoleon's armies and his representatives (often his relatives who ruled over portions of Europe such as in Italy and Spain) occupied vast regions of Europe, and instituted the Napoleonic laws, as well as the metric system and other components of the Revolution in those occupied lands and provinces. Laws are a text, culturally bound and tied to a society; they prescribe an ideal and they do not always reflect reality. Nevertheless an examination of gender issues in the Code reveals attitudes toward women that were to last for most of the nineteenth century. These laws, made by men, were severe or uncaring toward women. The Codes became the law of France, and also the law of areas of Europe conquered by France. Ideas contained in the law Code, like those of the Revolution, accompanied the administrators of the conquered territories and followed the soldiers wherever they went in war and conquests, spilling like plant seeds from the backpacks of the soldiers, sometimes falling on fertile soil. Beyond the actual adoption of the Napoleonic Code in other countries, this legal system that legitimized male power in the public and private spheres influenced other legal systems and cultures. It set forth ideas of citizenship and nationhood that excluded women, establishing the framework for attitudes and laws that circumscribed and prescribed gender roles in Europe and the United States for more than a century. What were some of these ideas that affected women?

Private property was the bedrock of French law as it was of Anglo-American law, and protection of the patriarchal family and its property became the hallmark of the Code. Legislators ordained that if the patriarchal family and the man's property were protected, then the social order would be stable; the family would become the basis of the social order dominated by male legislators, judges, juries, businessmen, and bureaucrats. Therefore, when a woman married, her loyalty was to her husband. She assumed his nationality, and she had to live wherever he chose and could not live apart. She could not file a legal suit, nor serve as a witness to any civil act – including births, marriages, divorces, and deaths. Men were the active citizens, and women the passive citizens, secondary to men. A married woman had minimal economic independence; her wages, by law, went to her husband and she could not have a business without her husband's permission; her profits became her husband's property.

In terms of sexuality, the Code treated men and women unequally. Men could commit adultery without moral or financial responsibility to the women they seduced or to the resultant children. There were no sanctions against male adultery unless he brought his sexual partner into his marital home. The Code punished female adultery by imprisonment and fines, with the sentence often at the discrimination of the husband, who could alleviate the punishment by taking his wife back. The Code explicitly forbad women and their children from seeking child support from the father for all children born out of wedlock. The intent behind such a measure was to ensure that a woman of the working classes would not pursue a man of property, especially a married man, and try to dissipate his family fortune on a child born outside the bounds of legal marriage. In forbidding paternity searches, the framers of the Code also sought to control women's sexuality. If a woman could not pursue the putative father of her child, legislators argued, then they would behave more morally and not engage in nonmarital sex, especially not with a married man. The Code, however, granted children permission to pursue their mother and claim maternal child support. The Code tried to enforce the male ideal of women's virtue. With the emphasis on property, in many aspects a married woman became her husband's property, not to buy and sell, but to preserve in order for her to bear him heirs that were undisputedly his. The liberal divorce law of 1792 became more restrictive with the grounds for divorce limited to three: conviction of either partner for crimes entailing a loss of civil rights or corporal punishment; brutality of one spouse to another, or adultery.

The Prussian Code (*Allgemeines Landrecht*) that had been developing since 1750 was finally completed in 1794 and it contained several articles that explicitly gave the husband rights over his wife. The Code declared: "The husband is by nature the head of his family. ... [A]s the wife enters into it of her own accord, she is in some measure subject to his power; whence flow several rights and privileges, which belong to the husband with regard to his wife. ... The husband has the liberty of prescribing laws and rules in his household, which the wife is to observe." She took his name and his status, and had to manage the household accordingly, and she could not have a trade for herself without her husband's approval. A wife also had to follow her husband wherever he should move and not leave his bed and board without his permission. Yet a wife also had certain rights and privileges. First, as part of his family she was entitled to a portion of his estate upon his death. She also had the right to seek security and defense from her husband, and he was obligated to support her. Based on the notion that the goal of marriage was procreation, the Code prescribed rights and duties of spouses to each other in terms of sexual relations. Neither spouse had the legal right "to continually refuse to perform the conjugal duty" except when a woman was nursing an infant, which the law required her to do; her husband had the legal right to determine how long she would breastfeed. She, however, could demand that he "pay her the conjugal duty, when he is not prevented by sickness or other accidents."[4] In Prussia, adultery was prohibited for both husband and wife. Enforcing many of these provisions would have been well nigh impossible. Nevertheless, this Code was yet one more example of how the public realm of politics and law interacted with the most private bedroom behavior. Its general tone was similar to that of the Napoleonic Code and this Prussian Code was well known among jurists in France.

The law Codes marking the end of the Revolutionary era attempted to restabilize the boundaries of women's lives that had become unsettled during the preceding decades. During those Revolutionary years two opposing movements to define women's roles emerged. One extolled the ideal of a virtuous wife and loving mother, devoted to the home. The other embraced the militant woman, acting in public with her writings and activities, endeavoring to further greater gender equality in education and civil rights for women as members of the social and political body. The nineteenth century was heir to both these ideals.

The Revolutionary and Napoleonic era suggested the terms of the debates that played themselves out all over Europe in the nineteenth century. It established a precedent for male dominance of rights and freedoms. It also carved out a public sphere for men in the world of business, politics, culture, and society while women were urged to relegate themselves to the interior world of home and family. Women often did not take this bitter pill that the Code and dominant male culture prescribed, and managed to ignore or get around the restrictions on their lives. The debates during the Revolution provided a new vocabulary and a new set of questions about women's rights, gender roles, the nature and limitations of citizenship, and education. It raised the important question of who constituted "the sovereign people." During the early stages of the Revolution, and in some of their writings, women were part of "the people" and even led in their demonstrations in demand of bread. After the Revolution, it became clear that women were not included in the sovereign people; laws denied women the rights of citizenship, relegating women to a non-political role, preferably in the home, as mothers raising good citizen-sons and dutiful daughters. Rousseau's ideas, rather than those of Wollstonecraft or de Gouges, set the framework for the dominant discourse surrounding women during much of the nineteenth century. While women's rights were limited in public policy and civil society, some argue that their role as Republican mothers improved the status of women, since it empowered them in the home and in the education of their children.

Nevertheless, many women ignored these distinctions, which were more applicable to the middle and upper classes than to poor and workingwomen who had to contribute to the family economy in business, commerce, industry, service, and agriculture – all in the public arena. The concept of a separation between public and private was irrelevant to these women. Moreover, the very men who wanted to confine women to the home needed these workingwomen outside the home to support their businesses and economic lives. The lives and goals of the *salonnières* differed drastically from those crowds of workingwomen clamoring in the streets. And the weatherworn peasant women had nothing in common with *salonnières* and shopkeepers of Paris, if they even knew of them at all. Over the course of the nineteenth century, however, middle-class men and women would attempt, with uneven success, to spread their ideas concerning gender roles to the working classes and peasantry. They would also adapt these ideas to changing economic, social, and political circumstances, eventually using them to argue for an increased sphere of responsibility and activity for women. The tumultuous years of the Revolutionary and Napoleonic eras had profound and long lasting repercussions for women's lives in Europe throughout the nineteenth century.

2
Reproduction and Sexuality

The French Revolution framed nineteenth-century European politics and culture, but issues of death, sex, and birth affected women's private lives. Throughout the century, women's private sexual and reproductive lives became open to public scrutiny, as economic and public policies blurred the boundaries between public and private. Bioreasoning, or thinking about women in terms of their bodies and biology, shaped Western European attitudes during the nineteenth century, affecting gender identities, sexuality, and ideas of reproduction and sexuality. Attitudes toward women's reproductive biology infused politics. Europe's new cultural elites believed that because of women's sexual and reproductive roles, their bodies could disrupt the social order and therefore needed to be observed and restrained, discursively and legally. Moreover, toward the end of the century, the biopolitics of each nation regarded power in terms of the quantity and quality of its population. Since women were the procreators, and responsibility for reproduction was gendered female, fertility rates loom important for a history of nineteenth-century women. The term "fertility rate" is defined as the average number of children that a woman gave birth to; concern with this rate indicates the essential role of women in national politics.

The population of Europe underwent two demographic transitions during the long nineteenth century. The population explosion from roughly 1750 to 1850 was the first. The second, starting around 1880 and known as the "fertility decline," reversed the trends of the first. These population movements provide a critical background for understanding women's lives. As attention to the nature of citizenship occupied the minds of many writers and politicians, so did women's role in creating citizens. Male doctors, politicians, religious leaders, and economists took a profound interest in the sexuality and reproductive capacities of women and had much to say about the most private matters of women's lives. When politicians paid attention to producing population, the status of women as mothers became a public concern; reproduction became a public responsibility.

Mortality

Mortality is not generally associated with women's sexuality and reproduction, but it figured in population growth and affected women in a myriad of ways, not the least of which was in their reproductive strategies, in watching their babies die, or in public attitudes toward them as mothers. A decrease in the

24

mortality rate was not the major explanation for the population explosion; mortality rates throughout the nineteenth century remained fairly high, decreasing only at the end of that century, and even then mostly in Western and Northern Europe.

Death did not hit people in all socioeconomic groups equally. The upper and middle classes fared somewhat better than the poor. Lung diseases, such as consumption (tuberculosis) or bronchitis, and fevers, such as typhus, typhoid, measles, smallpox, and scarlet fever were the most frequent causes of death. Furthermore, the cholera epidemics of 1832, 1849, 1852, and 1854 decimated large segments of the European population. Until the very end of the nineteenth century, famine caused suffering and death in the rural regions of Europe, especially during "the hungry forties" of 1846–48.

Infant and child mortality was especially high and did not significantly decline until the beginning of the twentieth century. Depending on region, one in four infants might have died before her first birthday, and one child in two before her fifth birthday. Yet, many women could have seen 10, or more, of their children live to adulthood. The underserved and poorer populations of Europe experienced a higher likelihood of infant and child mortality. In the mid-nineteenth century, the number of deaths of babies under one year was the lowest in France and the United Kingdom where fewer than one in five babies born were expected to die. It was higher in Italy and Germany where almost a quarter of all live births died. In Russia, almost a third of all babies born could be expected to die within their first year.

Infants primarily died from diarrhea and dehydration, predominantly in the hot summer months, particularly if the mothers did not breast feed. Cow's milk might have been left in bowls, bottles, or pots, collecting flies, other insects, and germs and becoming polluted, especially in the heat of summer. Drinking water was no better since it often came from contaminated streams. Lung diseases followed intestinal diseases as the leading causes of children's deaths. Until the twentieth century, there were no medical means of protection against childhood diseases, such as diphtheria (a real killer of babies), and no cures either. Mothers did what they could, whether following a doctor's advice or preferring their own folk remedies.

Many women, could not, or would not, keep their infants with them after birth. Women who worked in shops alongside their husbands and women of property and high social position who wanted to regain their figures faster and resume their social life often sent their babies to wetnurses, or brought a rural lactating woman into their own homes to feed their newborn. Babies sent away to a wetnurse had a higher mortality rate than those whom a mother breastfed. The middle- and upper-class women who used wetnurses preferred to import the best wetnurses to live in their houses and breast feed the infants, if they could afford it; others would export their infants to healthy, lactating women in the countryside. Many destitute and unwed mothers (in France, Italy, Spain, Portugal, or Russia) abandoned their babies at a foundling shelter, from where authorities shipped them out to wetnurses. The poorest wetnurses, those whom the middle classes did not hire, became the paid wetnurses of the hundreds of thousands of abandoned babies. The mortality of abandoned children remained significantly higher than that of other children. Although many wetnurses fed and cared for their charges well, some may have privileged their own babies, or had no breast milk and fed the infants indigestible cow's milk. Those wetnurses who did not privilege their own nursing babies may have seen their own baby suffer in order that the infant whom they took in for money lived. In England, in a system known as "baby farming," working mothers of ex-nuptial children paid another, non-lactating, woman a fee to take their babies and possibly find new homes for them.

Women not only watched their children die, but they also frequently did not live to see them grow up. Death in childbirth was not unusual; neither doctors nor midwives understood nor could do much about complications from childbirth. Caesarian sections were risky and excruciatingly painful until the advent of anesthesia late in the century. Neither doctors nor midwives understood the germ base of puerperal (childbirth) fever, and therefore could not take adequate measures to prevent it. In some cities, such as Paris, women who gave birth at home with a midwife's assistance had lower rates of death from puerperal fever than women who gave birth assisted by doctors in hospitals. In other countries, mortality from puerperal fever was less frequent among the upper classes who might have had a doctor deliver the baby rather than a midwife.

All women were susceptible to diseases such as tuberculosis. This disease could affect the rural woman living in a cold damp farmhouse, the urban denizen of a slum, a slender stylish middle-class woman, or an artist or artist's lover, such as Mimi in *La Bohème*. Marguerite Gautier, the heroic and ennobled consumptive in Alexandre Dumas fils' *La Dame aux Camelias* who is better known as Violetta in Verdi's *La Traviata*, lived the life of a courtesan who died from consumption. Syphilis (a sexually transmitted disease associated with prostitutes) was undiagnosed among middle-class women whose husbands brought it home to them. Women also saw their husbands die; widows outnumbered widowers only in part because widowers tended to remarry rapidly in order to have a helpmate in work and in raising the motherless children.

Mortality rates remained high until the end of the nineteenth century because advances in medicine and modern ideas of public hygiene became known and accepted only then. Pasteur's discoveries date from 1867 but most doctors did not acknowledge and accept the germ theory of disease and the pasteurization of milk until the late 1880s. Infant formula production began in 1892, but infant formula did not result in decreased infant mortality for all social groups because the poor women stretched it by mixing it with unsanitary water. Toward the end of the century doctors understood that microbes rather than miasmas contributed to contagious diseases, and they began to use antisepsis in their practices. Various vaccinations, such as that for small pox, also began to control disease and reduce mortality. These changes began in the northern and western areas of Europe, leaving high mortality in the eastern and southern regions. Until the end of the nineteenth century, a general improvement in diet was the main reason for any decline in mortality.

Historians can only imagine what it may have been like for a woman to watch as many as half of her children die before they reached their sixth birthday. It may have been that she valued all her children and the death of any one of them left her bereft. Or, death may have occurred with such frequency that a woman might have become inured to it. Moreover, given the lack of contraception during the nineteenth century, she may actually have been relieved to have one less mouth to feed. One theory postulates that because mothers watched so many of their babies die, they did not invest emotional capital in each child. Furthermore, the culture of the middle- and upper-class women that sanctioned having other women breastfeed their infants might reveal a minimal emotional investment in the children. However, many women practiced the precepts of Rousseau and breastfed and reared their own infants, revealing an emotional attachment that even the death of several could not allay. There is little evidence that women sought to limit their family size by selective neglect, favoring the survival of male children. Parents were not indifferent to their children, but saw them both in economic and emotional terms.

Fertility increase (1750–1850)

The population of Europe expanded from 1750 to 1850 largely because of an increase in the birth rate. Religious moralists and economists, most notably Thomas Malthus (1766–1834), believed that the population would expand in accord with the available supply of resources; there would then be a natural ceiling at the point where population size and the means of subsistence were in balance. He assumed that most births occurred within marriage and that population would be controlled by a high age at marriage. According to Malthus, if the population grew beyond what the land could bear there would be an increase in mortality. But, the natural ceiling on population growth did not materialize, and rapid population growth went hand in hand with changes in the economy. Malthus, and the moral reformers in his wake, took a moralistic view of limiting births, confining birth control to abstinence. They viewed any form of fertility limitation that allowed sexual intercourse as a threat to the moral and economic basis of society. Sexual activity and reproduction were linked until the end of the nineteenth century. A woman's childbearing period could last from menarche (usually between ages 12 and 17) until menopause, usually around 40 to 50 years of age.

Despite the lack of safe, efficacious, and affordable barrier contraception, women and men sought to control conception in a variety of ways. Without some kind of fertility control a woman's life would be one of almost constant childbearing, draining her both physically and emotionally as well as depleting the family's resources. Manuals on birth control existed, although they were not widely circulated. Francis Place's pamphlet on contraception, *To the Married of Both Sexes* circulated in Great Britain in 1823, and Robert Owen's *Moral Physiology; or a Brief and Plain Treatise on the Population Question* published in 1831 included a section on contraception. Abstinence and coitus interruptus were the main forms of birth control, but a man's withdrawal depended on his needs and his respect for the woman. The decision to employ some means to control the likelihood of pregnancy reflected the nature of the relationship – whether it were a companionate relationship based on love or a forced seduction. Although condoms had been known throughout the eighteenth century, they were rarely used. Casanova (1725–98) reputedly called them his "English overcoats." But not until after the vulcanization of rubber in 1844 did their use spread, mainly to prostitutes and their clients concerned about venereal disease; in the 1880s they became more widespread still. The cost remained prohibitively expensive, however, and until after 1920 they were associated with illicit sex and venereal disease.

Nevertheless, women sought to control their own sexuality and fertility. They inserted a sponge or pessary or douched with various herbs, both pre- and post-coital. Some upper-class women soaked the sponge in brandy, which acted as a spermicide. All of these methods had a limited success rate, with the vaginal sponge being the most efficacious, and reputedly used by noble women, the bourgeoisie, and prostitutes. Under Church teaching, some relied on a woman's "safe period," unfortunately miscalculated as in mid-month, just between the menses. Abortion, although illegal, was the form of family planning of last resort, especially when a family already included numerous children. Women did not write about abortion, per se, but used code phrases such as those in newspaper advertisements that promised a particular midwife or pharmacist could "restore menstruation." Abortion techniques were dangerous, and included tightly binding the abdomen, jumping from high places, taking hot baths, ingesting particular herbs and roots, and eating match heads that contained the chemical phosphorus that acted as an abortifacient. These herbs and chemicals could cause uterine contractions, but women had to estimate the quantity; too much could be poisonous to a woman's entire system. If herbs and other less invasive techniques failed, desperate women resorted to the insertion of a sharp instrument with the hopes that it would dislodge the contents of the uterus without perforating it or other organs. They could try to do this themselves, with the help of a friend, or by using an abortionist or midwife. Since midwives often served as abortionists, they received the sobriquet of "angel makers."

Women did not always understand their bodies, and some needlessly attempted to abort because they missed a couple of menstrual periods and erroneously believed that they were pregnant. A mercenary midwife may have convinced the woman to have an abortion, or she could have mistaken a tumor for a pregnancy. The more fortunate women who tried abortion attempted it before their fifth month of pregnancy. However, many attempted it in their fifth or sixth month of pregnancy because only then, after quickening (the sensation of fetal movement) might a woman be sure that she was pregnant; this was as true of nobility in England as it was of the poor shopwoman in France, or the Italian peasant. With quickening as the defining time for pregnancy, the courts took a woman's word about whether she thought she was pregnant. Toward the end of the century, a doctor's word became the basis for criminal judgments, muting the woman's voice. If abortion failed, or if women did not have the networks to try to abort, the truly desperate resorted to infanticide. Poor, single, unwed or widowed women, alone in the cities or countryside, without community resources or networks, were those most often prosecuted for infanticide. There is no way of knowing how many infanticides actually occurred.

Late marriages had been another means to control the number of births, and this marriage pattern prevailed in the north and west of Europe, across all socioeconomic levels, and decreased toward the southern and eastern regions of Europe.[1] People delayed marriage until they could establish independent households. The average age of first marriage for men was over 26 and that for women was over 23 years of age, giving a woman about 20 fertile years. In France, where fertility was not as high as in other countries, the average age of marriage was higher. The high age of marriage for women was more significant than that for men but would only control marital fertility, and not nonmarital fertility or pregnancies that resulted in marriage, known as pre-bridal pregnancies. Imperial Russia did not follow the Western European marriage typography. Here, family and social pressure favored early marriage and large patriarchal families, both during and after serfdom. Women in Russian villages usually married before they turned 20; men married at around 20.

Marriage patterns related to land holding and occupation. A sound economic basis was expected for family formation, and in Northern and Western Europe this usually meant marriage was delayed until a man could obtain land or earn an independent living. He either had to wait for his father to die or he had to make property arrangements with parents, siblings, and other relatives. Kinship alliances helped members marry and set up independent households. This might have meant providing a woman with a sufficiently large dowry to enable marriage. Again, the pattern for Russia differed. High fertility and cultural restrictions on family fission (sons did not separate from fathers, and a son's wife entered his household) along with patterns of family mergers made three-generation households possible. In Russia, a high mortality level in part offset the high fertility level.

These checks on population, whether by contraception, abstinence, or late marriage, were offset by better diets. A woman's fertility, in part, is based on the number of calories and types of nutrients she consumes in relation to her work; an absence of body fat is a contributory factory to amenorrhea. Notably, the introduction of the potato as a human food crop did much to increase fertility when people in Europe started cultivating and eating it in the eighteenth century. The potato was a relatively hardy crop, resistant to blight and to climatic calamities. This may appear to contradict the well-known Irish potato famine of the 1840s, but between 1740 and 1840 the population of Ireland quadrupled.

Historians relate social and sexual practices resulting in more children to the transition to capitalism; but it is difficult to determine if an increase in the birth rate led to economic changes, or the converse. Industrialization, or proto-industrialization, developed in different stages in various places in Western Europe starting around the mid-eighteenth century. Proto-industrialization was the development of cottage industries, often called the putting-out system, whereby entrepreneurs employed farming families to produce goods that would then be sold in regional or national markets. The relationship of family size to proto-industrialization is complex. To one extent, proto-industrialization developed because farming populations needed a means of keeping family economies stable when faced with an increase in population that was more than the land could support. Women engaged in cottage industries such as spinning while their children carded. Men wove, thus earning cash for their goods, which made their way to the market. Some historians argue that population pressure spurred industrial development, which in turn caused an increase in population pressure.[2]

Families that engaged in proto-industrialization relied on their labor in textiles and other manufacturing more than on farming, and tended to have a lower age at marriage; thus the woman could have more reproductive years within marriage and more children.[3] For proto-industrial families, obtaining land was not an issue in delaying marriage. Moreover, a family gaining most of its living from industry would benefit from more children, which meant more laborers.[4] The major drawback to having many children was the life-cycle poverty that could ensue when a woman had several young, nonproductive children at home, restricting her wage-earning work as well as creating more mouths to feed.

Cultural, religious, and community factors also played a role in reducing the age of marriage and increasing the numbers of children per family. Ideas about the ideal number of children for a completed family, the birth intervals between children, and even breastfeeding may have changed, resulting in more children. There is some evidence that families wanted a certain number of children, depending on their economy, culture, and occupation; when families reached an ideal size, couples stopped having children. The ideal family size among certain groups of the population, such as those working in industry, may have increased. In some places, spacing childbirth every two years was pronounced biologically "natural." Women achieved this spacing by abstinence, miscarriages (induced or spontaneous) or by breastfeeding. Some cultures established taboos, such as prohibiting sexual intercourse when a mother was lactating. These cultural practices may have shifted, resulting in more births.

Although childbirth was supposed to follow marriage, conception often preceded it. Various rural cultures even expected that pregnancy would precede marriage as a sign of a woman's fertility. When the family economy was predicated on the number of working hands, families and the community tacitly condoned pre-bridal fertility. To save the woman's family honor a marriage had to ensue if the woman were pregnant. In nineteenth-century cultures, it was always the woman who had to prove fertility, never the man. In these small, endogamous, rural communities, kin and neighbors knew who was courting whom. When the woman became pregnant, community pressure could force a marriage. With development of the market economy and increased migration, especially of men, the ability of the family and community to enforce marriages broke down. Knowing he could escape marriage, a man might have exercised less sexual restraint, and worried less about the consequences of his acts of seduction.

The number of births outside of legal marriage, generally called the illegitimacy rate, also greatly increased during this time period, in some places more than others. The religion of the area was not generally a factor. In areas of high religiosity, a woman who was pregnant outside of marriage could have gone to a nearby city to have the baby, thus inflating urban statistics and showing few ex-nuptial births in a highly religious area. In Paris, during the first half of the nineteenth century, 25 percent of live births were to a nonmarried woman, while in London that rate was only 4 percent. This had little to do with religion and more to do with culture, reporting, and public policy. In France, unwed pregnant women tended to leave their home areas and go to the cities. In

England, pregnant women arriving in the cities would be sent back to their parishes.

No one was happy with out-of-wedlock births, for moral as well as economic reasons. Politicians, doctors, religious leaders, and moral reformers criticized the women for their allegedly immoral sexual behavior. Furthermore, an unmarried mother and her baby posed financial problems to themselves and to others. An unmarried mother had to support that child, usually on her own wages. The luckier women could have help from the baby's father or from her family – if they had not abandoned their pregnant daughter because an ex-nuptial birth was a blot on the family honor. Often the burden for that child fell on the local parish, local nobility, or the government.

Historians have advanced several hypotheses to explain why an increasing proportion of women had babies outside of marriage. The most compelling explanation relates to change in the economy and community, as well as the increased vulnerability of women to men's advances and seduction. Increased male migration to commercial centers transformed what in the past might have been a pre-bridal pregnancy into an out-of-wedlock pregnancy. Single mothers maintained that the man had promised them marriage but then abandoned them as soon as they became pregnant. Migrant women were also more vulnerable. Newly arrived in the city, or in another household as a domestic servant, a lonely woman could have been seduced, or could have voluntarily entered into a sexual relationship based on a verbal promise of marriage, but had no one to enforce the marriage. Moreover, men were freer to seduce and abandon or neglect coitus interruptus than they had been. Having a child out-of-wedlock was often a result of their traditional behavior in more modern times. Finally, many births that the records show as illegitimate were to couples in long-term consensual unions. The mothers were not really single or unwed mothers; they were just women who did not have a legal marriage.[5] Among the middle and upper classes, either marriage was enforced, or a woman had an abortion, or had the baby. If the woman remained pregnant without marriage, a family would send their daughter out of their hometown to keep the secrecy of the pregnancy and preserve the family honor. Sometimes, men recognized their bastard sons. And, when counterculture romantics, radicals, or artists lived in consensual unions their children would appear as "illegitimate."

Fertility decline in the late nineteenth century

Toward the end of the nineteenth century women had a more decisive role in controlling their fertility. Seeking ways to limit the number of children indicates that they were well aware of their own sexuality when the middle-class dominant discourse of the era said that they were not supposed to be. Women's control over their own fertility also indicates a shift in the relationships of power between men and women in sexual behavior, within and outside of marriage. There is no historical certainty about why the fertility decline occurred, or which culture started it. Some historians postulate that it began with the upper classes and filtered down. Recent evidence, however, disputes that diffusion theory and sees family limitation occurring in different communities at different times, according to community cultural norms and occupation-related concerns.[6]

The term "fertility decline" indicates a decline in population *growth*, but not in total population. Nations, obsessed with economic and military competition, examined their numbers vis-à-vis those of other countries. French politicians, for example, looked at their own numbers in comparison with those of Germany. Whereas the population of France increased by 3 percent, that of Germany since unification in 1871, increased by 20 percent. This meant that politicians were putting pressure on women to have more and healthier babies, for the national strength. It also indicates that the most private sexual and reproductive lives of men and women became subjects for the pens and policies of male politicians. France had the greatest decline in both marital and non-marital fertility, but the fertility decline occurred in all countries of Western Europe starting around the 1880s. The birthrate in England fell from 35.5 per 1,000 women in the 1870s to 26 per 1,000 in 1910. The decline in the number of births was only partly a result of delayed marriages or increased age in first marriage.

Technological innovations played only a small part in the fertility decline. Barrier contraception such as condoms, pessaries, diaphragms, cervical caps, suppositories, sponges, and spermicides became efficacious and acceptable, especially among the middle and upper classes, spawning dissemination of birth control information, but it was only after 1920 that barrier contraception became affordable and widespread to all socioeconomic groups. Although men and women still used some of the "traditional" measures of birth control, such as abstinence, coitus interruptus, and abortion, they increasingly sought barrier contraception. Except for the condom, all these technologies gave the woman control over conception, and their use speaks of women's increasing role in sexuality and family planning.

Contraception became a household word at the end of the nineteenth century, especially in England with the 1877 trial of Charles Bradlaugh and Annie Besant for publishing information about birth control. Accused of publishing pornography, these two stood trial, but the trial was such a sensation that the sales of their book increased. At the same time, the neo-Malthusian movement throughout Western Europe fostered family planning. Unlike Malthus who advocated delayed marriages, moral restraint, and abstinence, especially for the poor whom he said were "breeding" to excess, the neo-Malthusians wanted to teach the poor how to use contraceptive devices. Neo-Malthusians were not necessarily arguing for women's choice, although some were, but they lectured the poor on limiting their number of children to result in healthier workers.

New technologies for birth control did contribute to family planning and the fertility decline, but why did these technologies develop and why did people adopt them? The arguments based on technology tell only a part of the story. Families adopted birth control less because of new techniques and technologies, and more because of changing economic and social conditions. The economies of scale and the shifting nature of industrialization to larger-scale industries requiring less child labor toward the end of the nineteenth century changed the economic value of children and favored small families among both the middle classes and the workers. The industrialists' decreasing need for child labor allowed the passage of effective child labor protection laws in the 1870s in England, France, and Germany that established a minimum age for child labor and also restricted the number of hours per day that children could work. Furthermore, a decade later, the same countries enacted compulsory primary education laws requiring boys and girls to stay in school until they were 12 or 13. According to one theory, since children could not work as many hours and had to attend school, they became economic liabilities rather than the economic assets they had been in traditional times. Moreover, the depression of the same decades created economic uncertainty and material hardships, so women who already had several children wanted to prevent more births. Before the economic changes of the late nineteenth century, more children meant more labor; but this no longer applied in most of Northern and Western Europe. Parents then started to limit the size of their completed families. Here, the phrase "completed families" corresponds more closely to the number of births because of the decline in infant mortality.

The long depression of the 1880s, especially in England and France, along with the desire to maintain a certain quality of life and the "paraphernalia of gentility" despite an increased cost of living and diminished resources also led couples to limit the number of children. This was a middle-class rationale, based on the increasing cost of ensuring the educational, professional, and business success of their children. English and French parents believed that they could maintain their status and even secure a better life if they had fewer children.[7] This was especially true in the rapidly growing urban areas. Furthermore, lower infant mortality led people to limit the number of children born since each child would have a greater chance of survival. Families did not need to bank on many children. This hypothesizes an ideal family size and cultural reasons as well as economic and technological for limiting the number of children.

Cultural changes toward the end of the century, including new concepts of motherhood, more affective parenting, new marital relationships with greater equality between husbands and wives – especially in the realm of children – may also have contributed to a fertility decline. Women, who bore the burden of childbirth and most of the burdens of childrearing, may have wanted most to limit family size, and were able to do so. The emphasis on the quality of nurturing and emotional motherhood (and fatherhood) that began with educated elites became culturally diffused. Having fewer children, and nurturing them, came to be the mark of civilization for all social groups. Evidence that working-class women emulated middle-class attitudes about family planning is sparser than evidence that they adopted family planning to fit their changing economic lives. Some families thought that having more than three children was immoral as well as materially unsound. With a new effort to gain respectability, families sought to limit family size.

By the end of the nineteenth century, women were taking control of fertility and of their own sexuality. The rhetoric of birth control gave women of all social classes a new vocabulary to articulate matters pertaining to their bodies and their sexuality. When a woman could plan her reproductive life with some hope of success and have some control over her body, sexuality became separate from reproduction, emancipating women from their biological destinies. This led some male politicians and doctors to condemn the birth control movement because they thought that birth control would lead to "female sexual excess" disrupting the social order and male control. In some countries where doctors adopted the "family planning" agenda, rather than use language about women's sexual freedom, which they may have found threatening, they used terms that would give the men some aspect of control. In other areas, doctors eschewed the birth control movement and it remained subversive and against the national interests.

Sexuality

Sexuality means more than reproduction; it is important by itself, but more significantly, it can represent a power relationship. Fear of women's sexuality was not new at the end of the nineteenth century, going back at least a century to Rousseau's writings. Borrowing from Rousseau's prescriptions, nineteenth-century men argued that biology and sexuality destined women to be mothers, safely in the home, taking care of their husbands and children. Although it is undeniable that women are the ones to have babies, sexuality is not merely essential; it is also socially constructed, relating to the concept of the self. Women's actualization of concepts of their "self" coincided chronologically with their control over their sexuality and reproduction during the last decades of the nineteenth century. Whether concepts of "self" preceded control over fertility or the other way around is debatable, as women struggled to define themselves and their sexuality.

The discourse on liberty, on individualism, and on natural law that pervaded the nineteenth century included a coded form of sexuality. The new, urban, middle-class men who rose to power set forth hegemonic cultural ideals as one way to delineate themselves as a group apart from the "other," which were women, the poor, and the colonized. Building upon their concepts of individual property, inheritance, and reproductive strategies to protect their property, they established a moral ideal and system of habits, delineating gender roles to affirm their own power and property transmission. They thought that they needed to govern and regulate women's sexuality. Thus, women's sexuality became a major subject of the nineteenth-century rhetoric of repression that linked morality with sexuality, for the good of society. Women, in this instance, were both powerful and powerless. They were powerless in that they were legally and discursively confined to a secondary and submissive role. Women were powerful because that same discourse that confined them to the private sphere also assigned them sexual power. Women bore children and were also supposed to be the moral influence in the family and society.

A middle-class fear of "rampant sexuality" among working-class women inspired moral tracts during the first two-thirds of the nineteenth century, especially in England and France, that criticized working-class women who bore children out of wedlock and had more children than they could afford. Middle-class men saw these children and their mothers as evidence of women's unregulated sexual behavior and passions that needed control. Women working outside the home, and not the men who helped create the children, were singled out for lack of morality.

At the beginning of the nineteenth century, moralists saw themselves as the dominant regulators of sexuality, both politically and discursively. By the end of the century that role had transferred to doctors and other medical practitioners who developed scientific analyses of sex and sexuality. With the increasing prominence of doctors, clinical descriptions of sexuality and sexual behavior superseded the moral categories. These clinical descriptions, however, contained implicit moral judgements, often defining certain forms of sexual behavior as "pathological." Whether cast in a moral or pathological framework, discussions of women's sexuality became part of the biopolitics of the nineteenth century.

When writing about morals and sexuality, historians have often referred to the nineteenth century as the Victorian era because Queen Victoria of England (1819–1901) ruled from 1837 to her death. That era had been associated with repressed female sexuality and with the idea that people did not talk about sex. By 1976, however, Michel Foucault had successfully discredited that interpretation of a sexually repressed society. On the contrary, historians now demonstrate that the bourgeoisie was preoccupied with sexuality as part of a concern with social order, hygiene, health, property, and power. Foucault argued that sexuality was not an exclusively private affair, but was rather the topic of an extensive public discourse whose purpose was not so much the regulation of sex as the production and deployment of power. The nobility had always been interested in lineage and power based on bloodlines. The propertied middle classes were just as interested; according to Foucault, "the bourgeoisie's 'blood' was their sex."[8] Foucault also debunked the long-held idea that a person's sex was essential, part of their biological makeup, while gender was constructed; he showed that sex could also be constructed.

Doctors and other social commentators allowed men sexual freedoms, which meant a double standard for men and women. Men were sexual beings; sex was natural for them and they did not have to confine their sexual ardor within marriage. For the idealized passive woman, however, sex was only to occur within marriage, and only for procreation. The domestic ideal placed women barefoot and pregnant in the private sphere of the hearth and home, with men shod in boots, free to roam throughout the public world. Dante Gabriel Rosetti's (1828–82) painting of the strong man in heavy boots, with the bound ewe in his cart, dragging a woman (presumably his wife) from her cowered position back to him, presumably to tie her up, as he did the ewe, presents an indelible image.

The ideal woman was the "Angel in the House," the title of Coventry Patmore's poem (1854–56) that became the popular phrase for the biblical Madonna-like wife and mother. Although most closely associated with England, the concept of "angel in the house" pervaded much of Western European writing; it helped the middle classes define family values. The middle-class angel, however, subordinate to her husband and devoted to him and her children, was not totally powerless since she held the keys to the household functions. Defining the middle-class woman as a Madonna placed her in opposition to a woman who openly had sex outside of marriage, thus establishing her boundaries in opposition to the "other," whom writers depicted as a whore; the "other" woman may have been a prostitute but was usually a working-class woman who had a child out of wedlock. Writers attributed to working-class women and women in the colonies the overt sexual drives that they deprived their wives, creating a double standard between middle-class and both working-class and colonial women. In one of the many paradoxes of the time, middle-class male writers exploited the working woman both sexually and economically, but also wanted her to adopt the moral standards of the middle-class angel. Becoming an "angel in the house" was difficult for poor women, given crowded living conditions and the necessity of working for wages.

Despite the idea that a middle-class woman was supposedly innocent in sexual matters, doctors published advice manuals on sex. Some, such as the English William Acton (1813–75), believed that middle-class women were passionless, but should make "unselfish sacrifices" to their husband's desires. To refuse a husband's sexual advances would endanger his health. Those "sad exceptional" women who showed sexual excitement could develop "nymphomania, a form of insanity." Other writers were not so sure about women's passion, or lack of it, but thought that women's sexuality differed from a man's. The French, such as Auguste Dubay (1802–90), appeared to be more accepting of women's sexuality and even their eroticism, telling men and women how to please each other, and enjoining couples to have sex regularly – but only within marriage and in moderation. In the case of the French, that advice may have been predicated on the doctors' desire to increase the low birth rate. Yet most sex manuals encouraged women to defer to their husband's interests and even to fake orgasm to keep him happy and the marriage stable. The manuals also defined ideal and acceptable sexual behavior as compared with deviant; they labeled the latter as promiscuous, nymphomaniac, or perverse.

The lived experiences of middle-class married women did not always correspond to the ideal. Women demonstrated amazing resiliency in not following the prescriptive literature; not all were the asexual Madonnas that they were supposed to be, and some showed an interest in their own sexuality and their own orgasms. Their desire to avoid sexual intercourse may have been less from prudishness and lack of passion than from their desire to avoid more children, vaginal or urinary tract infections, and venereal disease. Toward the end of the century a new genre of premarital guides emerged to inform women about sex within marriage, with the French physicians pre-dating the English by a decade in writing and publishing them. Chastity, however, remained the moral, religious, and sometimes legal imperative for all women before marriage. Paradoxically, middle-class men wanted working-class women as well as their sisters and daughters to be chaste until marriage, yet they themselves seduced women prior to marriage. In most cultures, paternity suits were either illegal or difficult, so men faced no legal consequences for their seduction.

Women wanted to know more about their own sexual bodies, including menstruation and amenorrhea, and doctors were willing to tell them – even if their own mothers could not. The onset of menstruation was an important milestone, fraught with perceived perils, fears, and myths. It began a period of medical and social supervision of a girl's life, because menarche ushered in fertility and sexuality. The few extant autobiographies of nineteenth-century women rarely mention menstruation for several possible reasons: because of the mystery, because of the taboos of talking about it, because of shame and modesty attached to discussion of private bodily parts, because it was considered an illness or a "curse," and in part because they just did not know how to deal with the changes in their bodies, including the development of secondary sex characteristics. Menstruation was also a time when they may have considered themselves dirty, as others considered them; the use of rags was the major way to absorb menstrual blood, which doctors believed should flow freely.

The literature of the time abounded with distinctions about the relationship of race and class to a young woman's menstrual cycles. Commentators believed that poor girls who worked in the textile and garment trades where they were physically active, or who lived in crowded, dirty, and immoral surroundings had an earlier onset of menarche, indicating excessive sexuality and "carnal instincts." To some extent nutrition and diet determined body fat and the onset of menses; in terms of diet, however, there was little difference in the caloric intake of rich or poor working girls since it was fashionable for young affluent girls to eat little, and for their diets to be bland and without much red meat, as the latter was thought to encourage passion and menstruation. Working-class girls just could not afford to eat meat, red or otherwise.

Concern with the menstrual cycle and amenhorrea influenced the range of permissible activities for women's minds and bodies. According to some misguided popular beliefs, intellectual exercises could endanger "normal" menses and could create uterine problems. One doctor singled out trying to solve quadratic equations as causing a lack of blood to the uterus and hence amenhorrea and sterility. Others faulted novels and the theater for exciting the passions; still others, especially late in the century, blamed bicycle riding. Women often wore restricted clothing or long layered skirts or tight corsets, although medical opinion was divided on the effect of tight corsets on menstruation and reproductive capabilities. According to some English manuals early in the century, affluent women were supposed to have little exercise, and they often developed tensions and related ailments. A French manual, on the other hand, advised some physical exercise, such as walking and jumping rope, to bring on the menstrual flow. Attitudes about menstruation did not significantly change even at the end of the nineteenth century. One English writer of 1895 referred to the *pelvic power* of girls up to the age of puberty when girls are superior to boys. With puberty, however, her mental and physical education is stunted. If not, her "brain saps the pelvis of its power." There is a balance, he asserted, between pelvic power and mental power, and after menarche, mental power takes a back stage to pelvic power.[9] Despite these prescriptions against intellectual activities, women wrote novels, became scientists, mathematicians, and musicians, and pursued education and even sports.

Doctors worried about problems of the uterus throughout the century. Women's emotional and physical ailments, such as neurasthenia and hysteria, were associated with the uterus, linguistically as well as medically. If a woman were excessively fat or thin, doctors blamed the woman's weight, as well as the excessive use of her brain, for uterine dysfunction. If working-class women failed to menstruate, however, doctors believed it was owing to bad diet, disease, and immorality.

Menopause, on the opposite end of women's reproductive, and hence sexual life in the minds of many, posed less of a problem to society. According to Marc

Colombat, the French writer on sexuality whose works were translated to English and widely read, a woman past menopause must not allow herself to feel love or passions because that would wreck havoc with her nervous system since she could no longer have children. Instead of love or sex, these women should develop their moral, religious, charitable, or grandmotherly qualities. Women went from being depicted as sexual objects to asexual beings in their forties.

Historians cannot safely say how much women knew about sex. There was no sex education in the schools and an imposed modesty may have kept many mothers from telling their daughters anything except what Queen Victoria apocryphally told her daughter on her wedding night: "Lie back, my dear, and think of the Empire." During the eighteenth and most of the nineteenth century, sexual violence normatively accompanied marital and non-marital sex. Some of this sexual violence was part of male culture. To overcome women's innocence and fear of sex upon marriage, toward the end of the nineteenth century doctors designed sex manuals to educate women and men, cautioning men that sudden violent sexual penetration of their wife might be inconsiderate. Nevertheless, women of all groups probably knew the pleasures of sex either from experience prior to or outside of marriage, or from within a love-based marriage, or from their own sexual instincts and experimentation. They wrote of their joys, their loves, and their bodies, often in letters to close female friends.

Courtship and mutual attraction were important parts of sexuality. In rural areas parties at the homes of rural nobility and propertied notables provided venues for courting under the watchful eyes of parents and relatives. Church services and activities also served as places of social and romantic encounters. For the farming communities, evening get-togethers provided sociability to adults of all ages as well as to teenagers with high hormonal levels. Ritualized courtship occurred at these gatherings, and if a couple went off together watchful eyes saw them leave. If the girl were to become pregnant, the community usually knew who the man was and could enforce marriage.

Rural courtship patterns remained when women moved to urban areas as new urban sites replaced the rural village celebrations. Elements of traditional behavior persisted in a modern environment. However, the community was less able to offer sanctions or enforce marriage. Affluent women continued to court and be courted at church and at social events, such as parties, the theater, and the horse races. Toward the end of the nineteenth century, schools and music halls became additional sites for courtship, even more distant from parental and community control. For many of these women, love and emotion competed with family interests, but a marital engagement had a high value as a contract not only between the couple, but also between families. For those who had to work, the workplace was a venue to meet others, as were the market, public street fairs and public balls.

All these modern places of encounter could encourage scenes of seduction, which were not necessarily followed by acts of marriage. The issue of seduction is a thorny one. Writers during the nineteenth century often blamed working-class young women for seducing middle-class men with the hopes of marriage above their station. Furthermore, they blamed the women, who were supposedly the guardians of morality, for failing to exercise self-control and to control men's passions. Nevertheless, at the same time that writers blamed women for encouraging seduction, they maintained that it was natural for men to seduce women and it was up to women to resist. Men wrote about women's "seductive charms," but men could seduce and get away with it. Furthermore, the lines between seduction and rape were legally blurry. Laws generally did not find rape a crime unless it were accompanied by kidnapping or the girl was under age.

The definition, boundaries, meaning of rape, and sensitivities toward it, varied over the centuries, depending on the age and vulnerability of the victim, the number of attackers, the degree of violence, and the social status of both the victim and the attacker. Showing greater suspicion of the women victims of rape than any understanding of them, judges assumed that women were inferior and weak-willed and that they voluntarily consented, unless there was visible evidence of bodily violence, such as knife cuts, witnesses to the woman's screams, or evidence that many men attacked her. Not surprisingly, women were reluctant to speak out.

Throughout the nineteenth century, tolerance of all forms of violent crimes, including rape, decreased, and societies abhorred sexual crimes against children more than against adult women. After mid-century new words and concepts accompanied the decreasing tolerance of violence, with "attempted rape," "indecent assault," "offenses against decency," and "moral violence" entering the vocabulary and jurisprudence, especially as pertaining to attacks on children. Nevertheless, doubts about the morality of the victim persisted, and doctors entered the scene to cast their opinion on the degrees of physical violence, the evidence for the women's acquiescence, and whether the accused rapist was an upstanding community member or a degenerate on the margins of society. When a woman was seduced, even violently, usually the man did not suffer the consequences, unless there were a broken marriage promise, the engagement had been made public, and the woman's family had lost honor and money in the marriage preparations.

Although the Madonna with child was held up as the feminine ideal, and women of all ages and sexual inclinations could have been objects of seduction or rape, other forms of female sexuality existed, namely same-sex relationships. Historians know even less about sexual relationships between women than they do about those between men and women. Yet we know that they existed. Contemporary novels and pornographic tracts included women who had sex with other women, and doctors and moralists worried about sexual relationships that could be forged among women placed in close proximity, such as prisons and boarding schools. Among the women who worked as domestic servants, seamstresses, and day laborers, sharing rooms and beds in garret housing in efforts to make do on their meager earnings, same-sex cultures emerged that could provide the basis for sexual relationships. In all-female boarding schools, women developed crushes on each other and on their teachers. One doctor wanted girls taken out of boarding schools at puberty since boarding schools "tear the veil of modesty, and destroy, for ever, the seductive innocence which is the most charming ornament of a young girl."[10] Lifelong friendships between women and homoerotic letter writing form part of our knowledge about women's often intense relationships with one another. They exchanged passionate letters, sharing emotions and love, mentioning erotic and tender moments and hopes for sharing a bed. Many eventually married men, while others lived their entire adult lives with a female friend.

Same-sex relationships came more prominently into the public discourse at the end of the nineteenth century with the emergence of the sexologists, notably Richard von Krafft-Ebing and Havelock Ellis, whose manuals established sexual taxonomies and labels. Homosexuality and heterosexuality are relatively modern social constructs. Prior to the nineteenth century, people did not classify themselves as either one or the other; furthermore, some loved both men and women and experienced fluidity in their sexual lives. In part, owing to the categorization of sexualities in the manuals, "normal" became defined as "heterosexual" in middle-class culture at the end of the nineteenth century. Krafft-Ebing labeled degrees of "homosexual deviance" according to standards of appearance and social behavior, ranging from women with a conventionally feminine appearance who had a sexual preference for other women who behaved like men, to women with a preference for men's clothes and behavior, to women who assumed a masculine role and appearance. Ellis associated lesbianism with modernity, declaring these women to be liberated, and sexually active but also "perverted" and "degenerate." He divided lesbians into two groups, those who were "inverts" or essentially lesbian and those who were potential lesbians, according to their situation.

The sexologists' labeling coincided with the emergence of the modern New Woman at the turn of the twentieth century. The New Woman was a term used to refer to women who postponed or rejected marriage in favor of pursuing an education and/or a career. If such women did marry and have children, staying home, as a submissive angel in the house, was not an option they chose. Rather, they entered the public arena as writers, students, actors, philanthropists, teachers, or political and social activists. They sometimes cut their hair short, wore pants, and smoked. These behaviors were gendered male, and led sexologists to label the New Woman as "unnatural." Physicians and sexologists classified these women as "lesbian misfits" and vilified them. Sexologists and other writers linked lesbianism with the New Woman and saw both as a negative sign of fin-de-siècle modernity. For women, sexuality became intertwined with their drive for equal wages or civil rights as well as their love for another woman. Although most sexologists adopted a negative view of same-sex relationships, the labels they provided allowed women a means of understanding themselves as different from mainstream society and led to the creation of communities based on sexual preference.

At the turn of the twentieth century, many sexologists and their contemporaries believed that same-sex relationships disrupted the natural order. The two-sex model of sexuality had become so dominant that it did not allow for other alternatives. There was no concept of psychosexual identity. In the first decade of the twentieth century homophobia became part of the backlash against modernity and became linked with the anti-Semitism and antifeminism in France, Germany, and elsewhere.

Society's attempts to control women's sexuality were not limited to supporting marital sex for reproduction, or labeling nonreproducing or lesbian women as deviant. Nymphomania entered the literature even in the early decades of the nineteenth century as a socially constructed criminal category of so-called deviant women, sometimes labeled as insane, who overtly enjoyed sex and failed to exercise the self-control that others asked of them. This term could apply to the women who committed adultery, to lesbians, to prostitutes, and to working-class women. In one of the many contradictions of the nineteenth century, Victorian writers envisioned women as sexually passive (especially in Great Britain) but always saw the danger that an aberrant few would be "hypersexual" – their passions uncontrolled either by the women themselves or, more significantly, by men in power. Moreover, constructing colonial and poor women as over-sexualized enabled middle-class white men to consider those women sexually available. Many men considered both the colonies and working-class neighborhoods zones of sexual "freedom," where the constraints of middle-class morality did not apply.

Victorian constructions of sexuality, fond of dichotomies such as the heterosexual and the homosexual, and the Madonna versus the whore, sought to control or regulate the lives of prostitutes. In some instances, writers linked prostitutes with lesbians and with working-class women as nymphomaniacs. Other novelists, such as Emile Zola (1840–1902), depicted prostitutes as forming lesbian relationships partially as an alternative to their brutalization by men; yet he also envisioned lesbianism among prostitutes as a form of depravity. No writers condoned either prostitution or lesbianism, but rather tried to establish sexual repression and purity codes as a distinguishing mark of a superior, white, middle-class, civilization, particularly aiming to repress the "primitive," unbridled, sexuality of working-class women and women in the colonies.

Social purity movements sought to further distance the white middle classes from others, and minimalize the risk of contagion, both of disease and of immorality. These movements focused on cleaning up and regulating prostitution and working-class women's sexual activities as a means of protecting middle-class men and their wives from disease. The most well known of these movements was associated with the Contagious Diseases Acts (1864, 1866, and 1869), which the British government enacted to regulate prostitutes in an attempt to control the spread of syphilis not only to the middle classes but to British sailors (see Chapter 4). The women's movement succeeded in getting these laws repealed in 1886. European governments generally did not make prostitution illegal; rather they considered it a necessary evil. In France, prostitution had been subject to regulation since the beginning of the century and in Germany it had been regulated since unification in 1871. Prostitution was a crime in Russia between 1845 and 1866.

By 1914, throughout Europe, in a merging of the public rhetoric and women's private lives, sexuality and childbirth dominated the political–medical discourse on women's lives as well as their lived experiences. The history is complex and replete with paradoxes and contradictions, as traditional customs adapted to modern attitudes and practices, not without a lot of tension. Historians, however, know more about what middle-class men wrote about women's reproduction and sexuality than about the women's lived experiences. It is almost a cliché to argue that in their lived experiences women did not always follow the prescriptions, and women sought ways out of the roles designed for them. Nineteenth-century writers and the political community wanted sexuality and reproduction to occur only within a family, but as this chapter has demonstrated, individuals engaged in sexuality and reproduction outside the family as well. Moreover, as Chapter 3 shows, families had many different forms and functions throughout the nineteenth century.

3
Family Life

At the beginning of the twenty-first century, social commentators lament the breakdown of the family. Focusing on modern single-mother and lesbian or gay families, they bemoan the end of the traditional family, usually idealized as the married, nuclear, heterosexual, coresidential, two-parent family. Historical research, however, reveals that throughout the nineteenth century a variety of family forms existed, ranging from single-parent families, to same-sex families, to mixed gender and same gender communities that functioned as families, to extended households of related and unrelated coresidents, to kinship groups either living together or not, to the legally married two-parent nuclear family with or without children. Because of the high death rates, single-parent families and blended families were quite common in the nineteenth century. A family could consist of kin who may or may not have been coresident and it could also be a household unit consisting of members who may have been unrelated by marriage or blood. A family was not just the heterosexual, married, two-parent, nuclear family living together, although nineteenth century writers defined the family as the conjugal unit. Families were historical constructions. Throughout the nineteenth century, family formations and definitions were fluid and over-lapping, depending on time and circumstances, including kin, coresidency, and nonconjugal relationships. The private realm of the family was complex and increasingly more public.

Political philosophers asserted that the legally married two-parent family was the basic building block of nineteenth-century society, and enjoined all to follow that model which they valued so highly. Although an epistemological model animated the discussion, there was a difference between the hegemonic discourse and how women led their lives. What an elite prescribed is not a good indicator of the variety of women's familial experiences; different types of families and familial arrangements coexisted. This chapter, therefore, does not discuss one model family, but rather different families and familial arrangements, including people who slept together, ate together, shared activities, formed communities, or were related to each other by blood or marriage. Families were emotional and cultural units, as well as reproductive or economic units.

Most historians of the family confine their studies to the conjugal coresidential family, and have engaged in a debate on the changes from the traditional extended family to the modern nuclear one, in terms of family size and culture during the early nineteenth century. Some scholars, such as Philippe Ariès, maintain that industrialization and capitalism, requiring small, well-disciplined nuclear families, provided the impetus for a transition in family structure and function from large kinship groups to the nuclear family in the early nineteenth century. Peter Laslett was among the first to put to rest this long-standing myth that preindustrial families consisted of large extended households with multiple functions and that nineteenth-century industrialization and individualism ushered in the dominant nuclear family, leading to the disappearance of the extended kin families of preindustrial times. No widespread demographic evidence indicates that industrialization and modernization transformed the family from large kinship groups of siblings, nieces, nephews, parents, grandparents, and in-laws, to small nuclear families of only parents and children, even in England where industrialization was earlier and more developed than elsewhere. Isolated nuclear families and extended households or kinship groups existed in both traditional and modern European societies. The average household size remained fairly constant, generally consisting of two generations: parents and children. Less frequently, and depending on region, stem families, or three-generational families including a grandparent, were the norm. Blended families created by remarriage also formed part of nineteenth-century family history. Local cultural and economic patterns loomed more important than structuralist models in defining a family, as people negotiated everyday practices in a web of emotion, duty, and reciprocity. In general, Laslett and others positioned Northern and Western Europe as the domain of nuclear families with Eastern and Central Europe dominated by extended or stem families.

Recent research, however, even indicates that the frequency of extended families increased during the nineteenth century, reaching as many as 20 percent of all households in some areas, including those of Northern and Western Europe, and especially in Central and Southern Europe, such as in Italy. Extended families served a variety of purposes, depending on income, culture, place, and needs of the members. One historical interpretation maintains that industrial working conditions and the urban poverty of the nineteenth century created hardships for families, and coresidence of kin was an expedient adaptation to hard times. With extended kinship families, relatives could supply childcare in exchange for housing; some members of the extended family could be employed while others were temporarily laid off, thus enabling the family economy to survive. This was part of the economics of scale that pervaded the nineteenth century. Other historians argue that rising living standards with an increasing life expectancy and a falling age of marriage led to more extended families. They linked extended families less to economic hardship than to the opposite, economic well-being. Furthermore, various kin continued to supply networks of support, or conflict, either as coresident or in the immediate neighborhood.

The debate on families, however, was more than just about the demise of extended families in favor of nuclear families. Historians and anthropologists continue to debate whether families based on emotional ties replaced those based on material interests, with many arguing that families of the past differed little from those of today or from the nineteenth century. They dispute the notion that material concerns connected preindustrial families whereas emotions bound the nineteenth-century family. They postulate that sentiment was always a factor of family life, despite hardships, numbers of children, and household size. As institutions, families preserved property and lineage and served as emotional and cultural units. Sometimes one or the other aspect of family relationships dominated. Preindustrial families, nineteenth-century families, and modern families all existed within the context of property, rights, duties, obligations, and emotions. Families also existed as a part of kinship groups, larger households, and communities.

Households, usually considered as those living under one roof, are not always identical to families, although there is considerable overlap. A household could have one nuclear family, but also a variety of sisters, cousins, and aunts, who would be part of a related family. Many households also contained domestic servants and lodgers, unrelated by blood or marriage. Although some households may have regarded their servants as "part of the family," historical demographers do not usually consider them as family members, but rather as members of a household. Throughout the centuries, households and families served a multiplicity of functions, from domestic activities, to communal agricultural endeavors, to production in the cottage industries, to places of religious worship, to communities of shared intellectual or political endeavors, to education. Households also served a civic duty as welfare institutions, by taking in needy kin and women in distress as well as by providing lodging and food for the frail and infirm. Privacy was generally lacking in these households of business, welfare, and sociability. The cultural demography of the time and place usually determined the family and household composition, size, and function.

The household continued to serve as the site of production and reproduction, for all social and economic classes, but especially among the rural populations. Family members worked together on related tasks, with little separation of domestic life and work life, virtually from sun up to sun down. For the urban middle classes, however, starting around the mid-nineteenth century, the workplace separated from the household, leaving the home a site of leisure and sociability and sometimes a retreat from manufacturing and the marketplace. Nevertheless, such middle-class nuclear family households usually contained servants. Other households continued to contain boarders, lodgers, and places for the elderly.

The nineteenth-century literary, reformist, and political narratives prescribed an idealized married, heterosexual family with children and a dominant paterfamilias. Indeed, in the vast majority of nineteenth-century families men and women shared power unequally. As industrialization developed, after about the 1830s, especially in the north and west of Europe the gender division of labor provided men with more highly remunerative jobs, and sometimes jobs with greater status. In some areas, such as England, families were based on the concept of the male breadwinner with a dependent wife, thus diminishing women's status and income. French families, however, based less on the male breadwinner model, recognized women's work for wages. Whether working for wages or not, women bore responsibility for childrearing and their family's well being, both biologically and socially. These beliefs about gender roles in the family were part of the ideology of domesticity. Domesticity assigned women a subservient role within the family, but also granted them an area of agency. Women decided on the household's purchases and expenditures, and on the education and occupations of their children. They were also in part responsible for the family's status in the community, often relying on kinship networks in making social and economic arrangements. Women managed the family and household, including kinship ties; hence women are essential in understanding the family. Women could negotiate power relationships, but fathers and husbands controlled the resources and had the law behind them to enforce their authority in the family.

The theories of sociologist Pierre Bourdieu may be useful for understanding the nature of families as sites for the transmission of capital, especially social capital, or knowledge about how the world functions and how to get ahead in it. According to this model, people contribute to family resources by their behavior and self-presentation in society, projecting an image that they have a variety of resources above what sheer economics might indicate, enabling the family to present a higher status. Women were central in this endeavor as they managed and distributed the symbolic, social and economic capital of the family. Furthermore, Bourdieu's concept of "practice theory" allows for flexible and reciprocal relationships between the individual and the social, cultural, and political settings in which they negotiate their lives. Practice theory places individuals as strategizing (sometimes not consciously so) and often struggling to find their way within a given situation. In return, the social structures become modified through the individual's behavior. Women negotiated and renegotiated power within the family and in presenting the family to the outside world.

It may also be useful to think of families as having aspects of *Gemeinschaft*, or a community based on emotional bond of mother–child and family. This is the women-centered aspect of the family relations. Families also have aspects of *Gesellschaft*, or a society consisting of a patriarchal social, economic, legal, and linguistic set of family relations in association with public institutions and the state.

Despite the dominance of patriarchal conjugal families in the discourse and in lived experiences during the nineteenth century, evidence of matriarchal families and women-centered kinship structures and households exists.

Women-centered household units

Women who did not marry, either by choice or by circumstance, had several options open to them, some not very desirable. Among the least desirable options for a middle-class woman who did not marry were serving as a governess, living as a maiden aunt and often infantalized in a sibling's household, or taking care of aging parents. For a poor woman the prospects were even more dismal, involving domestic service or perhaps unwed motherhood. Some women, however, usually those who were single by choice, formed women-centered households. Evidence from the Netherlands, France, England, Italy, and Russia indicates that unmarried women set up independent, or female-headed households. Historians have not devoted much attention to female-headed households, and the actual numbers and the nature of them are difficult to determine. Existing data indicate that women of a certain age, mostly over 30 and frequently over 50, headed them and that most included children.

No terminology for same-sex families existed in nineteenth-century official records, which usually defined families as conjugal and implicitly heterosexual.

Moreover, social restrictions in most countries prohibited single middle-class women from living apart from their parents' or siblings' families. If they had a partner and had established close emotional and sexual relations, they could not usually live together as a couple and maintain their respectability. Two women living together risked being stigmatized and harassed as prostitutes or radicals. Moreover, it was expensive for two women to set up an independent household. Women who loved one another often had to keep their emotions for each other in check when among others, and had little opportunity to live together as a couple in a separate household. Yet, when historians alter their angle of vision same-sex families come into view, revealing a few examples of the European equivalents of a Boston marriage; more undoubtedly existed but left no records. Around the end of the eighteenth and into the nineteenth century, two Irish and Anglo middle-class women, known as the Ladies of Llangollen, lived together for more than forty years in an out-of-the-way cottage in Wales. The French artist, Rosa Bonheur (1822–99), lived with her partner very much in the public eye. Some scant historical evidence also indicates that a woman might cross-dress in order to live as a married couple with another woman. More frequently, single women lived in communal households for companionship, support, and also affordability.

Convents could be viewed as the most acceptable and familiar form of women-headed communal households. The historical literature does not usually include them in discussions of families or households, but they often functioned as such. The members had superiors serving in parental roles, and they ate, slept, worked, socialized, and worshiped as a family. Convent families, as other families, came together for both emotional and material interests; the members even squabbled as a family. For Russian women, convent life was the only way to avoid a heterosexual marriage, and peasant women sought to form religious communities that served as families.

Religion allowed women to exercise some control over their lives, although sometimes they exchanged parental authority for that of a Mother Superior and the strict discipline of a convent. In Catholic and Protestant (predominantly Anglican) church communities, women left their biological mothers and sisters for spiritual mothers and sisters, and joined a new family under one roof. Convent life may have been a haven and solace for a single woman, and a place as personally supportive of her as any family could have been, offering her security that she otherwise could not have found. Many women entering the convent family broke ties with their parents; others kept some of those ties while forming a new family, much as a woman did when entering marriage in a patrilocal or patrilineal society. A woman usually chose the life of sisterhood, and to do this she needed an independent spirit, yet that independence could lead her to problems in this family that demanded obedience just as it did in the family she willingly left. The convent community of St. Mary the Virgin, Wantage, was described like a "well ordered family" that " 'has the feeling of being in a family rather than in a community of nuns.' "[1]

Single women, often religiously inspired but not sufficiently so to join a convent, formed other types of collective communities sharing characteristics of families and households. Middle-class women, usually over 30, at an age when their parents might release them from their natal home because they were beyond the marrying age, sought independent home-like living arrangements. Tending to adopt the model of the married families they came from, close female friends lived together and created homes for the needy, usually mothering poor and unfortunate women and children. These communities generally took the form of schools, sisterhoods, settlement houses, or female-headed, woman-centered households that took in needy women as lodgers, boarders, workers, or students. These households resembled traditional families in that they were loci of work and usually involved mothering – although not of their own children, but of poor, orphaned, and neglected young girls. Yet, they were modern in that they embodied women's choice and independence and did not normally include men. Women in collective households often combined a career (usually in education or social work) and family, without having a marriage and a husband. Rather, they developed close friendships, often romantic, with other women. Martha Vicinus has well documented these families in England, quoting an epigraph in the 1875 edition of *The Yearbook of Women's Work*: "We cannot make a home for ourselves, but we can make ourselves a home for others, and then by and by we find that their love has built our loving service into a shelter for ourselves ...[2]

A few radical Russian women formed different kinds of households and families. For example, in mid-nineteenth-century Russia two impoverished noble sisters chose not to marry in order to achieve independence and joined one of the mixed-gender radical movements of the time. Joining their comrades in Moscow, they ran a collective to help seamstresses break from their dependence on male employers. Trying to survive as a unit of production by the sale of the seamstresses' work, but always short of money, the members of the collective lived communally, sleeping and eating together, and supporting members who were temporarily too sick to work. This coresident household had the same attributes as other households, except it consisted of people unrelated by blood or marriage, and was headed by the two sisters who ran it.[3]

Evidence from Northern Italy and France reveals less formal women-centered family communities that included single mothers with small children living and working with other women in similar circumstances. Usually poor, these women found communal life a survival strategy to alleviate solitude and share the financial burden. Because social and economic wage discrimination did not allow single women to live independently, they resorted to forming communal households. In both rural and urban areas, female-headed households with children more commonly existed among the poor than among the middle and upper classes. Female-headed households, however, were more common in urban areas than in rural farming areas, and almost nonexistent in the large areas of Europe where sharecropping dominated. In poor farming and sharecropping areas, a man's labor was essential for the family economy. Female-headed households with children were less a matter of culture, but rather a necessary relationship between the community and individual as a means to scratch out a living.

Throughout the nineteenth century, single mothers formed a large segment of many urban populations, with data indicating that single mothers headed as many as 20 percent of all families with dependent children in England and

France. These same data, however, cannot distinguish single-mother families resulting from widowhood or marital breakdown from those who never married. Nor is it clear if those data include women living in consensual unions. Women were not single mothers by choice; rather, if they were not widows or separated they had often engaged in sexual relations with a man after a promise of marriage; when pregnancy ensued, the man fled. Unable to hold the child's father responsible, even if the women wanted to, for many single mothers their situation was the result of a marriage strategy that failed. During the first half of the century, politicians and reformers castigated single mothers as immoral. Toward the end of the century, however, they came to recognize the mother–child dyad as a family and provided welfare for them. Nevertheless, life was far from easy for the women. Sometimes they were able to make ends meet living with their child. Frequently, however, they needed to send their child to a relative so they could resume work. Sometimes they lived conjugally with the father of the child, or else with another man. In desperation, some just could not make it, and had to abandon their baby, send their child to a poorhouse, or go there themselves with their child.

Little is known about single mothers from the aristocracy or middle classes because of the shame and dishonor of their situation. The letters of a French family of the petty nobility at the end of the century reveal a family searching for ways to protect its reputation and also stand by an unmarried daughter, Marthe, who bore a son. Not abandoning the infant, Marthe paid a wet nurse, or foster parent, to raise the boy. After Marthe married someone other than the father of her child, and then divorced, she retrieved her son, who soon died of dysentery. At that point, Marthe went to live with a female friend in a cottage in the countryside, until she died of a respiratory disease at the age of 30.[4]

During the nineteenth century, legal adoption existed only for purposes of transmitting an inheritance, if the person adopting was too old to have biological children, and if the children were old enough to consent to the adoption. Despite the illegality of infant adoption until the twentieth century, families, and even single women, adopted children, de facto. These adopted children either added another child, usually an orphan of a kin, to those who already had children or they joined childless households creating what the culture referred to as "fictive families." Martha Vicinus describes single women adopting children. One "adopted an illegitimate daughter of one of her brother's junior cavalry officers"; another took a six-year old French girl provided by the Salvation Army. In one scenario a 51-year-old single woman, Mary Carpenter, adopted a child whose mother was still alive. Carpenter wrote: " 'Just think of me with a little girl of *my own*, about five years old! Ready made to hand and nicely trained, without the trouble of marrying, etc. a darling little thing, an orphan. I feel already a *mère de famille*, happy in buying little hats and socks and a little bed to stand in my own room, out of *my own* money. It is a wonderful feeling!' "[5]

More common were informal adoptions that occurred throughout Europe. Sometimes single women, usually widows, accepted as part of their family the illegitimate children of coresident daughters, or of daughters who left home to seek work. Other families "lent" children to relatives to relieve the overcrowding in their own households and to help out widows or other aging relatives. If the children were old enough, they could work for the grandmother or aunt; if not, families (usually single mothers, widowers, or widows) would pay the women a pittance to take in their young babies. Conjugal families and single women with some property were more likely to have these "loaned" children in their households than others. The social welfare function of the family helped children, grandchildren, and siblings who had fallen on hard times by taking in young children, or children old enough to work. This was a form of adoption in countries where adoption was not yet legal. Single women in the cities also temporarily lodged newly arrived kin in search of work. These were not legal families, but temporary family arrangements. Some adoptions were successful; others were dismal failures. Then, as now, it was difficult for single women of a certain age to raise a child alone, or even with a little help from her friends. Conjugal families helped.

Conjugal families

Consensual unions were not usually women-centered households unless they failed and the woman was left alone or with her children. Nor were they the legally married conjugal family that nineteenth-century writers extolled and many women sought. Yet, consensual unions tended to function as conjugal families, and some have referred to them as "common-law marriages."

From the eighteenth to the twenty-first century, the French have recognized what they call *concubinage*. In English that word has a pejorative connotation, but to the French it simply means a man and woman living together in a domestic partnership. Other phrases that best describe this are "cohabitation" or "living in a consensual union," whereby neighbors, friends, and families regarded the partners as a domestic couple. Not unique to France, consensual unions existed in all countries of Europe. These unions were love relationships as well as economic units. During the early nineteenth century, politicians and reformers bemoaned the alleged immorality of a woman living with a man without the so-called benefit of marriage, but gradually came to accept it as a fact of life; by the end of the twentieth century, the French made it a legal family form that applied to both same and different sex partners. For literary women and members of the avant-garde, living in a "free union" with a man made a statement of insouciance about legal marriage, they formed a union based on love as a means of escape from an arranged or loveless marriage in the era before divorce – typically before the 1890s. For women in Russia, living in a "free union" had the added feature of making a political statement against the institution of marriage. Many of the poor, however, lived in consensual unions for reasons of economic expediency and not personal politics. Although historians find evidence that generations of poor English women in consensual unions formed a "subculture of bastard-bearers," this was only the case for some. Among many couples, especially among the poor, cohabitation was a temporary expediency until the couple chose to marry, or could afford to do so.

Although a few women decided that marriage would inhibit their intellectual growth, and many more women who sought to marry did not, nineteenth-century commentators as well as contemporary historians concur that most women viewed marriage as their goal; it was the foundation of women's lives, and those who did not marry were marginal to normative society. The conjugal family was a public institution based on private lives.

Reverence for the married family with children pervaded nineteenth-century thought on the family. The revered bourgeois vision of an ideal family included a paterfamilias who expected to receive obedience from his wife and children. Victorian gentlewomen had to conform, at least outwardly, to expected behavior of docility, gentility, and motherliness. This ideal conjugal family formed the bedrock of the nineteenth-century social order, which extolled traditional family values in the face of modernity. Toward the end of the nineteenth century, the traditional ideals of patriarchy relented, or became more modern, to allow some equality for men and women, although that was often an equality based on differences.

Increasingly, love matches marked modern marriages, although throughout the nineteenth century, some parents continued to arrange marriages between their children. Couples had ample opportunity to meet each other in school, the workplace, and at social events that became commonplace toward the end of the century. Women had some autonomy in choosing a husband. Men and women tended to find each other based on mutual affection, but then they usually needed parental approval. Sometimes obtaining parental approval became difficult, as families sought to maintain or improve their socioeconomic status and feared a mésalliance. Families established economic requirements for prospective marriage partners, such as a dowry, land, or an occupationally generated income. Social, geographical, occupational, and status endogamy prevailed over much of Europe, with some differences in regional marriage patterns, which tended to relate to occupation and patterns of land holding. Kinship groups and community alliance networks often enabled people to marry and set up independent households. Their expected generosity helped people start new lives and the large weddings were community affairs, especially in rural areas. During the times of depression, however, tighter economies promoted smaller, more private weddings.

Within the family, the distribution of household resources varied by sex. After industrialization, men contributed cash to the household budget, but women managed the economic and symbolic capital, the household resources. They decided on the household purchases such as food, clothing, and other consumer goods. Moreover, the woman projected the family's image to the community by her dress, her social engagements, and the style of her home, and therefore managed the family's status. Families struck a balance in the contributions and interests of individual members and the family's interests and needs as a unit. However, there was unequal distribution of power in the gender division of labor and status of men and women within the family, as familial relationships reflected the asymmetry in the market. When a husband's income and occupational status was greater than his wife's, he had a more controlling voice in family matters.

The form and function of conjugal families continued during the century, with one major change. During the nineteenth century, mostly in Western Europe, work increasingly took place outside the home, resulting in a separation of home from workplace among families from most socioeconomic groups, especially after mid-century in the northern and western portions. As a result, middle-class families became idealized as a "haven in a heartless world" where the wife was to create an environment of calm and repose. She established family rituals to complement changes in the economy, setting a time for school, a time for visiting, and time for family togetherness. These nuclear families became based more on reproduction than production as they had been earlier in the century, or in the eighteenth century.

Having and rearing children has been the universal role of women in conjugal families, sometimes by choice, but until the twentieth century more often by default. Society had long glorified motherhood among the married and toward the end of the century many politicians and writers regarded women as reproductive machines or walking wombs. Childbirth conferred status and was also considered a woman's labor and duty. Giving birth was a family ritual, a rite of passage. Until end of the nineteenth century, a woman generally gave birth at home, surrounded by family and friends – to assist, support, and gossip – whether the mother wanted them there or not. Some of the more affluent enlisted the aid of a physician, but the greatest number used a midwife, sometimes one trained in a school for midwives but frequently a woman who learned her trade from others in the profession. After mid-century, childbirth gradually went from the hands of midwives to the hands of doctors, who had new drugs (such as chloroform) and instruments for delivery (such as forceps). Doctors had professionalized and sought to undermine the power of midwives. They fostered laws prohibiting midwives from using drugs or instruments, with the result that women who could afford to pay a doctor came to prefer the painless childbirth those men provided.

The poor, unable to afford midwives, or without a room of their own in which to have a baby, went to the public hospitals to deliver their babies. Esther Waters, the eponymous heroine of George Moore's 1894 novel, gave birth to an illegitimate child in a public hospital surrounded by women wailing in labor and a cast of insensitive nurses and doctors, very much similar to the historical situation for the poor and pregnant in Paris as found in the records of non-fictional women in the Paris maternity hospital. Because of the dangerous and morbid conditions in the public hospitals until the 1880s, women preferred giving birth with a midwife, if they possibly could.

Regardless of social or economic level, women bore primary responsibility for the material and moral well-being of their families. For the middle classes, this may have meant children, church, and kitchen, giving rise to a domestic ideology, perhaps best exemplified by the ideal Victorian family. In Austria, the name *Biedermeier* referred to a domestic interior prior to 1848 that provided a safe haven from the world; the French denoted the *foyer*, or hearth, as the warm center of family life. The domestic ideology discursively barred women from political, economic, or social power outside the family. Yet women embraced the domestic conjugal life, which caused them much work in managing the servants, fashioning the household, educating the children, and engaging in a flurry of activity – sometimes sewing, cooking, cleaning, caring for linen, polishing the silver, arranging flowers, and rearranging drapery and furniture to correspond to seasons. Ironically this very domesticity led to paths out of the home into charity and teaching. The growth in nationalism and the ideology of pronatalism at the end of the nineteenth century further valued motherhood. Working women, however, could not stay at home and tend to their husband's and children's well-being. Rather, they had to balance their productive and repro-ductive lives – either going out of the house to work, or else bringing piecework into their house. The family home was not necessarily a special retreat for men and women, and it was not a "home sweet home" for everyone. Although in the arena of domesticity women had a degree of power, the family was also a site of conflict and power struggles as men and women renegotiated mutual obligations as their situation necessitated.

Under the laws of each nation, and according to the notion of coverture in England, a married woman held few of the rights of a single woman. She had no rights to property and her legal identity became that of her husband's. The Married Women's Property Acts of 1870 and 1882 in England enhanced the equality of women within the family by recognizing that the husband no longer controlled his wife's person or property. However, the Acts did not give wives equality with their husbands, nor did married women have the personal legal rights of a single woman. Similarly, married women in France did not have equality with their husbands. Article 213 of the Civil Code said, "The husband owes protection to his wife; the wife owes obedience to her husband." Moreover, husbands had legal control of family property and the children. In the German lands, both the Prussian *Allgemeines Landrecht* and the Bavarian Code denied a married woman legal capacity and allowed a husband to admin-ister corporal punishment to his wife. In unified Germany, the husband retained legal control over his wife's property, unless she acquired the property by her own work. In German as in French law, he also determined where they lived and she took his name. In some instances, however, although the Civil Code granted the husband control over property, the Code allowed some local options in working out the specific details.

Undoubtedly, many women married and subscribed to the prevalent domes-tic ideology if for no other reason than it gave them some power within the home and a sense of belonging. Furthermore, given the middle-class culture of the time, it was practically the only avenue for social recognition; society expected marriage and motherhood for all women, and granted middle-class women precious few acceptable places outside of marriage.

Women also married for financial security since marriage created a functional economic unit. It was in women's material interests to marry someone with earning power or property, who did not squander his resources on drink or gambling. The middle and upper classes sought to maintain inheritance and pat-rimony through marriage and children. Poor women sought marriage and fam-ily life for solvency and for their economic survival. Paid less than men, they could ill afford not to marry. For the peasantry, marriage meant survival, and the best marriages consisted of unions not only of two individuals and two fam-ilies, but two contiguous parcels of land.

Women also married for love as companionate marriages increased during the century. Historical evidence is sketchy on whether the man's work outside the home led to less companionship between spouses and more camaraderie outside the nuclear family, or if work outside the home among the middle classes led to more quality time between spouses and within the family. Men went to their cafés, clubs, and pubs, often leaving wives to form their own friendship circles.

Marriage also provided opportunities for women to have new experiences, and to carve out areas of activity for themselves abroad. Wives of missionaries who otherwise could not travel went to other parts of the world, such as Africa and Asia. Wives of colonial administrators usually followed their husbands. Although some marriages tried to keep women in the home and garden, other marriages allowed women to go out in the world.

On the family's periphery

Most women preferred marriage to the alternative of remaining single. Most single middle-class women who did not form families of their own lived on the periphery of married families and of social acceptance. Referred to as "spinsters," because spinning had been the task of single women, or "maiden aunts" because they often lived in their siblings' families, they were marginal and powerless, lacking access to resources; theirs was a lifetime of service to others. Nineteenth-century commentaries referred to them as "redundant women" since the discursively prescribed place for women was with a husband and family. During the eighteenth century, and before the mid-nineteenth century, some single women could have had roles as shopkeepers, as small business owners and managers, and as independent workers. Although some women continued these economically independent occupations, the nineteenth-century social economies of family and domesticity pushed many of them to the margins of families. There they served as governesses, nannies, companions, or seamstresses, redundant in the families of their siblings or other middle-class homes. Some were doting aunts, while others were disdained and disdainful. They had to maintain their middle-class gentility while serving others. Some families treated them as servants or children, forcing them to join the young children at the dinner table rather than allowing them to eat with adult family members. Many of the single women were the caretakers of their parents. These were the true "angels in the house." But, when parents died, these single women could be destitute if the property were left to the sons. Many preferred marriage and their own household, no matter how patriarchal, to their infantalized status between adult and servant. Others, however, sought opportunities outside of the traditional family. Especially after mid-century, new educational and career opportunities allowed single women to lead meaningful and fulfilling lives.

Like her more wealthy counterparts, the poor single woman also bore responsibility for her aged parents, or worked as a servant for her siblings. More typically, however, poor single women found places as domestic servants living with neighbors and friends, on the periphery of other families. When they moved to cities they found employment in the families of strangers. The web of household domestic relationships included servants who helped with basic childcare as well as kept the fires burning, the stove heated, the marketing done, and the linen clean. Some of these servants had left their own families when these families could not support them and they were only 12 or 14 years old.

Domestic service provided young women with another family to enter – one that could keep an eye on them or exploit and abuse them. Young sons in the household could take sexual advantage of the servants; the families would ignore the woman's protests, and when she became pregnant typically turned her out. Most servants eagerly sought marriage for both material and emotional reasons.

Having at least one servant marked middle-class or elite status in most regions of nineteenth-century Europe. In England, having three or more servants marked a family's higher status. The less well-off families could afford only one servant who filled several jobs; she would be a maid of all work who also helped take care of the children. Widows or women of a certain age who never married also worked as servants. Servants relieved a middle-class woman of some of the more unpleasant domestic tasks she preferred not to perform, providing her with status and gentility in her household; but servants also created tensions and a loss of privacy. Middle-class households were not always the tranquil area of isolated privacy that the ideology of domesticity made them out to be.

Widows and elderly women depended on the property, pensions, or benevolence of others, sometimes also living on the periphery of families. Historical literature has tended to neglect elderly women, both in terms of how others perceived them as well as in terms of their own experiences. Since being and feeling old does not occur at a fixed age in a woman's life, the elderly are not a clearly defined group. For working women, the end of gainful employment marked old age in their life course, a stage of increased poverty and dependency. This could occur at the age of 50. Images of widows and elderly women fall into stereotypical groups: Some were wise grandmothers helping their daughters and obtaining joy from their grandchildren; others were shrews or shrewd; many were objects of compassion and respect; yet others were ridiculed as toothless, decrepit, limping old hags, having outlived their husbands and their usefulness to their children. Women sandwiched between taking care of dependent children and dependent parents could be found in the nineteenth century as well as in later times.

Married women in the upper and middle classes typically did not work for wages outside their home or their family business and faced a loss of income when their husbands died, especially if their husbands left them without a pension or savings. A widow depended on property from her husband's estate, which the marriage contract sometimes stipulated, in return for her dowry. A woman could become wealthy from her deceased husband's property and might have good prospects for remarriage. However, she might have preferred widowhood where she would keep both her husband's property and her independence. Her kin network, including her children, and the community exerted pressure against her remarriage in order to keep the property within the family. Widows were far less likely to marry than widowers – possibly out of personal preference, possibly out of family and community pressure, and possibly because if they were poor and old they would not be a desirable marriage partner for a family based more on material than emotional interests. In the absence of a sizeable estate from her deceased husband, a widow may have had to confront the need to work for wages, which meant a loss of status.

A working woman faced dire straights if her husband died. Usually he was the chief breadwinner and her salary had not been nearly equal to his. As a widow with young children, she could barely make ends meet. She needed help and turned first to her family. If her kin could not or would not help, for reasons of their own poverty or life-course crisis, a widow with young children became the most deserving of the poor, and might receive a pittance from charity or welfare. If she had adult children, her condition marginally improved. Daughters might include their widowed mothers in their families if their mothers were young enough to work, or if they could care for children. If the daughter worked and had children under age ten, the household was more likely to have a coresiding grandmother. An elderly widow could also care for a neighbor's children, in a system where individuals and the community interacted to mutual satisfaction. No matter what the social class, a widow's life with her daughter could be one of dependency and strife. Widows without families or on the periphery of families depended on others for lodging and sustenance; they filled the almshouses. Most of those seeking admission to poorhouses in England and almshouses in the Netherlands and elsewhere were elderly women.

Family breakdown

Until divorce became legal toward the end of the century in some parts of Europe, when family relations broke down a legal separation could result. The usual grounds for separation involved a woman's adultery or the continual beatings her husband brought down upon her. Separation existed in England, France, Italy, and Germany. The Russian Orthodox Church, however, did not permit separation, even in cases in which the husband beat his wife. If she fled, she could be found and returned home, where she might likely receive further beatings for running away. The powerful Russian Orthodox Church, continuing to hold marriage as a religious sacrament, opposed its dissolution. Nevertheless, the Church unwillingly granted a few divorces, averaging only 58 per year in the entire Russian Empire around mid-century. This is the rough equivalent of 8.6 divorces per 10,000 marriages. The predominant causes were desertion or exile to Siberia. Annulment was possible, although extremely rare, averaging 33 cases per year; most of these were for bigamy.

The drive to permit divorce throughout the nineteenth century and the creation of new laws permitting it during the second half of the century reveal that the celebrated middle-class home could also be a prison or madhouse. Divorce proceedings illuminate the underside of family life and the speciousness of the domestic ideology. Discussions surrounding divorce mention wives' "insubordination," which included "refusal to perform the conjugal duty." In England, the Matrimonial Causes Act of 1857, generally known as the Divorce Act, enabled a husband to sue for divorce on the grounds of adultery while the wife had to prove desertion, cruelty, incest, rape, sodomy, or bestiality. Prior to this Act, a person could divorce only through an act of Parliament; the 1857 Act made it a judicial procedure. This Act did not result in a flood of divorces as its critics predicted, in part because the procedure was difficult, the cost high, and the grounds limited. By the end of the century, the grounds for divorce had been extended and the cost and process reduced. In 1884 divorce again became legal in France (it was legal from 1792 to 1815, although it became more restrictive during those years). Women as well as men could obtain a divorce on the grounds of adultery, violence, cruelty, criminal conviction, and "serious insult." French couples responded by filing for divorce in relatively large numbers, at least compared with the English. The 1884 French divorce bill took years to pass because those opposed to it, as in England, believed that divorce would sanction sin and adultery, signifying the end of the "traditional" (i.e. conjugal) family. Unified Germany adopted much of the Prussian Code of 1784 that permitted divorce on 11 grounds, but instituted some restrictions and reduced the grounds to a few, including adultery, criminal conduct, violence, desertion, failure to fulfill marital duties, immoral conduct, or mental disease. Because of the strength of the Catholic Church, in Italy women could not divorce.

Advocates of divorce argued that it enabled people in a bad marriage to find new partners and have more babies in order to increase national population and strength. In part, states permitted divorce as a means of establishing secular control over marriage and its dissolution, taking it away from the church. It also contributed to the increasing role of the state in family life.

A woman who decided to walk out of a bad marriage had few options. The possibility of refuge in a convent existed for some women. Those less religiously inclined might find a family to take them in, or they could live with their lover, or they could emigrate, or they could try to make it on their own as writers or artists, or in a menial occupation.

Regional differences

The cultural demography of the time and place influenced the family form and function, and women's role within it. As industrialization spread from west to east and from north to south, women and families changed along with the pace of capitalism and industrial development. Broadly generalized, in rural areas where the household was a unit of production, families and households had a propensity to be complex and extended. In urban areas, nuclear households tended to dominate (although many had servants) and were less complex than rural ones. Part of the reason for the difference was economic and part was cultural. Yet local economic forces and the needs of the family economy directly influenced the types of family formations, with great regional variations even within one country. Households and families adapted to circumstances, as nuclear families coexisted with complex and extended families.

England experienced early and rapid industrialization, beginning in the eighteenth century, with initial textile production encouraging single women to live with their parents. In textile cities most women lived in nuclear families that might have also included kin, as economic circumstances changed. Although industry and factory work drew women away from their rural families, the largest percentage of these women lived as domestic servants. A typical family might include changes from nuclear to complex and back to nuclear, depending on the woman's life stages. For example, in mid-century Britain, almost one-fifth of all households included kin beyond the nuclear family. A couple would marry and form a nuclear family, perhaps living with the husband's family until the birth of the first child. Then, they likely went off to live on their own, where they might have several children. Eventually the older children would go off to form new families, with the daughters usually joining their husband's family, as their mother had done. At that time an elderly grandparent (usually the grandmother) would move in, often to look after the young children, especially if the mother had died. Then, changing circumstances might cause one of the children who had moved out of the parental home to return and perhaps take care of an aged parent. Since many families, and the law, were patriarchal, this meant that women followed their husbands to and from their husband's families. Patrilocality (by which a woman lived with her husband's family and he remained with his own father) predominated in Russia.

The separation of home from workplace, the most distinguishing feature of nineteenth-century family life, appeared early in the century in England, and by mid-century in France, Germany, Sweden, and elsewhere. This separation accompanied growing acceptance – at least on a discursive level – of the confinement of middle-class women to the private sphere of home and garden. Many women actually lived the approved family life, but women's lived experiences could deviate from the prescriptions. And, "home sweet home" meant little to working women who continued to strain their eyes doing piecework in candle-lit areas of their tiny rooms.

The economy of France maintained the family enterprise and family economy longer than in England. Napoleon may have said that England was a nation of shopkeepers, but throughout the nineteenth century that sobriquet seemed better to define France. Women in rural France lived in a variety of different types of households and families, ranging from the three-generational stem family around the Pyrenees, to large sharecropping extended families, to complex households with extended kin, to small nuclear family huts. Urban areas contained single-mother families and nuclear families with servants more often than the rural areas. The persistence of cottage crafts and family enterprises in France kept women working and families together; nonetheless it made infant care harder, sometimes necessitating sending babies to wet nurses.

In Germany changes came after unification in 1871 and the rapid industrialization that followed. As in England and France, stem families, nuclear families, and complex extended families all marked the nineteenth century; their frequency depended on the economy of the specific region.

Italy remained mostly rural well into the nineteenth century and women in these areas were part of patriarchal sharecropping families or part of agricultural wage laborers (*braccianti*). The sharecropping families remained male dominated, consisting of the father, his wife, their sons, and their wives. The households grew, divided, or recombined according to the size and number of kin coresidents. Large households customarily resulted in larger amounts of land to farm, thus sharecropping households had an incentive to include many children and relatives. In the same areas, the *braccianti* lived in nuclear housing, although the latter often consisted of ramshackle huts. Female households formed to share resources can be found among the *braccianti* of some areas.

In Spain, as elsewhere, family forms varied by region. Largely agricultural during the nineteenth century, the population included day laborers who usually had their own small family households and sharecroppers who lived in complex large family households. In a manner similar to other areas, new husbands might bring their brides into their own family households. Women followed their husbands in Spain, as in Italy, France, and other countries.

Eastern Europe and Russia present an entirely different picture, with agriculture predominating until well into the twentieth century. The Russian household, or the *dvor*, which included multiple buildings occupied by kin, most aptly illustrates the household as a residential unit combining both production and also family functions. Few of these households contained nonfamily members, although some comprised three generations and many siblings. Historians have discussed the *zadruga* as emblematic of complex households in the south Balkans. This somewhat corporate formalized, fortified, household structure along the Croatian military border is of less importance for understanding women and the family than the familial kinship *zadruga* found in the Southern Balkan areas of Serbia, Montenegro, Herzegovina, and parts of Bosnia. Rarely did non-kin live in the Southern Balkan *zadrugas*. Based on patrilocality and domestic groups around a core of males, it was an age-old structure still existing, although decaying, in the late nineteenth century. It varied in composition and size, with great fluidity in its structure, never static, but in a process of formation and deconstruction as people were born, married, or died. A *zadruga* usually involved two generations, consisting of two or three brothers and their families, or three generations comprising a father and his sons and their families, falling within the range of 9–15 people, with great variation according to the specific area of the south Balkans and the changing ecological conditions – increasing or decreasing in size and composition as economics and birth rates warranted. Even in the Balkans, however, the small household of a nuclear family existed in the same areas as *zadrugas*. Other parts of the Balkans had long houses and women's spaces where women related by marriage to brothers would prepare meals and where single women might sleep.

In conclusion, when examining the form and function of family life for women, it appears that "the more things change the more they stay the same." In Europe and the United States at the beginning of the twenty-first century, families of all types and shapes exist – from conjugal families, to same-sex families, to blended families, to families of mother and children, to communal households economically and culturally functioning as families, just as they did in the nineteenth century. Yet the discursive family model of the idealized conjugal nuclear family has persisted, in part because people think of families as including children, and providing for children has been one of the functions of both families and societies. Moreover, the Western European state constructed on the family model with a patriarch at the head of state and power flowing both horizontally and vertically along family, or family-like, lines, helped shaped ideas about the family. The conjugal family, and its reflection in the state, has been a model that assures power and property to a male head. Throughout, the state made family issues one of its major concerns, thus the public sphere infiltrated realms of the private family.

In the nineteenth century, the conjugal family model served as a bulwark of emotional security against the enormous social and economic changes of the time. Moreover, the nineteenth-century narrative built on a family model that had existed in the literature for centuries. The conjugal family, although not always a nuclear family, had long been the only discursive family type in Western Europe. In a large part that model resulted from the important issue of the transmission of property and inheritance, and also from the need to combine resources for raising children in eras before family planning and when women could expect sexual activity to result in children that they would bear and raise. When historians look behind the rhetoric, however, a variety of families become apparent during the nineteenth century. Family formation and behavior did not always pay attention to the instructions and the rules. Women established their own cultural norms, sometimes obeying the discursive prescriptions, and sometimes choosing to manipulate or violate them. The great changes in women's lives during the nineteenth century – their work, their education, the decline in the death rates and rise (and fall) in birth rates, the growth of cities, as well as changes in politics and culture – all had a bearing on women's families and living arrangements. In this chapter, we have defined the family to reflect the variety of cultural forms that women have used in negotiating family life, demonstrating that families were complex and intertwined with public presumptions and programs.

4
Working for Wages

Women worked. Some worked within their families while others worked for wages outside the home. Despite the dictum that work outside the home was for men and work inside was for women, during the nineteenth century women increasingly worked for wages outside the home. In many instances women and girls would begin their working lives at the same age as men and boys, around seven years of age. Young women would continue working for wages until after their marriage and the birth of their first child, or for their entire life with nary a break. Married women who did not continue to work for wages after their children were born became dependent on the male breadwinner, filling their prescribed gender role of staying home. Their domestic work was still work, however, since it included sewing, cooking, and marketing, and required the supervision of children and often servants. During economic downturns, or when their husbands were sick or disabled, these women also may have taken in homework, such as laundry and sewing, but such work would have been hidden from their neighbors, from the census takers, and from historians. Moreover, low wages and unemployment among men sometimes required their wives to work outside the home and undermined men's purported authority within the home. The dominant male discourse may have considered the concept of a woman worker outside the home as blasphemous, but that did not prohibit other men from hiring women for lower wages than they would have had to pay men.

Changes in women's work began with the industrial revolution and continued during the entire nineteenth century, not always for the better. In England and areas of Northern Europe the mechanized factory system expanded and the scale of industry increased. Concurrently, cities and the urban population grew. However, until the mid-nineteenth century most of the population lived in rural areas and only in England did 50 percent of the population live in cities by the mid-century. Areas of Southern and Eastern Europe remained rural, with pockets or crafts and small workshops surviving until well into the twentieth century. By 1914 in most areas of Western, but not Eastern, Europe women's primary occupations shifted from a preponderance of agricultural labor, domestic service, independent retailing, and piecework to increasing work in industries, in the new department stores, and in the growing service sector of the economy. With the enormous changes of the century, women experienced a tension between tradition and modernity as their relationship with their community shifted, and boundaries between public and private became more fluid. Women's work experiences also varied with the local nature of industrialization. Women left the fields for the factories sooner in England than elsewhere. Germany for example, did not experience intense industrialization until after unification in 1871. As a result, agricultural work predominated throughout the century.

For most working-class women, the need to earn a wage was a constant throughout the century. Middle-class women contributed to their family's economic well-being as well, although their work tended to be hidden because of the loss of status associated with it. By the end of the century, wealthy women who did not need to work for wages nonetheless championed increased work opportunities for all women. In part, this was because the definition of work was changing. Traditionally, in the family economy, as historians have labeled it, work was not a means to individual fulfillment or development, but instead each member of the family worked as necessary to keep the family alive or, at best, increase its fortunes. The concept of the family economy persisted throughout the nineteenth century. At the same time, however, a new idea of work was emerging, especially among men of the middle classes. According to this new understanding, work was something that allowed an individual man to exercise his unique talents, increase his skills and knowledge in an area, and make a significant contribution to society. This new idea of work was something that some middle- and upper-class women, seeking an avenue for their talents and energies, sought to make their own in the second half of the century. As Florence Nightingale (1820–1910) stated, "women often long to enter some men's profession where they would find direction, competition (or rather opportunity of measuring the intellect), and, above all, time [to think]."[1] The wealthy Nightingale had the education, contacts, and time to pursue her "passion," as she called it, of nursing. For the vast majority of women throughout the century, however, work was an economic necessity.

Rural work

Despite the changes during the century, the majority of women remained in rural areas engaged in farm labor and oftentimes cottage crafts. Down on the farm, women's contributions to the family economy remained essential. In most areas, farm families could not survive without women's work in the fields, in raising food for the family in their small courtyards, in taking in labor such as laundry, or by spinning and carding, or making ribbon and other articles associated with the textile and garment trades. Some women engaged in metallurgical tasks such as making nails or chain links, depending on the local industry. Women also raised cows, ducks, and chickens, and bred dogs. Since industrial capitalism varied by region, so did the nature of women's work, with the rural economy dominating Southern and Eastern Europe longer than it did in the north and west.

Work in rural areas varied by age and condition of the family economy, with young girls in some poor families beginning to work as soon as they could gather twigs for the fire or feed the chickens. Even girls and women who came from families with considerable income and who lived on landed estates occupied themselves with domestic chores. As Athénaïs Mialaret Michelet of France reported, " 'I had constant toil before me, strangely unbroken for so young a child. At six years of age, I knit my own stockings, by and by my brothers' also.' "[2] Girls and young women worked alongside their mothers in agricultural work and in the cottage crafts. They also tended their younger siblings while their mothers worked.

Adult women bore primary responsibility for the medical and moral health of their children and servants, and were in charge of the household and farm-yard. Women participated or supervised others in drying and canning food for the winter, cooking and baking, tending the sheep, chickens, cows, and pigsty, as well as the gardens and orchard. Louise Otto-Peters in Germany described the domestic tasks during her middle-class childhood: " 'Bread and cakes were made at home, all the preserves for the winter: fruit from the simplest dried kind to the most complicated jellies, meat in all its various preparations, butter and eggs – everything was prepared and preserved at home for the household's needs.' "[3]

Poor women also worked in the fields, sometimes their own, and sometimes for a neighbor or another villager. Some farm areas thrived and enlarged their land holdings, while others suffered a loss of land. In both areas, especially dur-ing the harvest season, women did field work for pay. In Sicily, for example, women picked grapes and olives for commercial farmers. The most customary task for women was gleaning in which they scanned the fields for the grain left after the harvest, which they could either use themselves or sell.

Women's rural labor reflected the dominant economy of the area. In areas of Northern France, Belgium and the Netherlands, Scotland, Denmark, Germany (Bavaria) and Sweden, and other dairy and cattle raising regions of Europe, women tended the cows, and made and sometimes sold butter and cheese. Traditionally, the dairy industry depended on women who were either farmers' wives or single young girls as paid dairymaids. Some women even established their own dairies and cheese-making enterprises. As dairying became more mechanized, however, the occupation became more masculinized. In coastal regions of Norway, Spain, Italy, England, and France, women engaged in fish-ing along with the rest of their families. Their tasks involved finding the bait, cleaning the fish, and sometimes marketing it. As fishing became more com-mercial, women moved into the factories that canned and packed the fish.

In Eastern Europe, still dominated by noble families owning large tracts of land, the rural laboring population lost common lands, as they had done in Western Europe, especially England, decades earlier. Women had few rights, and worked at available agricultural jobs. Serfdom ended in Austria in 1848 and in Russia in 1861; until then people could not leave the land except with permis-sion of the community. After emancipation, the men would migrate in search of better work, leaving their wives and daughters to do the farm work.

Women's engagement in the cottage crafts that dotted the rural countryside of Europe saved many a family economy, and provided some increased status for the women. As young girls, they cleaned and carded; as they became older they would spin. It was a major event in a young girl's life when she obtained a spinning wheel or loom. Although it was a welcome sign of her maturity and her increased contribution to the family economy, it also portended an increasing amount of hard work. Women cleaned the flax, carded, spun, or wove. Distinctions of the local economy and culture also enabled some women to specialize and become skilled in such crafts as embroidery in Hungary, or the fabrication of lace in regions of Slovakia, Russia, France, Belgium, and Ireland. In other areas, such as regions of Denmark and the Netherlands, rather than working in textiles, women contributed to other specialized crafts, such as making cheese or pottery. In areas where women specialized in remunerative commercial crafts, communities might then engage migrant laborers, sometimes from Eastern Germany, Poland, Portugal, or Southern Italy to do the fieldwork.

If the family were destitute and had no alternative, it might join gangs of agricultural laborers. Sometimes girls would join their mothers on a gang, but often they would go off on children's gangs. British records depict agricultural gangs of upwards of 10 girls and women supervised by a male gang master. Mothers tried to avoid having their children join agricultural gangs because it encouraged bad language and behavior and also contributed to physical deformities and illness; moreover beatings from gang masters were not unknown. Nevertheless, in areas of Europe with large fields, children as young as seven years old earned a pittance doing back-breaking labor from dawn to darkness that required bending down to weed or hoe the soil, or harvest low lying or root crops – such as turnips and potatoes – often in the rain. Middle-class writers accused women who engaged in agricultural fieldwork of being immoral, irreligious, and debauched homemakers, especially if they allowed their children to do such work. It was a labor of last resort, frequently just for widows and children.

Mining helped keep the industrial machines running, and women often went down into the mines along with their husbands and children. Work in the mines could begin as early as 4 a.m.; miners would get out 12 hours later, when it was again dark. Children less than 12 years of age did various gender-specific tasks that included removing water from the pit or pushing the carts full of coal or ore that could weigh about 800 pounds along narrow passages. Mine owners thought the young girls best fitted to those tasks because of their size, not withstanding the weight of the cart. Because mines were so hot, women and children wore pants and little else. Women mine workers said that they were not sexually harassed because male family members protected them. Mine workers faced excruciating health problems, such as lung diseases and physical deformities.

At the turn of the twentieth century, although migration and modernization may have marked much of rural life, in areas of France, Germany, Ireland, and Russia women continued their agricultural work and cottage crafts as before. The situation in rural areas was not one either of general progress or of gradual deterioration. Some farming families prospered while others sank into landlessness and poverty. The 1840s, especially 1846–48, which historians call "the hungry forties," were particularly difficult years of natural blights and famines, as well as of economic transformations such as the development of factories, roads and railroads. As a result, men migrated to seek jobs in the cities, leaving women to tend the farms; or else the women joined different, gendered, migration streams to domestic service and the textile workshops and mills. Toward the end of the century, the decade of the 1880s was also one of economic depression, particularly in Western Europe. The multiplication of roads and railroads facilitated increased migration and urbanization as capitalist economies further changed, employing more women in factories and in jobs outside the home. The population remained predominantly rural until the end of the century in most areas of continental Europe, however, despite the pull of the cities and push from the countryside.

In the cities

Even when women went to the cities, they did not always engage in modern factory or manufacturing jobs. Many entered the city to work in the traditional jobs of domestic service and laundry work, or they followed their husbands. The stay-at-home wives of male workers had responsibility for their families' health and for ensuring that the family could exist on his wages. They took care of the children, did the laundry and the mending as well as the daily shopping and the cooking – usually the preparation of a soup. Not having many changes of clothing, they did frequent washing outside the home in public fountains or sinks, allowing time for sociability while they worked and also for the gathering (and dispensing) of information and gossip. If a workingman's wife could not make ends meet on his wages, she would take in homework, such as washing, ironing, sewing, and other piecework, to supplement his earnings, or she might take in boarders, which provided income but increased her labors. Having a domestic servant marked middle-class status.

Throughout the nineteenth century, domestic service was the largest employer of women outside of agriculture, with the numbers of women in domestic service decreasing at the turn of the century and dropping precipitously after the World War of 1914–18. Women entered domestic service because of the middle-class demand for servants, the poor women's need for employment, and the social approval of this form of women's work. Domestic service lured young women whose families could not support them, or for whom there were no cottage crafts and no better opportunities at home. Sometimes domestic service started at age 12. The family who took a neighbor's or relative's daughter as a domestic servant in the rural areas could have provided a family environment, or mercilessly exploited her as a farm laborer, kitchen maid, as another person to spin and weave, or as an object for the sexual adventures of the master or his sons. The master and mistress usually also paid her some meager wages, either directly or by sending almost the entire sum to her family.

After some time in service with a neighbor, a characteristic trajectory for a domestic servant involved traveling to the nearest big city to work for strangers. A young woman in search of a job typically followed a migration chain, relying on relatives and family friends to help her find a position. Domestic service was the first job of girls and women newly arrived in the city. As an urban domestic servant, a young woman may have been the only servant in a household, or one of many. Regardless, she was often lonely, and vulnerable to the warmth and friendship of others, making her susceptible to seduction and rape. She was expected to send a portion of her wages to her parents, and also to save for a dowry, quite difficult to do on her meager pay.

A domestic servant's chores ranged from that of a scullery maid or maid of all work, to a cook, or a ladies' maid, or even a nanny for the children of the family. She could have cleaned the steps, boots, windows, and water closets. She could also have waited on the owners and done the marketing. She had no regular hours and was always on call, working more than 12 hours a day, with a day off, according to local custom, either once a week or once a month. She might sleep in a corner of the kitchen, in the cellar, or at the foot of her mistress's bed, ever ready to serve. In large cities, servants from several of the households in one building would share rooms, and sometimes beds, on the top floor of the building, which was usually hot in the summer and cold in the winter. A fortunate servant, or one who had risen in the service hierarchy of the household, might have had a room of her own or one to share with another female servant.

Domestic servants tended to see their position as impermanent, lasting until marriage. Cooks, who tended to be older and widowed, were an exception to this rule, and some women remained in service their entire lives. For some young girls domestic service was an avenue of upward social mobility. As she did the marketing for the family, she did the marketing for a husband, hopefully meeting and marrying the son of a local merchant, tradesman, or craftsman. The less fortunate would find a man who promised marriage. Upon that promise, she would consent to sexual relations. However, if she became pregnant she would generally lose her job, and sometimes her lover. If her parents would not take her back and she did not find another husband, she could face a life of menial piece work at best or, at worst, destitution and perhaps prostitution.

Domestic service was not the only occupation for single working-class women in the cities. The increase in manufacturing and trade that marked most of Western Europe included expanding textile and garment industries that employed increasing numbers of women and provided needlework at home for many, even if that "home" consisted of one small partially furnished rental room. Married and single women who had been in the cities several years had networks to find these jobs.

Urban work was also seasonal. In some cases, family members came to the cities during the winters when neither farming nor cottage crafts in their rural area provided subsistence. In other instances, the family's primary residence was in the city, and they would migrate to farms during the planting and harvest seasons. In the cities, family members would work together spinning and weaving during the winter months. One woman from the industrial north of France, Mémé Santerre, reported that as the youngest child she attended school for several years, but after school she sat at her loom from such a young age that she needed wooden extensions on the pedals in order for her short legs to reach them. In the summers her family became seasonal migrants to farm in the countryside, and their income from that, along with their payments for spinning and weaving, kept them going from year to year.[4] It was not unusual for young girls to work 12–14 hours a day at home, stretching and framing for weaving. Some girls went to work in the mills, as changing consumption and industrial patterns created a supply and demand for readymade garments.

As cotton came to replace linen in the nineteenth century, women discovered comfortable underwear, thus increasing the demand for lingerie and for women to sew it. Furthermore, with increasing industrialization, people substituted store-bought garments for those made at home, creating a demand for sewing and stitching. Needlework was women's work, although critics objected to women doing this work in shops outside their homes. Needlework had its own hierarchy, with women owning their own seamstress establishments in major cities such as Paris, London, and Hamburg. These women might employ several seamstresses, not all relatives, some of whom sewed at home, paid by the piece.

Women's work in the needle trades might have required skill, such as the fine needle work in lacemaking or embroidery, or it may have been unskilled labor, easily learned repetitive tasks, such as piercing buttons or twisting bows, putting eyelets in shoes or stitching garments. Women in both skilled and unskilled work received payment by the number of pieces and tasks they completed. Such piecework, also known as "sweated labor," constituted much of women's work in urban areas. Isabella Killick testified in 1888 before the British Parliamentary Select Committee of the House of Lords on the Sweating System. Her circumstances were similar to those of many women. She had worked alone for 22 years finishing the sewing on trousers, saying, "it is paid for now so terrible bad." She worked from 6 a.m. until 8 p.m., and desperately needed the work since her husband was sick and dying and she had three children to support, ranging in age from three to ten. During the three months a year comprising the off season, she did cleaning and laundry for others in order to try to feed her "three little ones." Her meals were meager, "Chiefly, I get a herring and a cup of tea; that is the chief of my living. ... I get meat once in six months."[5]

Members of the middle and upper classes sought to understand how women's industrial labor caused the dislocation of sanctioned gender roles. To many nineteenth-century social commentators, piecework had distinct advantages. Not only did it afford manufacturers a cheap source of labor, but also women and girls could do the work at home, supposedly after they had completed their domestic chores. Thus, this idealized form of work represented a socially approved form of female labor. In the early part of the century, middle-class writers romanticized the young, single seamstress, imagining her singing while sewing at her garret window, and living happily on crumbs, "like a bird." Later in the century, as scientific inquiry into all forms of work came into fashion, some commentators decried not the work itself, but the long hours spent on it. Some portrayed women sewing at home as victims of working-class men, whom they accused of being too lazy or selfish to support their wives.

For the women, however, such work was often all that was available, and it also allowed them to stay home with their families. This was also a disadvantage, since having young children around rarely afforded women enough time to gain a living, especially if those wages were not supplementary to the male breadwinner's but were the sole family earnings. Women had abysmally low wages and no job security. Moreover seamstresses often had severe eye problems from working in close conditions by candlelight. The sewing machine that made its way into the more affluent working-class homes after the 1860s did not increase wages sufficiently to enable women to pay off the sewing machines that crowded their tight living quarters. Generally, families working together as a unit persisted in the needle trades.

Other work was carried out in the home besides textile and garment work. Women picked holes in beads for jewelry, made boxes and cartons, and worked at other similar unskilled tasks. Men did metal and woodwork in their homes or in workshops attached to their homes. These men did most of the skilled work, but their wives did the final polishing of wood and metal in their rooms. Moreover, family businesses persisted throughout the century, with entire families living behind their shops, sometimes having their bed and cooking area curtained off from the business. These artisanal and "mom and pop" businesses consisted of cafés, woodworking, fruit markets, textile and garment shops, milliners, and other commercial enterprises.

Although family work and piecework done in the workers' living quarters persisted throughout the century, work outside the home in factories or shops increased, starting early in the century especially in England, Germany, Northern Italy, and France. With new machinery run by steam or waterpower, work moved from the home and countryside to the new factories. This decreased the profitability of cottage crafts and, as a result women sought employment in the new textile factories. There, the clock, the factory whistle, and the rhythms of the machines regulated the lives of men, women, and children, leading to new structures and cultures of daily life. This represented a big change from rural time where holidays, weather, seasons, and community activity, determined the workday and workweek.

Factory labor also led to shifts in gender roles. Men claimed the heavier and most skilled spinning and weaving. Women, however, also did some weaving, becoming a better-paid class of workers. The gender division of labor depended in part on skill, but in part it was custom. In some places women did highly skilled work in the textile and garment industries, but their wages were still less than men's. However, most women performed unskilled work for very low wages. Until late in the century, many families worked together, even in the factories and mills. Children helped their parents by doing menial chores and also learned the production tasks. Some of the more modern mills and factories separated families. In either case, family economies became structured around industrial wages, with men paid almost twice as much as women. Family relationships reflected this asymmetry of the market; the balance of power at home reflected the balance of power in the labor market.

Women's work outside the home differed according to marital status and the presence of young children. Single women from about 16 to 26 years of age predominated among the women workers in the textile mills, although in some places married women continued working, at least until they had children. A small number of women cotton spinners worked at the mills from age 6 to 60; most however became too ill to work this long. Adult women normally worked from 5 a.m. to 7 p.m. with less than an hour off for food, usually some bread, cheese, and coffee, which they brought with them. Accidents occurred frequently, in part because the factory owners situated the mules, machines that spun the thread, so close together that a woman could barely pass; her skirts often got caught, resulting in wrenched or dislocated limbs and permanent injury.

Work in the sweated trades and in factory mills continued unabated throughout the century. In France, Jeanne Bouvier (1865–1964), began her working life at age 11 in a silk factory when her father lost his job. She changed jobs many times. Upon moving to Paris she and her mother first found jobs as domestic servants. She then worked in the hat-making industry, but she lost that job. By constantly changing jobs, sometimes because she was fired, and sometimes because she was seeking better pay, she became indebted to relatives and unable to save. At one point she worked 12 hours a day as a seamstress for a dressmaker and after hours sewed for her own clients. As a result of this lack of sleep and overwork, she temporarily lost her health. But she wrote that she never succumbed to despair or prostitution.

Other women could not say the same. The "dead season" of unemployment stalked women workers in the garment and textile trades when consumers stopped purchasing. At these times, urban women workers faced serious problems. Some went back home to their rural families. Others, usually married women with children, took in boarders, hired themselves out as charwomen, or took in laundry and ironing. Still others engaged in commercial sex. Henry Mayhew (1812–87), the English social investigator and journalist, not known for his sympathetic attitude toward many aspects of workingwomen's lives, decried the extreme poverty of seamstresses that forced them into prostitution, especially during the dead season.

It is difficult to know how many women engaged in prostitution, or sex work, in order to keep starvation from their door during seasonal unemployment. Sex work was temporary employment for some women who lacked legitimate employment, or whose wages from piece work did not always suffice to feed and clothe themselves and their families. These women continued to identify themselves as laundresses or seamstresses, and not as prostitutes. Sometimes parents knew their daughter engaged in sex work, but they accepted it because she contributed to the family economy, enabling them to keep food on the table, and even have a little meat. Undoubtedly, some women stayed in commercial sex work because the money was good and they liked the finery, despite the humiliation and degradation; they got used to wearing gloves or eating meat. Commercial sex workers developed their own culture, one of mutual assistance as well as mutual antagonisms and violence. In Italy and France, prostitution was legal, and brothels supervised – often by the police. The Vice Squads had an important role in regulating prostitution, limiting it, and perhaps also making their own profit from it.

To the middle classes, prostitutes symbolized working-class women's rampant sexuality and all that was wrong with urban women's work. Middle-class policy makers failed to acknowledge that women might engage in sex work as a temporary measure when there was no other work. Because the middle class feared working-class violence, abhorred women's visible sexuality, and also sought to diminish the rising incidence of syphilis, politicians in most countries regulated prostitution starting in the 1840s, either by use of the Vice Squads in France and Italy or by legislation in England. The interest was not so much in the prostitute, herself, but in protecting the countries' men from venereal disease. The police in Italy, France, and Germany attempted to regulate the pay, living conditions, and clothing of prostitutes, registering them, and inspecting them for venereal disease. The police licensed prostitutes to work in brothels or in certain areas of the cities, forcing them to have regular medical examinations. If they were public women and not housed in brothels, the police required that they register and carry a card, which they had to submit upon demand. Furthermore, once registered, prostitutes had to appear at a dispensary for an internal pelvic examination every two weeks to see if they had a venereal disease. Yet, most of the women in prostitution escaped regulation.

In Great Britain, the Contagious Diseases Acts of the 1860s permitted the police to arrest women in some public places, give them an internal examination for venereal disease, and register them as prostitutes. This quickly led to police harassment of women, and effectively denied women the right to venture outside alone, particularly in naval towns. Domestic servants and other young women walking in areas where the police thought they should not be, doing the marketing, or dating a sailor, were subject to harassment and arrest as prostitutes. Ironically, to protect the health of the British Navy, these acts targeted the prostitutes for examination and regulation, not the sailors. Once a woman was registered, it was very difficult for her to resume legitimate work. Regulation had the effect of making prostitutes an outcast group.

Prostitution was not women's only occupational option when domestic service, needlework, factory work, or help from home were unavailable. Acting could provide a lucrative career for those attractive, and persistent enough, to land and capitalize upon a stage role. Most Europeans, however, considered actresses little better than prostitutes. Laundry work provided flexible hours and a meager income in lieu of other jobs or when a woman needed to supplement her husband's wages. It could also be seasonal or part time, take place in laundry establishments or in the homes of customers. A woman doing laundry might involve her children in sorting, hauling, wringing out, scrubbing, and delivering. In regions of Northern Europe that tended to be dark and wet during most of the year, wet laundry hanging from clotheslines took up much of the space inside the houses as well as between rows of houses. Many women kept up laundry work, even in old age, some standing in water up to their waists, some working in groups upward of 15 to clean linen in the sludge of soap, potash, bleach, dyes, and dirt. A woman in this occupation aged before her time.

Some women had more regular work, but still were subject to seasonal unemployment. In some areas, women worked in pottery shops where they were paid by the piece. Many who had worked in the trade since they were young girls had pottery dust in their lungs and had to stop work because of ill health. Other women engaged in ambulatory occupations, such as setting up a street cart and selling cockles and mussels, fruits and vegetables, and herbs and cabbages. These women, if married or mothers, still had responsibility for the home and children, and had to balance their productive and reproductive lives. Single women often shared lodgings to cut costs and were frequently suspected of prostitution.

Conditions for working women did not significantly improve until the 1880s, and scholars debate if they improved at all before the twentieth century. As a result of dire working conditions, men, women, and especially children in the mines and mills suffered from malnutrition and rickets; in addition, women suffered from deformed pelvises and amenorrhea. Furthermore, accidents resulting in loss of limbs were not unknown either on the farms, in the factories, or in the mines. Until the 1880s, modernization and industrialization took its toll along with the production of economic benefits.

Developing capitalism and industrialization, along with a myriad of concurrent political and social reforms, changed the nature of women's labor force participation in northwestern Europe especially in the decades before the War of 1914. Not withstanding the persistence of agricultural work and domestic service, women's factory work increased. Half of Berlin's working women worked in industry, most of them in workshops or in the sweated labor of homework. Increasingly, they entered the factories. Labor statistics reveal that young single women dominated women's labor force participation. Married women's work usually escaped the data collectors since they typically worked in their homes. Yet, toward the end of the century, increasing numbers of married women, including mothers, appeared in the workforce in England, Belgium, and Germany as the overall numbers of women in the industrial workforce increased. In Germany it rose from under 400,000 in 1882 to 1.5 million in 1895 and 2.1 million in 1907. In France, the numbers did not rise as significantly because of the slower nature of industrialization and the hidden labor of many women. In 1899 there were about 600,000 women industrial workers; that number increased to 758,000 in 1911. With the advent of gas and then electrical lighting, women as well as men worked nights, until labor legislation prohibited women's night work in industries and mines.

Public officials perceived women's industrial work as harmful to women's reproductive capabilities, to their morality, and to the sanctity of the ideal conjugal family. They therefore responded negatively to the increasing numbers of women in factories. Reports to the German Reichstag in 1890 and 1899, for example, strongly disapproved of married women's work. This criticism rested on the male breadwinner model that regarded women as producers of supplementary family income. However, many investigators realized that women's wages were often necessary to the family. Employers also welcomed women workers because they could pay them less than men. The women, themselves, accepted the male breadwinner ideal, in part because their conditions of work were so onerous. Married women tended to leave the paid factory workforce after the birth of their first child – if they could afford it.

Starting in the 1870s and 1880s governments of Western Europe, including England, France, Germany, and Sweden enacted gender-specific labor legislation in order to restrict women's work, particularly targeting women in their roles as present or future mothers. These laws began to have some effect starting in the 1880s. In England, the 1874 and 1878 Factory and Workshops Acts limited the number of hours that women could work per week to 54. The 1890s laws in many Western countries protected women from phosphorus and tobacco poisoning, since doctors and legislators understood that both led to infertility and miscarriages. Other laws in England, France, and Germany prohibited night work for women. Protective labor legislation, however, affected only women in certain industries, and those that employed a significant number of women workers. In Germany, laws of the 1890s called for the separation of men and women in factories, and limited women's work to 11 hours a day and made Sunday a day of rest. The German labor code of 1891 reinforced the male breadwinner model, while emphasizing issues of women's morality and hygiene. Although it condemned married women's work outside the home, it did not ban it, but ostensibly allowed time for married women to shop and clean their homes. Women doing garment work and needlework at home were excluded from German welfare benefits, as they were from protective labor legislation in other countries. In 1900 the Swedish Parliament prohibited women from working the four weeks following childbirth, but provided no economic support to the women, thus putting workingwomen in a real economic bind. France, also eager to protect women as custodians of their fertile wombs and as mothers, in the early 1890s limited women's nighttime work, their work in dangerous occupations, and the number of hours per day they could work. As a result of these protective measures, many women drifted into occupations that remained outside the new legislation, such as home production. Ironically, the measures meant to protect workingwomen forced them into unregulated jobs and actually worsened many lives.

Another irony of protective legislation is that while it limited working-class women's hours and the types of labor they could perform, it created new job opportunities for middle-class women as factory inspectors. Legislators and employers alike believed that women inspectors would be more likely to understand the concerns of female employees and less likely to be taken in by any lies they might tell. Although the number of posts were limited, large numbers of educated, middle-class women took the competitive examinations; in 1911, for example 150 French women competed for four positions. By 1914, the governments of England, Germany, Austria, Belgium, Finland, the Netherlands, and Norway also employed female factory inspectors.

Neither workingwomen nor feminists wholeheartedly supported gender-specific labor legislation, although working women's organized union activity was sporadic and minimal. Labor organization and union activity was difficult for women because of the temporary and changing nature of their work, their isolation, and men's resistance to having women join them in unions. Nevertheless, women sometimes demanded the right to work, and also to improved wages and conditions of work. The first significant women's protest activities occurred during the Revolutions of 1848. Then, in the 1860s, with the founding of the International Working Men's Association, or First International, the controversy over women's right to work again surfaced, dividing the workers' movement. A few courageous women, such as Jeanne Bouvier, joined trade unions in shops and factories in France, England, and Germany. In Germany, when women textile mill workers went on strike in Saxony in 1903 for a 10-hour workday, they devised the slogan, "One more hour for our families." For the women workers, as for the legislators, labor was intertwined with the needs of their families. Other changes of the 1880s profoundly influenced women's and girls' labor force participation.

Women's work and the family economy shifted with the advent of compulsory education, the changing nature of industrial capitalism and the development of the service sector. As consumerism increased, so too did the tertiary sector of the economy, with women increasingly present as sales clerks in department stores and as government employees. At the turn of the twentieth century, middle-class women filled many of these positions, as well as those of teachers, social workers, secretaries, nurses, and professionals such as doctors and lawyers.

Middle-class women and work

A strong cultural prohibition against middle-class married women working for wages outside the home did not mean that none of them worked; many did. In subtle and often hidden ways they contributed to the family economy. As historical research progresses into the lives of middle-class women, the image of the lady of leisure, spending her hours in frivolous pastimes, increasingly appears to be a myth. Recent interpretations have emphasized how activities that were not wage labor such as letter writing, paying social calls, or embroidering still contributed to the economic well-being of the family.

Leonore Davidoff and Catherine Hall's study of merchant families in nineteenth-century Birmingham demonstrated that making social calls, entertaining and writing letters served to maintain the family's network of contacts, which became crucial when the family needed to borrow money to expand the business or find new business partners, suppliers, and distributors.[6] The effort put into dressing well and maintaining a fashionable home also created a "social capital" that could be "borrowed against," as potential creditors looked to the wife and home as signs that the husband, the official head of the family enterprise, was a hard worker and successful business man.

As the home was crucial to the success of the family in the public world of business, the world of business shaped the upkeep of the home. Increasingly, household tasks were to be carried out with the same efficiency, thrift, and order that were necessary in business life. Household manuals such as Isbella Mary Beeton's *Household Management* (1859–61) or Henriette Davidi's *Die Hausfrau* (The Housewife, 1863) taught women how to maintain accounting books to record money spent on supplies and services, write up schedules for the regular performance of household tasks, and establish inventories of food, linen, and china. These new tasks introduced new responsibilities, as did the growing focus on cleanliness. Regularly washing rugs and bedding, polishing floors and silver, and cleaning rooms from top to bottom until they shone became a requirement for the well-maintained house. Women with servants still had to supervise this effort and the great majority of middle-class women had to participate actively in housework in order to maintain the necessary image.

Upper- and middle-class women often participated in their husband's work. Husband and wife, as well as friends and colleagues acknowledged these "shared" careers. The wives of politicians kept up important contacts, proofread speeches, and even campaigned for their spouses. Wives of clergymen met with parishioners, wives of authors typed articles and books, and wives of scholars engaged in research. Husbands took formal credit for the finished work, and thus much of women's contribution has been hidden. Yet letters, diaries, and marriage proposals reveal the extent to which women were integral to their husband's work. When Reverend Edward Stuart Talbot, warden of Keble College,

Oxford, proposed to Lavinia Lyttleton in 1869, he "asked her to come and help him in his greatwork."[7] In these upper- and middle-class households, a woman was not paid a separate wage for participating in her husband's career.

Many married women and their single daughters in middle-class families often needed to earn extra money, and thus engaged in unofficial, part-time work. Since this work was done in secret its extent is impossible to measure. Evidence from letters and diaries shows, however, that many women, especially those at the bottom or the middle of the middle classes, needed to work part-time in order to earn enough money to keep up appearances. Women tended to choose work that did not conflict greatly with accepted ideas of femininity. Thus needlework was a popular choice, for it was a skill virtually all middle-class women learned. Women sewing at home for a few hours a day could earn extra income, although the wages paid were pitifully low. In Germany, daughters and sometimes wives of junior and middle-ranking civil servants sewed for money secretly at home. In Central Europe, middle-class women dominated the sewing trades until the 1870s, when working-class women began to outnumber them. In Berlin, single, middle-class women sewed in shops in the early part of the century. In France, schoolteachers sometimes also earned extra money sewing in shops. Competition among women of both the working and middle classes kept wages for needlework low throughout the century.

In addition to sewing, middle-class girls were taught to draw, to play the piano, and to read and write. These skills, meant to demonstrate a woman's claim to being a "lady," served her well in earning money at home. Women drew on their skills to etch engravings and hand-tint prints, and used their musical skills to write, compose, or translate hymns, for wages. Knowledge of foreign languages, another skill developed by upper-class women, allowed them to translate foreign works. Some women also wrote children's books, a task that accorded well with their role as educator. Although more difficult to hide, taking in boarders, which required a woman to cook and clean for a person outside the family but still in the home, could be a last resort for a middle-class family, and especially widows, fallen on hard times.

Just as with work for women of the popular classes, work opportunities for middle-class women shifted over the course of the century. Research is beginning to show that both the nineteenth-century conceit that middle-class women did not work and a more long-lasting impression that they did not work until the end of the century are false. Instead work opportunities for middle-class women underwent a profound shift in the period from 1780 to 1840 as previously accepted tasks disappeared or were designated masculine. Another shift occurred in the period from 1860 to 1914, when new sectors of employment opened up to middle-class women. Thus rather than either a gradual disappearance of work opportunities over the course of the century, or a sudden opening up of possibilities at its end, we see middle-class women's work shifting from one sector to another in accordance with the development of capitalist industrialization and bureaucratic centralization. The ideology of domesticity was often used to make sense of these shifts.

By the middle of the century, middle-class women in retailing and manufacturing families had moved from being active participants in the business to managers of the household. In the early part of the century, most enterprises were small family firms, with the retail or manufacturing space adjacent to the living space. This arrangement allowed women's regular participation. In addition to housing and feeding apprentices and other employees who were not members of the family, women kept the books, served customers, worked the register, ordered goods, and oversaw the business in case the male head of the household was away, ill, or deceased. Reflecting women's active participation as providers of capital or labor, a study of wills in Birmingham, England, reveals that in the early part of the century men overwhelmingly left their business to their wives upon their deaths. She was expected to run it herself until her death or until a son was of age to take over. Even then, however, she would remain an active part of the enterprise. Sisters, female cousins, and aunts also worked in family businesses. And, in certain rare cases, single women went into business for themselves. Although legally they required a male partner to sign contracts, the informal nature of much business activity in the early part of the century allowed some women to bypass this requirement.

Before mid-century, then, women in business were not an anomaly. They ran manufacturing works, retail shops, family farms, and inns. This situation may have persisted in European countries where industrialization was less advanced; the fact that Eastern European female Jewish migrants to London tended to seek out small business opportunities before becoming acculturated suggests this was the case, at least among certain ethnic groups. In Western Europe, however, it was increasingly assumed by the second half of the century that women were incapable of running businesses on their own. To a certain extent this was accurate, not because of an innate inability, but due to both structural and cultural changes.

In the second half of the century, businesses were increasing in scale. Small family firms and farms were being absorbed or bankrupted by larger agricultural, manufacturing, and retailing concerns. These enterprises required a large workforce that could not be supervised by a few family members. Managers and supervisors took over the day-to-day work of making the business run, while clerks and accountants handled correspondence and financial records. Large commercial farms, often specializing in a single cash crop, required scores of field hands rather than all family members pitching in at harvest time, while department stores required an army of shop girls rather than a wife and daughter behind the counter. Mechanization in manufacturing meant that workers with specialized skills were preferred over female family members.

The separation of home and workspace also encouraged women's withdrawal from the business world. A combination of growth in the scale of enterprises and increased urban problems such as overcrowding, disease, and pollution, encouraged middle-class families to separate their residences from their place of work. For some, this meant a move to the suburbs that were springing up outside of cities like London and Birmingham. Here, large houses and abundant green spaces provided families with pleasant and safe surroundings. In other cases, middle-class families rented large apartments or single-family townhouses in urban neighborhoods where the working classes were not welcome, except as domestic servants. As the home became separated from the business, middle-class women could not easily lend a hand, and their focus shifted instead to home, children, and charity.

Women's legal and financial status also made it increasingly difficult for them to start or maintain businesses. In most of Europe, women increasingly tended to own only "passive" property that yielded income but could not be sold or borrowed against, such as annuities, insurance, or trusts. This reflected a growing practice of husbands preferring to will the family business to a male relative or business partner, stipulating that his widow should be provided for through property held in trust. Trusts were usually controlled by male relatives or friends of the family. If a woman received property from her father and her husband were still living, he usually controlled the trust. Without his express permission and active participation (since women could not sign contracts), a woman's lack of control over her own property meant that it could not be used as collateral in order to obtain loans that might help her in business. The recognition that, from a legal and economic point of view, "marrying is like dying," as English writer Margaret Oliphant (1827–97) put it, led a group of middle-class women in England to organize a campaign to reform the laws governing married women's property.[8] This cause would be taken up throughout Europe in the second half of the century with varying degrees of success.

As a result of these changes, business and employment opportunities for women had greatly diminished by the mid-nineteenth century, especially in Western Europe. Still, many women needed to earn a living. Decreased opportunities within family businesses coincided with changes in marriage patterns. In England, the 1851 census revealed a growing number of unmarried women. In Germany, the marriage age was rising for middle-class women, leaving women in their early twenties with little to occupy them. And as awareness grew among middle-class women of the plight faced by working-class women, they began to argue that all women deserved the opportunity to earn a living wage. In her 1866 *La Femme pauvre au XIXe siècle* (The Poor Woman in the Nineteenth Century), the first French woman to earn the baccalauréat, Julie-Victoire Daubié, eloquently pled the case of poor women of all classes. Like many other European women, she used the ideology of domesticity to argue for women's work, arguing that a lack of alternatives degraded marriage. Similarly, Louise Otto-Peters (1819–95) argued in 1847 that more women should be allowed to work so that "marriage in Germany might rediscover its natural rights, and not merely be reduced to a 'welfare institution' for the female sex."[9]

Ironically, as middle-class women were beginning to debate publicly the question of female employment, employment opportunities were slowly expanding in new directions. This was due both to the efforts of women to enter fields previously limited to men and to structural changes in the economy and the state. Teaching, in mid-century often considered a last resort for middle-class women and one that maintained her in a dependent state, employed more women and became a more attractive career option in the second half of the nineteenth century. Nursing, journalism, and civil service employment all expanded in the period after 1860 as well.

Throughout the nineteenth century, teaching very young children and older girls was a task that women were expected to perform in their own families.

Moreover, some middle-class women volunteered to teach in Sunday schools and charity schools. In case of economic necessity, therefore, women could teach the children of others in exchange for wages without departing far from the domestic ideal. The most acceptable situation for a middle-class woman would be to teach inside her home or the home of others. A woman could open what in England was known as a Dame School inside her home. Although often these schools offered little more than supervision of children whose mothers were at work, the proprietress was expected to teach a little bit of religion and reading to the young girls in her charge. Single women served as governesses in the homes of others. Although a governess, by virtue of her class background and education, had greater status than did a domestic servant, her situation was difficult. Like a servant, she was subject to the needs and desires of her employers, who could be considerate of her person or abusive. Governesses had little free time, and were typically paid low wages. Yet, because this position allowed them to maintain some aspect of their class position, it remained an option for middle-class women for much of the century.

Middle-class women could also teach outside of the home, in a school for girls. Because few records were kept and schools tended to shut down when their director married, retired, or died, it is difficult to know how many private schools for girls existed. Evidence suggests, however, that employment in a girls' school was an option for middle-class women in many European cities. A well-educated middle-class woman was often sought by school owners as someone who could enhance the school's reputation. Women who taught at private girls' schools served at the pleasure of the owner who, in addition to paying low wages, could exercise enormous control over her teachers. Since, in the first half of the century, women who turned to teaching usually had few alternatives, they had little recourse if they were badly treated.

As demand for female education grew especially after the 1880s, opportunities for teachers improved along with their working conditions. The growth of female education was a response to women's demands for education and also to changing economic structures. In Russia, the abolition of serfdom meant that many noble families were no longer able to maintain their standard of living. Noble girls who previously received only a smattering of education while awaiting marriage now needed to find employment. Teaching seemed the natural choice, and the number of schools for girls grew as demand for education increased. Students could, upon graduation, hope to find a position teaching the next generation of female students. Economic restructuring also impacted middle-class families. As opportunities to contribute to the family income by helping in the business dwindled, women needed to look outside the family to earn a wage. Education was both a crucial tool to find employment and a source of employment in itself. As a result, all over Europe the number of female teachers grew in the second half of the century. In Prussia, the number of female teachers increased by a factor of 20 between 1833 and 1900. In France, 89,665 women were working as teachers in 1897. The number was even higher in England, where in 1911 women constituted 72.8 percent of all teachers.

Even as teaching outside the home became more acceptable for middle-class women, wages and status continued to lag behind those of men. Female teachers in Great Britain, Germany, and Austria, could not teach in state schools if they were married. They were often constrained in both their pedagogy and their private lives by the expectations of parents, employers, and public officials. In order to improve the lot of female teachers, women such as Emily Davies (1830–1921), who organized the Association of Female Teachers in 1866, sought to join with others to further their cause. Because so many women were employed as teachers, these associations could become quite large. Helene Lange (1848–1930) was one of the cofounders of the General German Association of Women Teachers. Founded in 1890, it gained 3,000 members after a few months, and 16,000 by 1900, making it the largest women's professional association in Germany.

In addition to equal pay and pensions, female teachers wanted better training. Here, their interests often coincided with those of the state. In nations such as France, Great Britain, Germany, and Italy where the suffrage was expanding, politicians became convinced of the need for state-run primary education. To staff these schools, they established or supported training schools. As a result of the passage of the French law of August 1879, which required a Normal School for women in every department, 64 new training schools opened.

Better training and government oversight also led to a rise in status in nursing, making it, by the last part of the century, a career that middle-class girls could contemplate. Throughout the century, most nursing was done by Catholic nuns or Protestant deaconesses. In 1898, for example, the Institute for Deaconesses at Kaiserwerth had placed 13,309 women as nurses in hospitals, poorhouses, infirmaries and orphanages. Nursing in these communities was closely tied to a religious vocation, and required joining a community of religious women. Nurses who worked outside of these communities were working-class women who many in the middle classes considered to be untrained and of loose morals. The professionalization of lay nursing was one of the goals of the wealthy Florence Nightingale, a woman whom contemporaries called one of the best educated in Europe. Despite the objections of her family, Nightingale pursued the interest in nursing that she developed when young by reading hospital and sanitary reports. She also visited the order of the Sisters of Charity in Paris and the Institute of Protestant Deaconesses in Kaiserwerth, both of which were known for their nursing. She visited hospitals throughout Europe, including the Middlesex Hospital in London, where she worked during a cholera outbreak in 1854. Later that year, war broke out in the Crimea, and Nightingale set out with 38 nurses to work in the military hospital at Scutari, across the straits from Constantinople. Within a short time of her arrival, Nightingale's insistence on light, air, and hygiene lowered the death rate from 42 to 2 percent. Her connections with high-placed people, including Queen Victoria, allowed her to pursue her passion for nursing reform after the war. Her example, as well as the institutions she helped found, such as the Nightingale School and Home for Nurses in London, made nursing a more respectable career for women. By 1911, 77,000 women were employed as nurses in England.

The Crimean War also proved a turning point for nursing in Russia. Front-line hospitals were staffed by female nurses; their contributions proved the value of medical training for women. In France, nursing was dominated by religious orders throughout most of the nineteenth century. Even at the end of the century, when the Republican government undertook an effort to replace religious women with lay women in the classroom, concerns about the low birthrate made legislators reluctant to expose women who could become mothers to disease. Nonetheless, despite the dominance of female congregations in nursing, lay hospital staff grew from 14,500 in 1880 to almost 95,000 by 1911.

Journalism was another career path that gained in popularity over the course of the century. Journalism required no apprenticeship, and could be easily done at home and part-time, if desired. The common practice of publishing articles anonymously, or with only the author's initials, also helped women in that they could do this work secretly. Women who moved outside the home to practice journalism still adopted strategies meant to emphasize their feminine identity: they cultivated a modest demeanor, dressed well, and displayed perfect manners.

Opportunities for women in journalism increased along with the growth of the press. As the numbers of periodicals and their circulation increased, specialized niches, such as papers for women, for children, or devoted to religion, offered women opportunities for publication that coincided with the domestic ideal. While many women restricted their journalistic careers to such periodicals, others used them as stepping-stones to other opportunities. In Russia in the 1880s, for example, renewed government censorship of political journalism meant that magazines considered to be less serious, such as those devoted to fashion, took center stage. Many of these magazines were published by women, such as Sofiia Mei's (1821–?) *Modnyi Magazine* (Fashion Magazine). A similar situation occurred in France in the 1830s and 1840s, when government surveillance of the press led to a flourishing of fashion, art, and literary reviews that were more open to female contributors.

While the bulk of female journalists worked in the nonpolitical press, others made politics their life work. In England, Harriet Martineau (1802–76) wrote over 1600 leaders for the *Daily News* between 1852 and 1866. She believed that although she did not have the vote and could not run for office, her work as a journalist gave her a means to shape political debates. In France, Marguerite Durand's (1864–1936) *La Fronde* confused critics who expected this paper, written, edited, and typeset by women, to be devoted to fashion and society issues. Instead, it discussed all the pertinent issues of the day, including politics. In order to cover the news, Durand had to receive permission for women to enter areas normally off-limit to them, such as the stock market or the Chamber of Deputies.

Women also served as foreign correspondents. The Russian Anastasia Vasil'evna Kairova (1845–88) reported from Serbia, Constantinople, Athens, Vienna, and Budapest for *Golos* (Voice). She was part of the first wave of Russian women foreign correspondents who came into existence with the outbreak of the Russo-Turkish War of 1877–78. Her identity as a woman remained a secret, since she signed her articles with her initials and used the masculine pronoun to refer to herself. Yet she sometimes referred to herself, in her articles, as being "in costume," thus hinting at her true identity. Other female foreign correspondents included Emily Crawford (1831/32–1915), whose "Letter from Paris" was published in every issue of *Truth* from 1877 to 1915, Lady Florence

Dixie (1857–1905), who covered the Boer War for London's *Morning Post*, and Jessie Meriton White (1832–1906), who served as the Italian correspondent for the *Daily News*.

Although women journalists often did not have access to the exclusive men's clubs and governmental bodies where they could speak with news and opinion makers, they created their own networks for information and support. Salons brought together individuals from the arts, politics, and business, and many women journalists were active members of salon culture. In England of the early 1820s the salon of the Countess of Blessington (1789–1849), who edited *The Book of Beauty* and contributed to *New Monthly Magazine* was attended by titled aristocrats, politicians, and writers. Avdot'ia Panaeva (1819/20–1893), on the editorial staff of *Sovremennik* (The Contemporary), also hosted a salon in Saint Petersburg. Other sources of information and professional contacts could be cultivated through family connections, letter writing, religious organizations, and, by the end of the century, feminist organizations. Women just entering into journalism sought out powerful male and female patrons like Charles Dickens or W.T. Stead in England or Eugenia Tur (1815–92) in Russia, who published many works by women authors while a literary critic at *Russkii vestnik* (Russian Herald) in the 1850s.

By the end of the nineteenth century, many women considered journalism a glamorous field, one that allowed them to seek not only financial gain, but also personal fulfillment. A freelance woman journalist explained the attraction of the career: "I do my work when and how I like, the sole condition being that my copy shall be good, and punctually delivered. When I see the tyranny to which governesses and nurses are obliged to submit, I count it a great gain that in journalism the woman is entirely her own mistress as regards the ordering of her life."[10] Journalism provided middle- and upper-class women with an opportunity to comment upon society and politics. Furthermore, as Mary Louise Roberts has argued, journalism opened up to women "environments in which they were not subject to the naturalized limits imposed on the self."[11] Whether submitting articles anonymously or writing as a woman about areas such as politics, female journalists could call into question accepted ideas concerning gender identity. That not all chose to do so can be explained perhaps by the criticism that faced those who did. Anna Volkova (1847–1910), editor of *Drug Zhenshchin* (Women's Friend) dreaded the reactions of others when they found out her profession: "A woman is supposed to be interested in fashion, pies, pickles, jams and other things, with embroidery, if you will, and nothing else ... if she takes it into her head to become interested in something else, then that's the end, she's dead; offensive gibes, little smiles flavored with sarcasm, that's the helping hand from society."[12]

In addition to teaching, nursing, and journalism, middle-class women who sought full-time employment could increasingly turn to the tertiary sector. Service jobs – whether in retail, private industry, or government – proliferated for women in the last decades of the nineteenth century. The increased scale of enterprises demanded a growing white-collar sector of clerks, secretaries, and typists. And retailing, which was shifting from small shops to large department stores, provided opportunities for female shop assistants. Because women employed in the tertiary sector needed to be well dressed and well spoken, and to posses a minimum of education, these jobs were seen as acceptable for middle-class women. As the scale of enterprises grew and the work process was divided, opportunities for advancement diminished, making clerical and sales jobs less attractive to men. Although many women worked their entire lives, employment in the tertiary sector was usually considered a stopgap for women waiting to marry, who would not therefore need, it was believed to move up the career ladder. This attitude also led companies to pay women less than men in comparable positions, and in some cases to grant them less time off. At the same time, employers took measures to ensure that women would find these positions acceptable. In some cases, working arrangements kept women and men separate. The Prudential and Pearl Insurance Companies had different hours and different entrances for men and women so that the two sexes would not have to mix coming to or going from work. The Bon Marché department store in Paris placed women in separate offices from men. Some employers granted women pensions and other benefits.

In addition to finding opportunities with private companies, women were employed by the postal, telegraph, and telephone services. In France, women began working for the postal service in 1835, in England in the 1840s, in Germany in 1873, and in the Netherlands in 1878. The French Postal Service introduced day care and maternity leave after 1903. Women also served as factory inspectors, and social welfare workers. These jobs were highly sought after, as were those of office clerks and secretaries. Unlike shop assistants, who tended to come from the lower ranks of the middle classes or even the upper levels of the working classes, clerks and civil servants tended to be from solidly, or even upper, middle-class families. In 1895, most of the 13,044 female office employees in Germany were the daughters of civil servants, doctors, or businessmen. The young women seeking these jobs possessed a good education, and were attracted by the higher status of these positions, despite the routine nature of much of the work. In 1874, 700 female candidates applied for five positions at the British post office.

With such competition, it was necessary to prepare oneself for employment in the tertiary sector. Many German girls graduated from one-year private commercial schools that sprang up in various towns and cities after 1860. Women could also seek help from employment agencies, such as the Lette Association for the Advancement of the Employment Skills of the Female Sex. Established in Berlin in 1866, the association helped middle-class women find jobs as governesses, nurses, embroiderers, and bookkeepers. This association, modeled after the English Society for Promoting the Employment of Women, spurred imitators throughout Central Europe. In Russia, Nikolai Chernyshevskii's novel *What is to be Done?* inspired a generation of young women to form collectives when it suggested that girls from the Russian nobility forced to find work in the cities might be better off if they joined together for mutual support. Young women could also consult career guides, such as the French *Noveau guide pratique des jeunes filles dans le choix d'une profession* (New practical guide for girls in the choice of a profession, 1891) or the Dutch *Wat kan mijne dochter worden?* (What can my daughter do? 1878), which included options such as stenographer, postal worker, and telegraph operator.

While teaching, nursing, and the tertiary sector employed large numbers of women by the end of the century, a small number of determined individuals entered the liberal professions as lawyers, doctors, and pharmacists. On the eve of the First World War, women made up 10 percent of the medical profession in Russia, numbering 1,500 doctors. France had fewer than 600 female doctors, while Germany and Great Britain both numbered around 500. The relatively high numbers of women doctors reflect the argument that like nursing, practicing as a doctor could be a natural extension of women's role as caretaker. Furthermore, female modesty might be offended when a male doctor examined a woman patient. The law was a much harder profession to enter. In France, the first woman lawyer qualified in 1890, but was not allowed to practice until 1900. Some women who obtained legal degrees worked as law clerks, never even seeking admittance to the bar. Despite their difficulties, however, the existence of women lawyers and doctors reveals that some women were able to create fulfilling and meaningful careers by the end of the century.

In 1852, Florence Nightingale complained that women have "trained themselves so as to consider whatever they do as not of ... value."[13] While many women throughout the nineteenth century struggled to reconcile their work lives with the ideals of domesticity, this chapter has sought to demonstrate that women's work was indeed valued throughout the period. Not only did women themselves value their work – for the wages that allowed them to support their family, for the contribution they could make to their families or society, or for their own personal fulfillment, but society valued it as well, if only as a source of cheap labor. Although women often toiled in dangerous conditions, and were always paid lower wages than men, the growing interest over the course of the century in the nature of women's work meant that individuals, groups, and even government committees, drew attention to the issues faced by women workers and sought ways to remedy the problems. They did not often agree on the causes of these problems, or decide upon a course of action, much less implement it, but nineteenth-century men and women were aware that women worked.

The types of work that women did changed with the onset of industrialization and the creation of modern, capitalist economies. This caused some to identify certain types of women workers – such as seamstresses with their sewing machines or middle-class office workers in their long, straight skirts and white shirtfronts – with modernity. At the same time, employers, commentators, and women workers themselves expended great effort to make it seem as if the work done by women was part of a tradition of domesticity. Similarly, while women's work often took them out into the public sphere of business and politics, and into public spaces such as department stores, schools, and offices, women workers continued to be identified with the private sphere of the home and family. From labor legislation that considered all women as actual or future mothers to the acceptance of female doctors on the basis that they could protect women's modesty, late nineteenth-century Europeans continued to identify women workers with the private sphere even as they were present every day in the public.

Associating new work opportunities with domesticity allowed Europeans to make sense of a shifting economy. At the same time, the consequences of women's work – including greater economic independence and a more visible public presence, gave it the potential to undermine dominant cultural beliefs. Similarly, education could both challenge and reinforce dominant cultural beliefs and the gendered social order. Government leaders, feminist reformers, and individual women all contributed to expanding educational opportunities for women in the nineteenth century. Some argued that education could help women become better mothers while others maintained that education was necessary for women to thrive as individuals in their own right. Questions of women's education, like questions of women's work, thus occupied the minds of many men and women during the nineteenth century.

5
Education

In the middle of the nineteenth century, French writer Jules Michelet declared, "every woman is a school." He meant that every woman had both the capacity and the duty to teach her children. This idea of woman as educator was one of the most profound and long-lasting legacies of the Enlightenment. It altered ideas about education everywhere in Europe. However, while the idea of woman as educator of her children gained widespread acceptance throughout Europe, the consequences of that idea for educational practices, institutions, and curricula were less clear. Although women were considered "natural" educators, the extent and type of education they themselves required were widely debated.

Education could be acquired formally – in schools and universities – and informally – in the home, through self-study, or by attending public lectures not linked to a degree program. Before the nineteenth century, what education girls did acquire was obtained either in the home, in privately run day or boarding schools, or in schools run by religious orders. These forms of education persisted throughout the nineteenth century. As late as 1914, 21 percent of female academics at Oxford University in England and 8 percent of female students had been educated at home. While private secular and religious schools tended to offer little in the way of a serious education in academic subjects such as geography or history, education acquired at home could, in the right families, be quite advanced. For most women, however, a limited education diminished their ability to adequately educate their children. Women who urged educational reform in the nineteenth century thus argued for the importance of access to formal, secular education.

Women sought access to formal, secular education both because state-run schools often had to meet minimum standards and because the degrees acquired through state-run institutions were necessary for certain careers. Access to formal, secular education increased over the course of the century, but it did so for a variety of reasons, not all of which had to do with improving women's minds and professional status. For example, as states sought to strengthen loyalty to the nation and expanded the suffrage, they came to consider increased access to state-run primary education important for its ability to inculcate pupils with nationalist sentiments. The changing structure of European economies, as the predominance of agriculture gradually gave way to more urban and industrial economies, also prompted increased interest in education. These industrial economies demanded a white-collar workforce educated enough to file, type, and carry out basic accounting tasks. It also required a disciplined labor force that could follow directions. Moreover, economic and cultural developments made the situation of unmarried women precarious; these women needed to make a living, and education could help them do so. Finally, access to formal education increased as women argued that they should be able to obtain the intellectual fulfillment and satisfaction of a professional career that education made possible.

As these various reasons for the expansion of formal education imply, access to education was not in itself emancipatory. Education could allow women to become more independent of others, both intellectually and financially, but it could just as easily serve to reinforce notions of sexual difference associated with domesticity. Furthermore, education did not necessarily become more emancipatory over time. In the 1870s, when upper middle-class women were beginning to gain access to universities for the first time, states were passing legislation meant to establish public primary schooling. Women who attended the university considered their education to be vital to their independence; girls in primary schools were taught to obey their husbands and the state. The story of women's education in the nineteenth century is thus complex and, at times, contradictory.

This complexity derives in part from tensions within the debate over women's education that emerged during the Enlightenment. Before the Enlightenment, education in general was the preserve of the elites. Elite women obtained a minimal education acquired either at home or in schools run by religious orders. Debates over women's education, which date from the Renaissance, focused entirely on whether or not elite women should be educated in the same subjects men studied, such as philosophy and classical languages. These debates did not focus on access to state-run educational institutions, since such institutions did not exist.

The debate over women's education changed somewhat with the Enlightenment. Enlightenment thinkers argued that education was necessary for all individuals, as it would emancipate them from the Church, tradition, and superstition, allowing them to make their own decisions. This was believed necessary for progress and human happiness. They argued that governments had a responsibility to establish schools for their population, schools that would teach people useful information that they could apply in their everyday lives. In the absence of such schools, Enlightenment thinkers focused on alternate means of spreading education. The multivolume *Encyclopédie* (1751–72), for example, was meant to provide individuals with practical information that could be used in a variety of trades, while members of debating societies and other associations sought to educate themselves by interacting with others.

In France, women who ran salons, or *salonnières*, considered the preparation they did for the gatherings they held in their homes to be an important education, for both themselves and others. In order to guide the conversation, *salonnières* read widely and corresponded with the leading thinkers of the day, trying to put their fingers on the pulse of intellectual debate. Conversation among intellectuals, and correspondence with like-minded individuals in other cities and countries encouraged reflection and comment on the topics the *salonnières* selected. Salons served as informal institutions that could educate adults in the new ideas that were part of the Enlightenment. The education of children remained in the hands of mothers, fathers, private tutors, and religious orders.

Other European nations adopted the French model of salon culture in the late eighteenth century, and the ideas about education associated with it. In Poland and Russia, the adoption of salon culture meant that women became less sequestered in the family. Expected to hold their own in intellectual conversations, women realized, some with great relish, that they needed a better education. In response, Catherine II of Russia established the Smolney Institute for Girls of Noble Birth in 1764. The Smolney Institute only educated 900 girls out of a population of 40 million, yet it was a small step forward in girl's education.

Catherine II's initiative was unusual. Most governments did not take action on girls' education until the upheavals caused by the French Revolution made a variety of changes possible. In France, the Revolutionary government declared the need for elementary education for both boys and girls. This goal, thought to be necessary for the formation of new citizens, was never carried out due to a lack of resources. Similarly, in Bavaria, the Enlightenment-inspired Prime Minister Maximilien von Montgelas mandated school attendance for both boys and girls aged 7–16 in 1802. However, Montgelas also secularized the convents and closed their schools, which meant that venues for obtaining this education had disappeared. The Teacher Training Institute that the Bavarian state founded in response included a few women among its primarily male student body. Graduates of the Institute were meant to serve as a secular teaching force. Their numbers were so few, however, and the need for teachers so great, that Ludwig II restored the religious orders and their schools in the 1820s.

The initiatives taken by Catherine II, the French Revolutionary government, and the Bavarian Prime Minister are the products of one strand of Enlightenment thought, a strand that emphasized the importance of education for both men and women. The Marquis de Condorcet, for example, argued that any perceived deficiencies in women's intellectual ability were rooted in their inferior education. If women were to be denied citizenship on the basis of an inability to reason, he maintained, "we must also deprive of the franchise the part of the people which, devoted to incessant labor, can neither acquire light nor exercise its reason, and soon we should come, step by step, to such a pass as only to permit citizenship in men who had gone through a course of public law."[1] Condorcet argued that given the same education as men, women would be just as able to develop intellectually and contribute, through their accomplishments, to the public good. This same assumption underlay educational reforms in Russia and Bavaria.

A second strand of thought about girls' education emerged from the Enlightenment, one that was opposed to the point of view expressed by Condorcet. French writer Jean-Jacques Rousseau best expressed this strain of thought in his treatise on education, *Émile*, published in 1762. In *Émile*, Rousseau proposed a method of education that would preserve what he believed to be the natural goodness of humanity. Rousseau focused most of his attention on the education of boys, through his description of the education of the fictional boy, Émile. He argued that teachers should seek to inspire a boy's natural curiosity, allowing him to explore and play, and raise questions on his own, and that they should frame lessons as solutions to practical problems. In this way, Rousseau believed, boys would be educated not in order to serve or please others, but in order to seek out knowledge and apply it to practical problems of public import. Rousseau spent less time discussing the education of his fictional female character, Sophie, but it was clear from what he did say that her education would differ greatly from that of Emile. "A woman's education must...be planned in relation to man," he wrote. "To be pleasing in his sight, to win his respect and love, to train him in childhood, to tend him in manhood, to counsel and console, these are the duties of woman for all time, and this is what she should be taught while she is young."[2] Rousseau argued that nature should determine the education of both boys and girls. Girls should thus be allowed to run about and play when young, because it would make them strong for childbirth. At the same time, girls needed to be taught to restrain themselves. Girls learned to be docile when they interrupted their play when asked, without complaint. Mothers had the task of demonstrating how each lesson applied to the creation of a happy and pleasing home, thus making clear the practical import of their education. While boys were to focus on attaining an understanding of the physical world, girls were to pay attention to human relationships. They were to calibrate their words and conduct to the opinions and feelings of others. And rather than acquire an abstract knowledge of humanity, they were to learn what made those with whom they lived happy or sad, virtuous or corrupt. In this way, Rousseau argued, a woman could fulfill her true mission: to subtly and gently guide her husband toward virtue in all things, without usurping his authority.

Rousseau's ideas on education were extremely popular among many upper- and middle-class families. These families named their children Émile or Sophie, and adopted many of the educational methods Rousseau advocated. They also shaped state-run education. In Russia, Catherine II died in 1796, and the direction of the Smolney Institute passed to Empress Maria Feodorovna, wife of Paul I. The empress had been raised according to Rousseau's model, and thus shifted the curriculum of the Institute to prepare women for the home, rather than the salon. This shift was part of a larger cult of "pedagogical motherhood" in Russia that emerged in the late eighteenth century. Although the symbolic importance of the mother was a long-standing tradition in Russia, this new set of beliefs put the emphasis on a woman's practical duty to educate her children. Advice literature and literary texts could help teach her how to carry out this duty.

This emphasis on the Russian mother as educator contradicted traditional family practices, in Russia as in Western Europe, where children, especially children of the elites, did not spend time with their mothers until, as teenagers, they were ready to enter society. Before this, they were raised by servants, governesses, and in boarding schools. These ideas also threatened the traditional authority of the husband and father in the family, which was considered to be absolute. Proponents of pedagogical motherhood, by contrast, argued that women could and should play the role of moral guide in the family. This emphasis on women's importance as moral educator helps to explain why many women were attracted to the ideas expressed by Rousseau. Although at first glance the education of Sophie seems to limit her to the home, it also allows her an authority there that she had never before possessed.

Rousseau's ideas on education spread for other reasons as well. The Revolutionary and Napoleonic wars led to a rise of nationalist sentiment throughout Europe. By the early nineteenth century, countries such as England, Russia, and Poland, along with many German states, repudiated the salon and the *salonnière* as a symbol of all things French. Instead, they emphasized the simple virtues of the English, German, or Russian maiden. In Poland, partition among Prussia, Russia, and Austria in 1795 meant that all sovereign institutions were abolished. Out of necessity, Poles turned to the private sphere for their sense of identity, and argued that nationalist sentiment resided in the Polish mother, whose duty it was to teach it to her children. Rousseau's emphasis on women as guardians of moral virtue was easily adapted to nationalist ends. Mothers were thus urged do their patriotic duty by educating their children in the virtues of the nation.

Rousseau's ideas also became attractive when states realized the difficulties involved in reforming the educational system. In Bavaria, for example, the goal of educational reform for boys was clear: a better education would create boys better suited to work in the state bureaucracy. But the goal of girls' education was less clear, since their main role was still that of wife and mother. Many worried that too much education, or the wrong sort of education, risked ruining them for that role. Rousseau's emphasis on educating women for family life appealed to those worried about how to shape girls' education. Furthermore, in the wake of the French Revolution, governments worried that education might lead to instability. The lesson of the Enlightenment – that individuals should learn to make their own decisions – appeared to result in bloodshed both in and outside of France. Rousseau's belief that women should be taught to respect authority, and that they should exercise their moral authority to encourage their husbands to do the right thing, convinced many that educated women could be a source of stability.

The growing conviction that a certain type of education for girls could benefit the nation as a whole did not lead to the immediate foundation of state-run school systems. Many obstacles still existed, including insufficient resources, uncertainty over how much education girls needed, and opposition from those who believed that the study of academic subjects – as opposed to sewing, for example – would be dangerous for women and their families. Nonetheless, as the conviction grew over the course of the century that there was a link between political stability and education, states took an increasing interest in girls' education. Women educators advanced this process by taking the initiative in forming schools for girls of all ages.

Education in the home

Throughout Europe, girls received their first education in the home. The quality, extent, and content of their education depended upon their parents' knowledge. Girls in urban working families or rural farming families whose parents might not know how to read and write were nonetheless taught some religion, as well as skills related to their family's means of earning a living.

Education was secondary to work, however, as families sought to ensure that their children could contribute to the family economy by learning a trade.

Education for upper middle-class women and noble women also took place primarily in the home throughout most of the century. Education among the elites varied more widely, by geographic region and family background, than education among the popular classes. Until well into the nineteenth century, most Russian noblewomen did not know how to read and write. The focus of their education was on religion and obedience to one's husband.

In England, on the other hand, most upper middle-class women were expected to acquire a solid education, one that was more than merely decorative and that included real accomplishments. Mothers were central to this endeavor, yet other instructors could supplement their efforts. Fathers frequently participated in their daughters' education, and families hired tutors and governesses in specialty areas such as foreign language or music. However, even among girls of the English upper middle classes, there were very few subjects that every girl studied. Reading, writing, basic arithmetic, religion, and needlework were the staples in every well brought-up girl's education. Beyond this, however, educational levels varied widely. Many young women studied history, botany, and literature. Some mastered several foreign languages, while others obtained great proficiency in composing music or painting landscapes. Girls from scientific families were more likely to study sciences such as astronomy than those from other families.

Among the upper classes, education was meant to prepare girls for marriage and family life. As they grew into adults, women were expected to continue their education. Women's skills in languages or art could help fill their many leisure hours, and save them from boredom. They could also be used to enhance family life. Women composed music that was performed in family recitals, and painted portraits of family members. They also made good use of their education when the time came to teach their own children.

While most girls were educated primarily in the home, this was not the only locus of female education. Women supplemented their home-based education with lessons and lectures outside the homes, as well as with periods in boarding or convent schools. When Professor James Thomson of Glasgow, Scotland, began offering courses in geography and astronomy in 1833, the number of well-dressed ladies who attended surprised him. Likewise, John Ruskin's art history lectures in Oxford in the 1870s drew crowds of four to five hundred listeners, of which about one-third were women, although women could not yet obtain a degree at Oxford. As these examples indicate, girls and women living in large cities and university towns had the greatest access to informal education. Women also took the initiative in forming groups where they could learn from each other. In Russia, noblewomen in the countryside formed groups during the 1850s where they could debate questions of social and political reform. Their urban counterparts began to audit university lectures in 1859.

Education that began in the home could lead women far from it. The Englishwoman Elise Paget grew up in Oxford, where she became a talented painter. To advance her artistic education, she traveled to London to copy paintings in the National Gallery, and to Paris. When a family was either unable or unwilling to undertake a girls' education, privately run boarding schools or convent schools stepped in, giving girls the basic skills they needed for family life. However, just as education in the home varied greatly, so too did boarding and religious school curricula. It was not until the end of the century that governments began to oversee girls' private education. Before this time, the uneven and unregulated status of girls' education meant that the educational level attained by women varied enormously. This situation began to change when those who were better educated took it upon themselves – either for financial reasons or out of principle – to educate others.

Schools and the state

From the 1830s to the 1860s, many middle- and upper-class women took the initiative in moving education outside the home and into schools. These initiatives were motivated by a desire to provide girls with a better education. However, they were also linked to larger tendencies within European society. The expansion of girls' schools was due in part to demographic and economic changes, as growing numbers of single women sought employment in education. Ideological motivations contributed as well: governments fearful of revolution encouraged religious-based education, while liberal and conservative middle-class women alike came to believe, for different reasons, that working-class mothers could not provide their daughters with an adequate education. Feminists argued that traditionally raised middle-class mothers did not do much better. Finally, whether initiated by the state or against it, nationalism provided an important impetus for creating new schools.

Private schooling had traditionally offered an alternative or supplement to education obtained in the home. Traditionally, aristocratic families did not place great stress on educating their children at home. Daughters in particular were only interesting when they reached marriageable age, and could be used to consolidate a family's fortune. Up until that point, daughters spent much of their youth in convent schools, where they were educated in religion, basic reading, writing and arithmetic, needlework, and music. In the eighteenth century, privately run girls' schools began to offer parents an alternative to the convent school. These schools included both day and boarding schools, and were geared to both working and upper-class girls. In England, Dame Schools, day schools run by individuals in their homes, catered to working-class girls; the better ones taught them reading, writing, math, and domestic skills. Dame Schools continued to flourish until the 1880s. Boarding schools for middle-class girls also remained popular throughout the century. Girls in these schools were taught the skills believed necessary to a middle-class lady, much as they would have been in the home. French actress Sarah Bernhardt wrote of her two years in boarding school, "I learned to read, write and do arithmetic. I learned many games I didn't know. I learned how to sing rondos and how to embroider handkerchiefs for Mama. I was relatively happy because we went out on Thursdays and Sundays and these walks gave me a feeling of freedom."[3]

Whether religious or private, in most cases, girls of different classes attended different schools. An important exception was the parish school system in

Scotland. Fueled by the Protestant belief in universal education, yet not as concerned as the Church of England schools with the link between education and rebellion, Scottish parish schools educated boys and girls of all social classes together. Middle-class boys attended these schools the longest, as working-class boys and girls left to work and middle-class girls left to attend to family duties. Yet all were exposed to a variety of subjects, and by the end of the eighteenth century, most of the population of the lowlands was literate. Over the course of the nineteenth century, more emphasis was placed on different curricula for boys and girls – a change that working-class parents protested. However, girls of all classes continued to learn together.

Statistics on the number of private schools in existence in the nineteenth century are hard to come by. The statistics that do exist suggest that more girls were attending school over the course of the century. In Russia, for example, 2,007 girls attended school in 1802 and 4,864 attended in 1834. In the German states, secondary girls' schools increased from 342 in 1850 to 869 in 1901.

In some cases, schools were founded because women needed to support themselves. Middle-class women had few career options open to them until the end of the nineteenth century. The belief that women were "natural" educators led those women who needed to find work into teaching. Many women worked as governesses, helping to supplement the education a family could provide a girl in the home. The English writer Charlotte Brontë, who worked both as a governess and as a teacher in a private girls' school, used those experiences in her fiction. In *Jane Eyre* (1849), she described the difficulties governesses faced in a household where they were to cater to the whims of spoiled children and dismissive parents. The orphaned main character, Jane, was also forced to endure the snubs of local gentry ladies, who saw her as no better than a hired servant. From middle class or even, in countries such as Russia, noble background but forced to earn a living serving in the home of others, governesses occupied a position that combined educational accomplishment and economic and social dependency. It was a situation many found hard to bear. Governesses also expressed concerns that they were forced to teach children lessons that they did not believe. Aleksandra Ivanova (1844–?) wrote to her sister Ekaterina, "Can working as a governess really be considered earning an honest living? Either teachers have to teach children things that they don't believe themselves, or they must teach them to lie, by telling them to hide their ideas from their parents for fear of punishment."[4]

Women could obtain greater intellectual and social freedom by opening schools of their own, which increasing numbers chose to do. This was an expensive alternative, however. Opening a private girls' boarding school in Paris in 1860 required about 50,000–60,000 francs, while governesses in the best families made about 800–1,500 francs per year and were employed at most for only 10–12 years. Given that most women who went into teaching did so because they did not come from wealthy families, opening a school of one's own was a great accomplishment.

However, due to the uneven education most women possessed, sending one's daughter to a private boarding or religious school was no guarantee that she would receive a better education than she would at home. Indeed, middle- and upper-class families who wanted their daughters to learn more than basic reading, writing, arithmetic, and needlework often preferred to hire male tutors. This same assumption meant that men dominated the teaching staff at many private boarding schools as well. Religious orders, whose staff was female, had, by and large, no pretensions to serious academic preparation. Teachers at schools run by the Congregation of Notre Dame, for example, attempted to instill in their students "love for work, order and economy, modesty, docility, gentleness, goodness, simplicity."[5]

While such goals were consonant with the view that education was a preparation for family life, many girls and their families increasingly argued that education was a necessary prerequisite for earning a living. By mid-century, novels such as *Jane Eyre* had raised awareness of the difficulties facing a woman who had to earn a living. As the demand for employment rose, young women sought training as teachers, and new secondary schools opened to train them. Different European countries followed slightly different timelines in this matter, and yet everywhere secondary education outside the home became more common for middle- and upper-class girls over the course of the century.

France and some of the German states were the most advanced in this respect. In France, the first private teacher training school, or Normal School, for girls opened in 1838. Many more private schools to prepare girls to be teachers opened over the course of the 1850s. Bavaria and Prussia were also leaders in secondary education. The situation in these states was even more unusual, in that the state played a leading role. In Bavaria, the Max Joseph Institute for aristocratic girls aged 7–17 opened in 1813, the Nymphenburg School for daughters of professionals and higher civil servants aged 6–15 opened in 1817. The elitism of these institutions led lower civil servants and artisans to establish the Advanced Girls' School for their daughters in 1822. They wanted the school to focus on academics. Whereas French teachers who emphasized religiosity and feminine accomplishments ran the Max Joseph Institute, and the Nymphenburg School focused on piety and patriotism, the Advanced Girls' School was to offer an education that could be of practical use. As part of this mission, in 1826 the school absorbed the Teacher Training Institute that had been created in 1814. Although Prussia did not develop such an extensive school system in the beginning of the century, the state did sponsor teacher-training seminars as early as 1832.

More advances in secondary education were made during the 1850s and 1860s. Precursors of things to come, Queen's College and Beford College – both private schools – opened in London in 1848 and 1849 to train teachers. In 1850, Frances Buss opened the North London Collegiate School; this was followed in 1853 by the Cheltenham Ladies' College. Much later, in 1869, Hitchin and Girton College of Cambridge University opened, and in 1872 the Girls' Public Day School Company was established to open fee-paying boarding schools. The woman who headed this organization, Maria Grey, also established the Skinner Street Training College (later the Maria Grey Training College) for teachers in 1876. These schools were all private, although after 1869 they were eligible for taxpayer funds according to the Endowed Schools Act.

Other countries followed similar patterns, with varying participation from the state. In Germany, 60 state higher girls' schools were established in 1850.

State-run girls' gymnasiums – the first of which was located in Baden – began to open in 1893. Privately run, but state-authorized gimnaziia, or secondary schools, were established in Russia beginning in 1858, although special courses for teachers were not approved until 1870. Privately run courses at the secondary school level were opened in Cracow in 1868, and teacher-training seminaries established in 1871. In Austria, specialized state-sponsored schools – one for daughters of officers and another for those of civil servants – had opened in 1775 and 1786 respectively. These schools provided training for governesses. Aside from these special schools, no public secondary schools were founded in Austria until 1885. However, private schools were established in the 1860s, and by the mid-1870s some had begun to receive government subsidies.

Many of these establishments were founded in response to the demand for teacher training. The opening of secondary schools in Russia was a direct response to the diminished prospects of many noble girls following the emancipation of the serfs in 1861. The loss of land and of rights to free labor and dues led many families to a gradual impoverishment. Poorer nobles encouraged daughters to work; they were also less likely to take in unmarried female relatives. By 1866, 13 *gimnaziia* had opened; by 1881, 331 were in operation with a total of 69,700 pupils. In St. Petersburg, 50 percent of the pupils enrolled were from noble families. Similarly, in England, the 1851 census, which revealed that women outnumbered men, raised concerns about the role of "surplus" women – women who could never hope to marry. Teaching was considered an acceptable alternative to raising a family, and increasing numbers of middle-class families sought an education for their daughters in case they found it necessary to support themselves.

The link between secondary education and teacher training led to greater state involvement in countries that actively promoted a state-run elementary school system. France was the leader in this regard, passing laws in 1833, 1836, 1848, 1850, and 1881 that mandated primary education for both boys and girls. As a result, the French government expressed the greatest interest in women's education. The Duruy courses, established by the French Minister of Education Victor Duruy in 1867, were modeled after private secondary courses but were meant to ensure that the training of primary school teachers was both consistent and strong in sentiments such as nationalism. While these courses largely failed due to Catholic opposition, secondary public schools established in 1880 were more successful, and fulfilled the same function. On the other hand, the Austrian government did not begin regulating girls' secondary education until the late 1890s, and then only under pressure from women's organizations that wanted to see more stringent academic standards enforced.

While the primary motivation for opening a secondary school for girls was to satisfy demands for teacher training (and to employ already trained teachers), ideological considerations were also important. In the city of Dortmund, in Prussia, the anti-Catholic policies of the German government led to the closing of schools run by Catholic orders. Several Catholic girls' schools, all run by laywomen, opened between 1874 and 1892; all were harassed by authorities. In 1892, the nuns were allowed to return. The Catholic secondary school henceforth coexisted with the Municipal School for Protestant and Jewish girls.

In Poland, the situation was even more dramatic. Poland was partitioned in 1795, partially reconstituted under Napoleon as the Duchy of Warsaw and after 1815 as the Kingdom of Poland. In 1830, the Kingdom of Poland lost its autonomy and came under Russian control. The province of Galicia remained under Austrian control (it gained partial autonomy in 1867), while Western Poland was run by Prussia. While Prussia was relatively tolerant of efforts to establish schools that could teach Polish history and the Polish language, the Russians vigorously combated such schools. As a result, they went "underground"; an illegal network of schools, largely run by women, kept Polish nationalism alive. The women who taught in these schools faced exile to Siberia, while parents of the girls who attended faced steep fines.

Political and ideological conflict could thus make it difficult to keep a private school open. Financial pressures also took their toll. In the months following the 1848 revolution in France, many private girls' schools closed as parents found it increasingly difficult, given the unfavorable economic situation, to pay their fees. Many also looked to religious schools for a more conservative education. Private schools, which faced competition from each other and from religious institutions, were often considered less stable, even though religious schools could be closed when the political wind shifted. Thus the movement toward religious schools in France was reversed in the early 1880s, when new school laws sought to limit the role of nuns in girls' education. By the late nineteenth century, when most countries in Europe had achieved a measure of political stability, state-run schools offered the advantage of a greater sense of permanence.

In 1860, Russian writer Nadezhda D. Khvoshchinskaia published *The Boarding-School Girl*. In this novel, she argued that boarding-schools taught traditional respect for authority; her character's real education came when she met a male intellectual who opened her eyes to the reform movements shaking Russia. In fact, most secondary schools for girls were established for reasons other than developing women's intellectual capacities. Education was not meant to create female intellectuals, but rather to prepare women for family life or for employment as teachers. It was also meant to further certain political or ideological beliefs. This was even truer in the case of the working classes.

Educating the people

The advances made everywhere in Europe in secondary education for middle- and upper-class girls were not matched in elementary education for girls of the working classes and peasantry. Whereas states could and did play a role in girls' secondary education, the real impetus in most cases came from middle- and upper-class women themselves, who sought to further the educational and employment opportunities of future generations. Middle- and upper-class women focused on secondary education because it was assumed that most mothers in these social groups could provide an adequate early education for their children. Women, and governments, only became interested in education for the lower classes when political instability – a hallmark of the nineteenth century – seemed to indicate that lower-class mothers were not doing their job.

The goal of elementary education for workers and peasants was to create better workers and more obedient subjects or citizens. Virtually no thought was given to opening up secondary education to workers and peasants, especially girls.

With the notable exception of Scotland, education was segregated by class throughout Europe. Most people believed that the daughters of workers and peasants required a much simpler education than those of the middle and upper classes. Indeed, in many countries, schools for lower-class children did not exist until after mid-century. Two exceptions were England and France.

In England, little formal provision was made for working-class children until the passage of the 1870 Education Act. This law allowed local authorities to open schools funded by tax revenue in England and Wales. Compulsory attendance was mandated in 1876, and schooling was made free to pupils in 1891. Before these laws were passed, the absence of schools, the voluntary nature of education and the fees necessary to attend school meant that educational opportunities were limited for the children of the popular classes, especially those from poor families. Work came first, and even those children who did attend school would be kept home when work needed to be done.

Before 1870, Dame Schools, Sunday schools, and charity schools provided the only opportunity for some sort of education. These schools offered a very limited curriculum. The first Sunday Schools were founded by Hannah More and her sisters in the late eighteenth century. Believing that the poor should be able to read the bible (but not write), they established informal lessons on Sundays in rural mining districts. Networks of schools were established by Protestant dissenters beginning in 1808 and by the Church of England beginning in 1811. These schools focused on religious instruction, reading, writing, basic arithmetic, and sewing for girls. All of these schools charged fees, although beginning in 1830 they were able to offset these fees with grants provided by the government.

In France, various regimes repeatedly called for widespread elementary education. In 1816, the Restoration government called for each commune to establish a boys' primary school; this was extended to girls in 1819. The same regulation was issued by the July Monarchy in 1833 (1836 for girls), 1848 (for both sexes), and 1850 (for both sexes). However, no resources were allocated to these schools and the laws were not enforced. Elementary schools did open in some areas, largely run by members of religious orders. The same limited curriculum as that in English voluntary schools was followed. In some areas of France, up to 80 percent of girls had no formal education before 1850.

This situation changed following the passage of the Ferry Laws in 1881–82, which mandated the creation of free and secular public schools, and made schooling compulsory for children aged 6–13. Following the passage of these laws, many parents enrolled their daughters in Catholic schools, fearing the evil influences they might encounter in the state-run schools. However, since the female teachers in secular schools had received a traditional education that emphasized religion, they needn't have worried. Furthermore, the Ministry of Education mandated that the goal of girls' primary schools should be to teach pupils about "cares of the household and women's work."[6] The textbooks used in these schools emphasized women's domestic role.

Interest in educating the children of workers and peasants increased in the second half of the century. In Germany, middle-class women began establishing Sunday Schools for working-class girls in the 1850s. These schools taught practical skills like knitting, sewing, cooking, and infant care. While the girls worked, the teachers read them "morally uplifting stories."[7] These efforts were replicated in other countries as well. The impetus behind this expansion of education was to create a moral, hard-working, and obedient working class. It is no coincidence that such schools began to multiply after the Revolutions of 1848, when the demands for greater rights made by working-class men and women had frightened many in the middle classes. Such efforts made even a limited education more available to girls; yet, since these schools were largely organized and staffed on a voluntary basis, curricula were neither standardized nor regulated. In Germany, children's education was only standardized in the early twentieth century.

Middle-class women also took an interest in establishing vocational schools for girls. In Berlin, the Association for the Further Education and Intellectual Exercise of Working Women established a vocational school in 1869. That same year, Wilhelmina Schmidt opened the first technical school for women in Warsaw. It taught bookkeeping, bookbinding, retouching, and typesetting. The expansion of white-collar employment prompted the establishment of the Higher Grade Schools throughout Great Britain at the end of the century, which prepared girls for the commercial sector. Yet more traditional areas of employment were not neglected. The Association of Berlin Housewives set up a school to train domestic servants in 1876, while the first school of cookery opened in England in 1873. Since working-class women did not enroll in significant numbers, the school changed its mission to the training of middle-class women to become domestic science teachers.

Other efforts to educate the poor were more revolutionary. In Russia, Alexander II approved a Sunday School movement that sought to educate workers and peasants in their duties to God and the state. In the 1860s, women who belonged to the nihilist movement, a movement that rejected tradition in order to build a new Russia, sought to bring education to the people. Newly educated themselves, they were inspired by socialist and reformist ideas to teach rural women the basics of reading and writing, as well as to provide information concerning hygiene and health. While women in the countryside had to depend on those who came to them for an education, working women in cities had more options. They could attend special women's classes established at working men's colleges or participate in courses for working mothers established by middle- and upper-class women active in philanthropy.

By and large, however, educational opportunities for daughters of the working classes and peasantry remained limited in the nineteenth century. Even in France, where a system of free, secular, and compulsory primary education did exist by the end of the century, the curriculum of these schools tended to stress hard work, patriotism, and domestic virtues. Education was only emancipatory for a very small group of European women: those who attended universities.

Advanced education for women

Anna Korvin-Krukovskaia's father refused to allow her to attend boarding school, stating, "If you don't understand that it is the duty of every decent girl to live with her parents until she is married, I won't even argue with you, you stupid child!"[8] Given that secondary education for middle- and upper-class girls, like primary education for working-class girls and peasants, was not meant to be emancipatory, we might wonder at her father's attitude. Of course, he could have worried that education, even what little she might have received at a privately run boarding school, might lead her into new paths. In fact, while many middle-class girls attended secondary schools in order to train as teachers, others sought knowledge for its own sake. Louise Michel, a governess, school teacher, and participant in the Paris Commune, asked, "Do men sense the rising tide of us women, famished for learning? We ask only this of the old world: the little knowledge that it has."[9] This hunger for knowledge would lead growing numbers of middle- and upper-class women to fight, in the second half of the nineteenth century, for a university education.

The establishment of a greater number of secondary schools did not automatically lead to access to a university. Secondary schools for boys were meant to prepare them to pass the entrance exams necessary to matriculate. This was not the case for girls. Latin, which was necessary for admission to the university, was not taught in France, while in Germany, girls received no instruction in science, math, or classical languages. Furthermore, in most countries, women were not allowed to take the required entrance examinations. In 1861, Julie-Victoire Daubié was able to become the first French woman to pass the baccalauréat examination only because the Empress intervened on her behalf. More women took this examination in the 1860s. In 1863, Emily Davies, founder of Hitchin College, convinced authorities at Cambridge University to allow girls to take the examinations, but they had to take them separately from the men and with a chaperone. Austrian women were permitted to take the Matura beginning in 1872, while no German woman was allowed to take the Arbitur until 1895. Similarly, although the first public girls' secondary school opened in Cracow in 1896, girls were not allowed to take the final examination until 1907.

Simply being allowed to take the required examination did not guarantee admission to the University. First of all, just because women could take the exam didn't mean they did. Since most secondary schools did not teach all the required subjects, girls had to obtain the necessary training somewhere else. For example, although French girls could take the baccalauréat in the 1860s, no state-sponsored courses in classical languages were available to girls until after the First World War. Emily Davies' Hitchin College in England was an exception. She insisted that her students study the same subjects and take the same exams as boys did, not without much opposition. A more common attitude was that of Anne Jemima Clough, principal of Newnham College for Women. Clough believed that women were not yet ready for the University, and that women's secondary education had a long way to go to prepare them. She advocated the creation of informal university-level lecture courses for women.

Even Clough's position was too radical for many. Many individuals believed that advanced education, especially if it took place in the university, would be dangerous for both women and society. Opponents of university education argued that women would be a disruptive influence at the university, that intense study would render them sterile and/or revolutionaries, that granting women degrees would create competition between the sexes in the professions, and that higher education was not a good investment when it came to women, because they would quit when married. Elizabeth Garrett (1836–1917) exemplifies the difficulties women experienced in trying to obtain an advanced education. After applying unsuccessfully to one school after another to study medicine, she learned that there were no regulations barring women from studying pharmacy. She went through five years of courses and apprenticeships, often paying steep fees for private lessons when admission to general courses was closed to her. Shortly after she passed the exam, the Society of Apothecaries closed that avenue to other women, declaring that candidates who received any part of their education privately would not be allowed to take the exam. The British Medical Register never recognized Garrett's medical degree, which she eventually received in Paris. She did, however, practice as a doctor, specializing in women's health. Garrett's case demonstrates how both university authorities and professional associations were prepared to go to great lengths to deny women the diplomas they needed to exercise a career.

Despite Garrett's difficulties, medical schools were among the first institutions to allow women to enroll and graduate. This was the case in large part because women were able to argue effectively that women doctors could better serve women patients; male doctors, they maintained compromised the virtue of female patients. Thus as early as 1861, Nadezhda Suslova, the daughter of a serf, was able to enroll in the St. Petersburg Medical Surgery Academy. By 1864, the year it closed, over 60 women were enrolled, with no real opposition to their presence. Suslova then enrolled at the University of Zurich, where in 1867 she became the first woman in the modern era to earn a university degree. In the early 1870s, long before women were admitted to general university studies, several American women were in Austria pursuing advanced medical studies.

These early examples inspired more women both to campaign for admittance to a university, and to pursue alternative paths to an advanced education. English, French, and Russian women in the 1860s, German women in the 1880s, and Austrian and Polish women in the 1890s all campaigned for the right to matriculate. They created associations and signed petitions, such as that signed by almost four hundred Russian women in 1867. They also sponsored university-level courses for women. These were courses taught by university faculty, but open to the public. Paid series of courses, such as the Alarchin courses in St Petersburg, the Lublian courses in Moscow (both established 1869), and similar courses in Prague (1890) and Vienna (1892) opened to women without entry requirements. In 1882, Jadwiga Szczawinska, a Polish woman, created an illegal series of University-level courses for women who could not afford to travel abroad to study. Called the "Flying University," courses were held in private homes to avoid arrest; by 1893, 300 students were attending. Women also increasingly audited university lectures.

Yet although these initiatives allowed women to achieve a greater educational level, they did not lead to official degrees. Official degrees were necessary for women to be recognized in their chosen professions, and obtaining an official degree was only possible if women were allowed to matriculate. Although this change took the longest, from 1865 onward, when women began studying for degrees at the University of Zurich, growing numbers of women pursued formal higher education. By the 1870s, women had obtained formal admission to the Universities of Paris, Edinburgh, and London, and to universities in Ireland and Denmark. By the turn of the century, many more universities admitted women, including the University of Wales (1894) and of Baden (1900). Oxford and Cambridge held out the longest. Although they established women's colleges as early as 1868, they did not allow women to graduate until 1920 and 1921, and did not grant them degrees on the same terms as men until 1947. As the doors opened, women needed courage to face the taunts and criticisms of others, and the self-doubt that led them to question their abilities. Furthermore, until the professions practiced equality in hiring, a university degree was no guarantee of employment. Simply entering, much less graduating from, a university was an enormous accomplishment for a woman in the nineteenth century. As Gary Cohen has argued for Central Europe, "For a woman to matriculate in a university was still an extraordinary phenomenon in Austria or Germany before World War I, an act that required special dedication from any woman student and unusual support from her family. [...] The families of the early women students had to believe in the value of university education for their daughters and bear the financial burdens at a time when few learned professions would admit women."[10] As this quote indicates, even by the end of the century, when primary schooling had become common, secondary schooling widespread, and higher education a possibility, families still played an enormous role in determining the educational opportunities of their daughters. Although education was increasingly moving outside the home, no young woman could hope to obtain a degree without the support and consent of family members, especially parents. Thus education continued to be shaped by attitudes toward women's role in society even as structural changes in female education took place.

The expansion of female education in the nineteenth century was complex and uneven. The degree of education any woman could obtain depended on a wide variety of factors that included state policy, her class background, where she lived, her family's attitudes toward education and her own inclinations. While some women obtained an extensive education that allowed them to accomplish a great deal, others were barely literate. Despite this variety, however, it was increasingly accepted over the course of the century that neither of these two extremes were appropriate for women. The woman of genius was portrayed as a masculinized anomaly, while the illiterate mother was considered unqualified to raise her children. For the majority of Europeans, being a good wife and mother meant obtaining just enough education to be able to communicate intelligently with one's spouse and raise one's children to be good citizens. However, despite this widespread conviction, once women gained access to education, they were able to use it for their own ends. Women's education thus developed as a result of widely held communal beliefs and individual needs and desires. Although in theory it was meant to enhance private life, it could be used to enable women to function professionally in the public sphere. And, while many associated increased access to education – especially higher education – with modernity, the well-educated mother was herself a new phenomenon.

While increased access to formal, secular, education occurred as growing numbers of schools at all levels opened their doors to women, education was more than what happened in the classroom. Indeed, for most of the nineteenth century, as this chapter has emphasized, women gained an education through informal channels. This informality in the realm of education was mirrored by informal training in the arts and sciences. Artists and scientists in the nineteenth century tended to be both self-taught and self-sufficient, working by and for themselves rather than for universities or corporations. Although the term "amateur" is often taken to imply a lower level of skill, many amateur women scientists and artists were extremely talented. Furthermore, because many male scientists and artists were also amateurs in the nineteenth century, women were able to make important contributions. In using their knowledge – often obtained in the family or on their own – to write novels, paint foreign landscapes, or solve mathematical equations – female artists and scientists also contributed to the education of others.

6

Culture, the Arts, and Sciences

In the nineteenth century, the arts and sciences were important in providing individuals with a way to understand and talk about their society. The novels, poems, paintings, and musical scores that artists created were subjects of discussion, serving as catalysts in debates concerning the direction of social, political, and economic change. Artistic movements such as Romanticism and Realism stirred great passions, leading sometimes to angry exchanges as one manner of representing reality clashed with another. In a period in which the industrial and political revolutions, begun in the second half of the eighteenth century, still had to play themselves out, the arts could serve as a battleground for definitions of what society could and should be.

Science was similarly linked to social and political transformation. The objects of study chosen by scientists, their methodologies, and their conclusions all influenced, and were influenced by, contemporary debates concerning the organization and direction of society. The biological sciences were used to legitimize both democracy and racial inequality; they were tools in the battle for improved public hygiene and a prop to the development of political anti-Semitism. Discoveries in the physical sciences changed the way in which Europeans understood their world, sometimes causing great unease as a result. As science increasingly accompanied, and for many replaced, religion as the primary source of truthful knowledge about the world, scientific theories and discoveries took on growing importance in the discussion of social and political issues.

As the arts and sciences gained in importance in contemporary debates, questions of who should participate in artistic and scientific pursuits became more pressing. Long-standing beliefs concerning women's inferiority in both artistic creation and scientific exploration gained new currency in the nineteenth century. In both the arts and sciences, many saw women as occupying a passive role, serving as either a consumer of artistic works or a subject of scientific observation, rather than a creator of knowledge. Nonetheless, growing familiarity with the arts and sciences, improved education, and the need to earn a living drew increasing numbers of women into the arts and sciences as the century progressed. While many argued that women in the arts and sciences were dangerous anomalies, others stated that women could offer different and rewarding insights into the questions of the day. In the midst of these debates, female

101

artists and scientists struggled with the challenge of defining themselves both as creators of knowledge and as women.

One realm in which women had traditionally played an important and active role was popular culture. Women and men shared equally in popular festivities and pastimes. Whereas in the first half of the nineteenth century women and men were active participants in the creation of popular culture, by the end of the century, the growing influence of new mass cultural forms transformed individuals of both sexes into consumers and spectators of culture. At the same time, the new emphasis on the consumption of culture made women – traditionally identified as consumers – more important.

The growing influence of the arts and sciences

Both the arts and sciences have long had the ability to arouse great debate. In the seventeenth century alone, the quarrel of the ancients versus the moderns divided the dramatic world, while the Inquisition tried astronomer Galileo Galilei for arguing that the earth revolved around the sun. Yet for most of human history, a very small number of individuals pondered these questions and shared in the emotions they aroused. This began to change in the eighteenth century when rising literacy rates, a growing, and increasingly wealthy middle class, and an aristocracy interested in reform gave rise to an educated public. Through meetings in coffeehouses, tablesocieties, Masonic lodges, and salons, through specialized journals, newspapers, and letters, this public discussed and debated new artistic works and new scientific experiments.

In the aftermath of the French Revolution, these discussions took on a greater political importance. Although before the Revolution individuals had frequently imagined different ways of organizing society, the French revolutionaries took these imaginings out of the utopian realm and put them into practice. Once attempted, the possibility of creating a different society could not be derided as impossible. The literary and artistic movement of Romanticism drew upon the emotional upheaval of the Revolutionary period to produce among its adherents a tortured longing for a different society. Whereas Romantics looked to the past, to nature, and to the exotic as models of difference, scientists looked to the future. Scientists drew inspiration from the revolutionary conviction that society could be improved through human efforts. Continued growth in literacy rates, a gradual expansion of education at all levels throughout Europe, an expanding publishing industry, and the increased popularity of cultural activities such as attending a concert or visiting an art exposition, gave artists and scientists greater opportunities than ever before to expose their work to the public eye and to public debate. At the same time, as the public became more educated, more men and women alike wished to participate directly in these dynamic and vital areas of human endeavor.

By the beginning of the nineteenth century, more individuals were able to engage in artistic pursuits or scientific investigations than ever before, both as amateurs and as professionals. Several changes that took place over the course of the eighteenth century contributed to the growth of opportunities. New opportunities for making a living presented themselves to both artists and scientists. Western Europe in particular grew wealthy as a result of the "triangular" trade in slaves, plantation-grown tobacco, sugar and coffee, and manufactured goods. The middle classes grew in number and wealth and they, along with the aristocracy, began spending some of their money on the arts and sciences. Individuals commissioned paintings for their homes, and attended private concerts. They bought scientific journals, paid dues to scientific societies, and conducted experiments in animal husbandry on their estates. This trend became even more pronounced by the beginning of the nineteenth century. The expansion of the publishing industry made books, musical scores, and prints of celebrated paintings available to a larger public than ever before. This public also enjoyed the arts in growing numbers of theaters, concert halls, museums, and art expositions. Likewise, both specialized journals and the popular press discussed scientific discoveries, and in some countries the study of science was integrated into the university curriculum. In the first half of the nineteenth century, then, the arts and sciences escaped the confines of royal and aristocratic patronage to become topics of public interest and debate, and objects of public consumption. It now became possible to imagine that an individual could make a living by either appealing to the public taste, or by making a discovery that would be recognized to advance knowledge or be of great public utility. This new possibility opened up the door for men and women of more modest means to pursue their interests in the arts and sciences. For women, however, this door was often hard to pass through.

Challenges to women's participation

Many commentators assumed that artistic and cultural creativity were male characteristics. Women, it was argued, could inspire and appreciate, but could not create. Similarly, the tough social questions of the sort that artists and writers tackled in the second half of the nineteenth century were deemed inappropriate for women, whose presumed intellectual inferiority and natural modesty prevented them from being able to address such issues competently. Rather than creator, women were commonly seen as muse, reader/spectator, or subject of study.

One of the central currents of Romanticism, a highly influential literary and artistic movement in the early nineteenth century, was the idea of the female muse. In opposition to classically trained painters and playwrights, whose work, in both form and content, was shaped by norms assumed to be universal and regulated by Royal Academies, the Romantics celebrated the cult of individual, masculine genius and female inspiration. As a painter or poet's "muse," women prompted the artist to see the world in a new way. Working off this inspiration, the artist then used his inherent genius to create an original work of art. Some women embraced this role of muse. Caroline Schlegel-Schelling (1763–1809) became part of a circle of German Romantic writers. She was instrumental in helping her first husband, August Wilhelm Schlegel, translate Shakespeare into German. Similarly, the English Pre-Raphaelite poet and painter Dante Gabriel Rossetti drew innumerable portraits of his wife, Elizabeth Siddal (1829–62), whom he compared to Dante's muse, Beatrice. Reportedly, when Rossetti met Siddal, he "felt his destiny was defined."[1] Rossetti sketched so many portraits of Siddal after meeting her that a friend denounced his "monomania." Although Siddal was herself a painter and poet, her identity as an artist was long overshadowed by that of Rossetti's muse.

The widespread acceptance of the notion that female inspiration was necessary to the creation of great art led writers, painters, and composers to invoke both the muse and the feminine more generally in legitimating their art. Novelists in particular saw women not only as the inspiration for their works, but as the audience as well. It was widely believed that novels, with their focus on the everyday lives of ordinary individuals, were read overwhelmingly by women. Indeed, when the novel emerged as a new genre in the eighteenth century, women both wrote and read these works in great numbers. By the early nineteenth century, the novel gained a respectability that it had not before possessed. As a result, although women were still considered to constitute the major audience for the novel, increasing numbers of men tried their hand at this genre. To appeal to women, male novelists created stories that featured female heroines and sometimes even adopted the female voice. They also argued that they possessed a "feminine" sensitivity that made them able to penetrate the secrets of the human heart, an ability previously accorded primarily to women. At the same time, critics of the novel argued that novels excited the already unstable emotions of female readers, leading them down the path of debauchery. Such criticism led even some fans of the novel to believe that women, by writing about situations designed to appeal to the emotions and doing it for money, placed their virtue in danger. Women novelists tread a line, some believed, that brought them dangerously close to prostitution. Accepted during the eighteenth century when the novel was considered a lesser genre, women novelists in the nineteenth century found that they faced increasing opposition from much of their male competition. While many women persisted, others turned to writing children's literature, devotional literature, or conduct and housekeeping manuals, all of which carried less prestige.

The questions of both prestige and prostitution also shaped attitudes toward women in the fine arts. The prestige accorded to certain genres of painting meant that women found it difficult to compete or be taken seriously. Historical painting, for example, remained prestigious throughout the century. These paintings required the study of anatomy and life drawing in order to render the human subject effectively. For much of the century, however, women were barred from the study of both anatomy and life drawing, making it difficult for them to compete with their male colleagues in this genre. Women focused instead on still lifes, landscapes, and portraits, and were numerous among painters of miniatures. Those women who did attempt historical paintings, like the English Anna Jameson (1794–1860), were ruthlessly attacked by critics who tended to focus less on the image and more on the sex of the artist.

Over the course of the nineteenth century, the female subject, and especially the female nude, took on a growing importance in painting. At the same time, female models were increasingly associated with prostitution. Ironically, modeling had always been a respectable career for men, and classical painting's emphasis on the male nude meant that employment opportunities were plentiful in the eighteenth century. However, in the nineteenth century, as Romanticism and genre painting gained ground, costume was more important than the human form, and opportunities for male models diminished. The female nude, on the other hand, increased in importance, thus creating a need for a greater number of female models. Unlike their male counterparts, however, female models were considered to be immoral women, barely one step up from prostitutes. This association between the female model and prostitution, an association that was made explicit in certain paintings in the last quarter of the century, such as Edouard Manet's controversial "Olympia," rendered women's role as spectator difficult. Were female viewers of such artworks supposed to identify with the woman on the canvas or the man who painted her, or simply cover their eyes? The implications of viewing such works were troubling for women whose identity was based in the ideology of domesticity.

One of the forces behind a growing demand for female models was the emergence, in the second half of the nineteenth century, of a new artistic movement, called Realism. Influenced in great measure by the increased authority of science, Realism made evident a new role for women in the arts: that of subject of study. Realism moved away from Romanticism's imaginings of a different and better world to focus on the world as it was. While Realists also championed reform, they believed, like scientists, that change would come about through a minute examination of existing conditions. The improved understanding gained by such examination could then serve as a springboard for reform. Realists tended to focus on the more troublesome areas of contemporary society, and they were particularly interested in the problems that women faced.

In the nineteenth century, society came to believe that the maintenance of women's virtue and dignity was a necessary task of civilization. The existence of immoral or degraded women thus became a sign that society was not functioning correctly, and, for many, a warning that civilization itself was in danger. In an effort to improve society, Realist writers and painters turned their attention to female poverty, adultery, and prostitution. They examined in minute detail the nature of women's misfortunes and the causes of their downfall. Realist writers of the mid-century tended to place a fair amount of blame on functional problems of society, unlike earlier nineteenth-century writers who blamed women's misfortunes on the sexuality and depravity of the women themselves. French novelist Gustave Flaubert, for example, created in *Madame Bovary* (1857) a heroine whose tragic death was caused by a good dose of bad judgment and misplaced ambition, but also by a society that limited her possibilities for excitement and self-realization. A country girl wed to a stable but dull small-town doctor, Emma Bovary's desire for recognition, passion, and adventure led her to commit adultery, ruin her finances, strike her daughter, and eventually, take her own life.

Many of the late-century successors of the Realist writers, the Naturalists, focused on inherent – often genetic – flaws in women's characters. In French novelist Emile Zola's *Nana* (1880) the main character, a high-priced courtesan, is the product of generations of drunkenness, immorality, and violence. This background predestines her for a career as a prostitute, which she uses to gain wealth and influence in society, corrupting all those who come in contact with her, before sinking into the mire of Paris. This focus on inherently flawed women gave rise to a strong wave of misogyny in the arts, particularly among the avant-garde. Dutch author Joris-Karl Huysman's *A Rebours* (*Against Nature*, 1884) contains a nightmare sequence in which the main protagonist is chased by a horribly syphilitic female monster. As in this novel, women were often portrayed as dangerous bearers of decay, diseased harpies whose influence on society threatened an end to civilization. Such portraits were created in the midst of both a growing movement for women's emancipation and a rising incidence of syphilis. Painters and writers increasingly linked female emancipation, death, and the end of civilization in their works.

While such images became more popular in late nineteenth-century arts and letters, they were not the only images circulating. In Norway, the playwright Henrik Ibsen made waves with works that drew attention to the frustrations caused by the limitation of women's sphere. *A Doll's House* (1879) tells the story of a woman trapped in a marriage to a man who continually denigrates her intelligence and attempts to limit her autonomy. The female protagonist leaves her husband at the end, and although Ibsen's ending was ambiguous enough to allow for the possibility of future reconciliation, the play shocked audiences and critics alike.

As muse, reader/spectator and subject of study, women were omnipresent in the arts in the nineteenth century. They were also present as writers and artists. Those who believed that women's nature excluded artistic creation did not simply ignore the evidence of active women artists in their midst. Rather, they attempted to criticize their efforts with the charge that their participation in the arts stripped women of their femininity. Throughout Europe, the stereotype of the bluestocking or "bas-bleu" gained ground. The term bluestocking, originally applied to a small group of female intellectuals, expanded in the 1830s and 1840s to mean any woman who tried her hand at writing for money or recognition. Bluestockings were accused of being self-interested and ambitious, two traits that clashed with accepted notions of femininity. They were ridiculed in print, as well as in cartoons that depicted them with flat chests, stringy hair and haggard faces. Invariably, the supposed humor of these cartoons lay in the premise that the bluestocking believed she was beautiful, thus drawing a connection between her delusions of beauty and her delusions of literary talent. Some argued that the mental activity necessary for writing could destroy women's sanity and reproductive health. Critics who used the bluestocking stereotype always made an exception for one or two women, who expected neither fame nor fortune for their efforts. These women wrote out of purely feminine motivations to educate and bring beauty into the world, or to earn a little extra money for their children. In short, critics allowed for the possibility of the female writer, as long as she remained an amateur.

In addition to attacks on their femininity, women artists and writers faced institutional obstacles. Women found it difficult to receive formal training. The Royal Academy in London did not admit its first female associate member until 1922, and its first full member until 1936. While art schools taught their students to paint in the celebrated genre of the history painting, women often had to confine themselves to less highly regarded genres such as domestic scenes and miniatures. Those women who dared attempt the more valued genres were looked upon with disapproval. Anna Mary Howitt (1824–84), an English painter, was roundly criticized in 1856 when she submitted a large historical oil painting to the Crystal Palace Exhibition. Despite such criticism, even being accepted for exhibition was a success, for juries were composed of men. Similarly, art collectors, who also put on exhibitions, and, in the literary trade, publishers, were men. Women artists and writers thus had to overcome not only a lack of formal training, but also any prejudices that men in the art world may have possessed. If they succeeded in showing or publishing their work, they faced the scrutiny of male art and literary critics.

Women in the arts

Given these challenges, one might expect that very few women succeeded in the arts and letters. The ideology of domesticity, artistic and literary movements such as Romanticism and Realism, and male control of the institutions of the art and literary world seem to present an insurmountable barrier to women's participation. The reality, however, is more complex. Significant numbers of women pursued artistic and literary careers in the nineteenth century. Women who were active in the arts found ways to compensate for the challenges they faced on both an institutional and an ideological level. They founded informal support groups and formal institutions for learning their craft and showing their work. They found friends and mentors, both female and male, who offered them guidance and opportunities. And while many women worked as professionals, many more pursued the arts as amateurs. Their contributions were often welcomed by individuals who believed women brought a different perspective to issues. The editor of the English *Quarterly Review*, for example, urged Elizabeth Rigby, later Lady Eastlake (1809–93), to contribute to his publication, stating, "I had long felt and regretted the want of that knowledge of women and their concerns which men can never attain, for the handling of numberless questions most interesting and important to society."[2]

Women entered the arts for a variety of reasons. Most were drawn by a sense of vocation, but many were motivated by economic necessity as well. Despite the large number of obstacles women faced, the tremendous increase in demand for the written word in the first half of the nineteenth century opened up opportunities for women to earn a living by writing. In England and France, technological advances in paper manufacturing and printing lowered the cost of books in the early nineteenth century, at the same time as literacy rates were beginning to rise. Books thus became less expensive and more people were able to read. Even in countries where literacy remained low, such as Russia, educated noblewomen wrote for readers like themselves. The expansion of publishing also led to an increased demand for book illustrations, a field that employed significant numbers of women. Women artists also benefited from the growing popularity of art collecting in the nineteenth century. Again, this trend was most pronounced in Western Europe, with its larger middle class, but was evident in Eastern and Southern Europe as well. Women were active as landscape painters; for example, the English artist, author and feminist activist Barbara Smith

Bodichon (1827–91) gained fame in both England and France for her Algerian landscapes. Women also painted portraits, often of other women artists and writers. Portraitist Margaret Gillies (1803–87) was among a group of feminists and artists who exchanged portraits and photos of each other. A few women were able to earn money through the sale of their paintings; others supplemented income earned from their artwork with employment as art teachers. Pursuing a career in literature and the arts did not necessarily undermine the standards of domesticity, despite what many critics said. While some women sought exposure of their work, others found writing and illustration appealing because they could be done in the privacy of one's home, and, if so desired, pseudonymously. Similarly, many women pursued the arts as amateurs, creating stories and paintings meant to be enjoyed by family and friends.

Writing and painting thus became increasingly important as career paths for growing numbers of women. According to the English census, the number of professional women painters recorded jumped from 278 in 1841 to 1069 in 1871. Income gained through artistic and literary pursuits was especially welcome to women whose family situation left them with no other means of support. After the English writer Anna Jameson separated from her husband in 1838, for example, she was able to support herself from her writing. Yet legal restrictions created hardships for some writers and painters. French writer Flora Tristan (1803–44), who also tried to support herself through her writing, faced the challenge of a legal code that stipulated that money earned by a wife was the property of her husband. Her estranged husband succeeded in gaining control of much of her income, leaving her in near poverty despite her literary successes. The difficulties faced by women artists who did not control their earnings prompted Barbara Bodichon, ironically a woman of independent means with a most understanding husband, to draft a petition to Parliament calling for the passage of the Married Women's Property Act (1870), which would allow women to control their wages. Writing could be an important means of support, but only if a woman could retain control of her earnings, and only for those women who had received some sort of education.

Most women writers and artists born in the late eighteenth or early nineteenth centuries received informal training, often from family members. The reason behind such training varied, depending on the socioeconomic status of the family. Noble and middle-class girls were taught to draw, sing, and play the piano as a badge of wealth and rank. Although they were encouraged to become highly accomplished, they were taught to be modest about their talents, making use of them only to entertain close friends and family. Many of these women participated in the arts as amateurs throughout their lives, while others became professionals. Emilia Pardo Bazàn (1851–1921) was born to a moderately wealthy family in Spain. Her parents encouraged her intellectual interests, and, by the 1880s she had become a popular Naturalist writer and literary critic who focused on the status of Spanish women.

In the artisanal and working classes, some girls were taught to write and paint as a means to earn a living. French painter Rosa Bonheur convinced her father, also a painter, to allow her to study painting with her brothers, rather than be apprenticed as a seamstress. The Stannard family in England trained all its children in the arts so that they could contribute to the family income; while the boys learned landscape painting, the daughter, Eloise (1829–1915), became a still life painter.

Many writers also received informal training, especially in the first half of the nineteenth century, when few educational opportunities for women existed. The Brontë sisters, Charlotte (1816–55), Emily (1818–48), and Anne (1820–45), received most of their early schooling at home, under the direction of their father, the Reverend Patrick Brontë. Family participation in the arts could also supplement the limited education that existing schools provided. The grandmother of German writer Bettina von Arnim (1785–1859) was the novelist Sophie von LaRoche (1730–1807), while her brother, Clemens Brentano, was a poet. Her convent education was thus accompanied by interactions with other writers, including a correspondence with Johann Wolfgang von Goethe.

The earliest opportunities for formal training arose in England. With women of all classes active as painters, many considered women's admission to the prestigious Royal Academy both necessary and justified. In 1860, Laura Herford submitted her drawings to the school with only her initials and was admitted, much to the consternation of the school's directors once they learned the true sex of the painter. While the Academy began admitting women on a regular basis not long thereafter, no woman was allowed to attend life-drawing classes until 1893.

The difficulties in gaining admission to the best art schools led women to create their own institutions. Eliza Fox-Bridell organized an evening class on drawing from life for ladies, and the Female School of Art introduced classes using draped models in 1863. Despite continued criticism that female artists were women who neglected the higher calling of motherhood, better training resulted in improved technique and led one male observer to state in 1869, "female artists cannot justly be ignored."[3]

Women also established networks and support groups. The circle around Barbara Smith Bodichon was made up of women writers and painters who conversed and wrote with each other about their work and the struggles they faced. These informal networks gave way in the second half of the century to more formal institutions, such as the English Society of Female Artists, founded in 1856 by Harriet Grote (1792–1878). This organization became a forum for art classes and art exhibitions for women. Such organizations, both formal and informal, provided an important cultural function for women as well. In the midst of a general culture whose dominant message was that women could not succeed as artists and writers, these groups and institutions provided an alternate reality, one in which many women pursued their artistic calling with passion and determination.

These societies were all the more important in that women who were successful in showing or publishing their work faced the challenge of defining themselves and their artistic activities in relation to accepted notions of femininity. Since society viewed women artists as an anomaly, and the wife and mother as the norm, women artists found themselves needing to create a model of identity that could take account of both their sex and their vocation. Women writers sometimes apologized to their readers, begging their indulgence for untrained prose. Thus Russian writer Mariya Izvekova wrote in 1806, "I am sure that [...] the esteemed public will generously forgive the inexperience of a young girl who has written this Novel without the guidance of teachers [...]. I did not at all intend to publish it [...]. I am not so vain as to be insensible to its faults."[4] While possibly an attempt to deflect criticism, this apology also reflects the real anxiety women felt when venturing into the art and literary world. This anxiety was caused by uncertainty concerning how their work would be received. It was also the result of engaging in activities that challenged their notion of what was acceptable for women. Some responded to this challenge by rejecting the norms of domesticity altogether. The American sculptor Harriet Hosmer (1830–1908) became the center for a community of Anglo-American artists and writers in Rome. She believed that marriage and artistic careers did not mix for women. Members of the group of women artists and writers that formed around her became infamous for dressing in masculine clothes and forming romantic relationships with other women. Even Hosmer, however, referred to her works as her "children."

While cross-dressing could serve to make an ideological statement concerning the relationship between art and femininity, it could also serve a practical purpose. French painter Rosa Bonheur, who received the coveted Legion of Honor award for her paintings of animals, was given permission by the Paris police to wear men's clothes so that she could visit slaughterhouses in safety. Similarly, French novelist George Sand (1804–76) wore men's clothes to enable her to move about the city freely, observing and drawing inspiration for her literary works. Sand, whose real name was Aurore Dupin, published all of her 80 novels under a male pseudonym. Other writers, such as George Eliot, the Brontë sisters, and the journalist Delphine de Girardin (1804–55), who wrote under the name of the Vicomte de Launay, avoided, at least at first, criticism of their work on the basis of their sex by using a male name.

Women artists faced the question of how to explain their experience of the creative process. Marian Evans, the English writer more commonly known as George Eliot (1819–80), was inspired by painter Barbara Smith Bodichon, and apparently based the heroine of her novel *Romola* on her friend. Bodichon was inspired by nature, while her friend Anna Mary Howitt (1824–84) was, in the case of one painting at least, inspired by a vision. Inspiration was one part of the process; the work to bring that inspiration to fruition was another part, and women sometimes had to transgress accepted norms to get that work done. During Bodichon's stay in Louisiana, for example, her husband Eugène took care of all the shopping and cooking so that she could work. Women artists who lived with other women who were not also artists, such as Rosa Bonheur, could also often free themselves from worries over domestic tasks. Other women engaged in love affairs without marrying, thus maintaining some degree of autonomy. For many women artists and writers, finding the time and space necessary to do their work meant that they led unconventional lives.

One measure of this lack of convention was a willingness to adopt new methods of artistic expression. Photography was a new field in the nineteenth century, one that was praised for its ability to depict reality with scientific precision. Its association with scientific realism and the ability to manipulate heavy equipment and mix potent chemicals seemed to make photography a man's field. Yet women also adopted the new medium. Lady Clementina Hawarden of Scotland was an amateur photographer who posed her subjects in the windows and balconies of her home. Julia Margaret Cameron (1815–79) came to photography late, when her daughter gave her a camera for her forty-eighth birthday. An indefatigable amateur, she converted her garden greenhouse into a darkroom and studio. Her dreamlike images of young women and her starkly lit portraits of famous men were meant to encourage reflection on mortality and to capture the inner essence of the spirit. Cameron compiled albums of her photographs, which she gave as gifts to friends and family members. Although her "feminine" style placed her outside the mainstream of photography in her time, she did obtain praise for her work both then and in the early twentieth century, when her work was rediscovered and hailed for its modern feel and attempt to uncover the psychological depths of an individual.

Virginia Woolf, Cameron's great-niece, argued that the camera transformed her great-aunt from a housewife into an artist. Becoming an artist was no easy task for a nineteenth-century woman, and Cameron, like many of her peers struggled to define herself in both roles. That she chose photography as her medium did not make the task any easier, for its association with science made it an even more unlikely arena for a woman. Yet, in the sciences, as in the arts, women broke beyond the bounds of their culture's expectations to attain remarkable achievements.

Women in the sciences

Women researchers made several scientific advances in mathematics, physics, and the biological sciences. One of the most prominent mathematicians, Marie–Sophie Germain (1776–1831) as a teenager became so excited by the study of mathematics that her parents took away her candles and clothes and put out the fire in her bedroom so that she would get some sleep. Nonetheless, young Germain persevered in her studies, often wrapping herself up in a blanket and reading by candles she had smuggled in. In order to study mathematics, she had to overcome more than her parent's concerns. Women were not allowed to obtain a formal training in mathematics, so she made friends with a student at the Polytechnical School who was willing to lend her his notes. She sought out male mentors, corresponding with them at first through a male pseudonym, and only revealing her sex once she gained their trust. Despite a training that had some holes in it, owing to the fact that she was self-taught, she continually attempted to solve difficult mathematical problems. One of her attempts was the solution, known as Germain's Theorem, to a portion of an equation called Fermat's Last Theorem. This difficult equation was only fully solved by a computer in 1993. Her work won her the respect and admiration of many of her peers. In 1822, she was admitted to meetings of the Academy of Sciences. Germain never married; her father's money allowed her to pursue her love of mathematics until her death.

The situation of Marie-Sophie Germain was similar to that of many women in science. These women often demonstrated a talent for their area of expertise at a very young age. They were aided in the pursuit of their studies, and the development of their work, by family members and male mentors. Despite obstacles, their achievements often brought them respect and recognition. Although the ideology of domesticity, with its emphasis on the opposition between a female "nature" and a male, public world of "science," strongly defined European culture, women could and did achieve prominence in the sciences in the nineteenth century.

In the eighteenth century, Jean-Jacques Rousseau had argued that women were less suited than men for scientific investigation. The emotions and intuition that made them excellent wives and mothers, he believed, prevented them from achieving the objectivity necessary to scientific study. This argument would continue to be made throughout the nineteenth century. Indeed, opponents to women's scientific education argued that the intense study necessary in fields such as medicine could seriously disrupt women's nature. The increased flow of blood to the brain that intense study was believed to require would divert blood from the reproductive organs, resulting in disastrous consequences, including sterility and madness.

Instead of studying science, women were to be the objects of study. It was a commonplace of the mid-nineteenth century that male medical students ran the risk of entering into the autopsy theater on any given morning and seeing, dead upon the table, the body of a young woman he had once loved. This young woman, abandoned by the student, turned to prostitution and, after dying an early death, was given up to science. Students of the human mind flocked to the presentations offered by Dr. Charcot, where young madwomen writhed and moaned for their audiences. Women, associated with nature, were, like any other natural phenomenon, the object of scientific study rather than its agent.

Yet despite the existence of ideological and institutional barriers to women's activity in the sciences, a small group of women were involved in scientific study and experimentation. Their actions can be explained by a combination of structural and personal factors. Among these factors, was the acceptance of amateurs in the scientific community. In the early nineteenth century, the professionalization of the sciences had only begun. A lack of agreed-upon professional standards, and methods to enforce them, created openings for women. Medicine, for example, was still relatively disorganized in the mid-nineteenth century. Medical practitioners had varying levels of education and disagreed upon theories related to the causes of disease and their treatment. Women, who had long occupied a traditional role as healers and midwives, were still active. In most areas of Europe, midwives learned their skill from watching and assisting other midwives. Some became highly skilled, in great demand as midwives to nobility. Until the end of the nineteenth century, and the invention of anesthesia, most babies were delivered at home by a midwife. When doctors professionalized at the end of the century and made themselves uniquely able to use anesthesia and instruments in childbirth, they tried to undercut the midwives. Nevertheless, schools for midwives had existed since the early nineteenth century.

Little or uneven professionalization thus allowed women who had traditionally been active in the sciences to remain active. Similarly, the lack of institutionalization made science more accessible to women. In our day, science is done in expensive laboratories, usually located in major research universities or corporate research facilities. Carrying out scientific experiments in this setting means obtaining years of educational training, including apprenticeships in the laboratory, and then being hired as a scientist. This institutionalization of science was very much a twentieth-century phenomenon. In the early nineteenth century, most scientific investigation and discovery was done by amateurs, often working in their own homes. Employment opportunities for scientists were few, and most relied on the support of their families or of patrons in order to carry out their work. Patronage was based on personal relationships, often cultivated by women. This "domestic ... production" of science, the norm for most of the nineteenth century, was much more conducive to including women than the later institutionalization of science would be.[5]

Over the course of the century, institutionalization and professionalization gained ground, making it harder for women to gain access. As professional standards gained acceptance, women found it more difficult to obtain medical and scientific training, which henceforth was located in universities. Yet this shift to a fully institutionalized science was still incomplete, leaving plenty of room for amateurs in the scientific community and making it possible for women to gain entry. Exceptions to sex-based restrictions were often made for talented women scientists, especially when a woman's male peers in the scientific community pled her case. Ironically, formal training became more important in the late nineteenth century just as women were starting to gain access to higher education. Thus, while obstacles still remained, the nineteenth century produced a number of remarkable women scientists.

The best known of these women is without doubt Marie Sklodowska Curie (1867–1934). Curie came from a family where science was a subject of interest and study; her father was a physicist. This was true of many women scientists. Irish astronomer and photographer Margaret Huggins (1848–1915) was taught astronomy by her grandfather, an amateur in the science. Clémence Royer (1830–1902), who made a name for herself in anthropological and eugenics circles after translating Charles Darwin's *Origin of the Species* into French, was taught math by her father. Florence Nightingale (1820–1910), a talented statistician as well as nurse, was first taught mathematics by her father as well. Nightingale's method of statistical compilation for hospitals was widely adopted, and she became a fellow of the British Royal Statistical Society.

Curie was unable to attend the University in her native Poland, so, after working for several years, first as a tutor, and then a governess, she went to Paris to enroll in the Sorbonne. Other women who became scientists in the second half of the nineteenth century also had to leave their native countries to attend the University. Russian mathematician Sofia Kovalevskaia (1850–91) was studying University-level math at the age of 15 under a private tutor hired by her father. When she desired more formal training, she had to move to Germany. After studying first at the University of Göttingen and then at Heidelberg, she completed her doctorate at Berlin, where she became good friends with Julia Lermontova (1846–1919), who received her doctorate in Chemistry at the University of Berlin in 1874, the same year as Kovalevskaia.

Women who came of age earlier in the century were denied University training altogether; like Germain, they tended to be self-taught. Some have argued that this lack of formal training could work to a woman's advantage. Self-educated Augusta Ada Byron, Countess of Lovelace (1815–52) devised what is recognized as the first computer programming language after studying the newly invented Jacquard loom, which became the basis for computer data cards of the twentieth century. That loom, designed for weaving prints of flowers and plants, gave rise to the Analytical Engine, whose basic function was to execute whatever program its operator designed for it to calculate. She designed what is now accepted as the first computer program for the Analytical Engine to perform a calculation, by means of repeated instructions in a "loop" or "sub-routine." Her work remains so important that in the twenty-first century, computer scientists named a computer programming language, Ada after her. Similarly, when physicist Hertha Aryton (1854–1923) began studying the electrical arc, she was unfamiliar with accepted explanations, and thus devised novel ways of explaining it. Her pathbreaking work was recognized by colleagues who asked her to present and publish her work on this subject.

Even with University training, some women scientists almost abandoned a research career. When Curie, a strong nationalist, finished her studies, she intended to return home to teach science to young people. Kovalevskaia had contracted a fictitious marriage to allow her to move to Germany, a common practice among progressive Russian young people at a time when restrictions on women's mobility were great. After obtaining her degree, she returned to Russia where she attempted to live the life of wife and mother with her husband. Eventually realizing she was deeply unhappy, she began again to pursue a career in mathematics.

Curie changed her plan of leaving Paris after meeting physicist Pierre Curie. She and Curie agreed that they would marry, but still devoted their lives to their scientific pursuits. They kept their household possessions to a minimum so that housework would not take too long, and allowed Pierre's father to take over most of the child-care duties. Similarly, other women scientists had to find personal situations that would allow them to continue their research. So that both Kovalevskaia and Lermontova could continue their research, they combined their households and left the house and child care to Lermontova's sister, Sonia. Germain never married; nor did self-educated astronomer and mathematician Caroline Herschel (1750–1848), who lived and worked with her astronomer brother William, carrying on their research alone after his death.

Marriage to a fellow scientist with progressive ideas concerning women's role was often the most advantageous situation. Margaret Huggins married an astronomer, and the two pursued their research together, producing several joint-authored papers. Hertha Aryton collaborated with her husband in physics. Eventually, as he became ill, she pursued research on her own, presenting and publishing several individual papers.

Marrying a scientist gave some women entry into the scientific community. Ayrton was able to establish her legitimacy as her husband's "assistant," and then later used that legitimacy to obtain an audience for her own work. A male mentor could provide the same function. Kovalevskaia and Lermontova were looked after, while at the University, by mathematician Karl Theodore Weierstrass and his wife. It was Weierstrass who convinced the University to confer the doctoral degree upon Kovalevskaia (after she wrote three dissertations!). Later, one of his students, Gösta Mittag-Leffler, helped her obtain a teaching post at the University of Stockholm, where she became the first tenured woman professor in Europe.

Sometimes, mentors could provide women scientists with a way to escape the dominance of a scientific husband. The German Amalie Dietrich (1821–91) knew nothing of botany until she married her husband Wilhelm, who came from an illustrious line of botanists. She served as his assistant, carrying his heavy equipment and enduring his insults and neglect. Eventually, she left him, and found employment as a collector for Caesar Godeffroy, the head of a new museum of the geography, natural science, and ethnology of the South Pacific. She obtained this position with the help of H.A. Meyer, a businessman who bought one of Dietrich's plant collections and took an interest in her. Her first assignment, in Australia, brought her tremendous joy, "No one circumscribes my zeal. I stride across the wide plains, wander through the virgin forest. [...] When I wander over great spaces without let or hindrance, I think no king can feel so happy and so free as I. It is just as if Herr Godeffroy had made me a present of this vast continent."[6] Dietrich, known for her extensive collections, had two species of wasps, a moss, and two species of algae named after her.

Given the right circumstances, a woman scientist could make tremendous contributions. Marie Curie won the Nobel Prize with her husband and another scientist for their work on radiation in 1903 and in 1911 she received a second Nobel, making her the first person of either sex to win two Nobel Prizes for science. In 1906, after her husband died, fellow physicists convinced the Sorbonne that rather than offering her a pension, the University should hire her to fill her late husband's position, making her the University's first woman professor. Such accomplishments took remarkable talent and hard work; they also required a certain type of professional and personal situation: a supportive family, the time and money to acquire an education, a personal life conducive to research, and male mentors who could open doors.

Yet what of all those women who did not benefit from such circumstances? Helen Beatrix Potter (1866–1943) recorded her frustration in her private journal at her inability to have her theories and drawings on fungi recognized. While we will never know how many women mathematicians, physicists, and chemists might have made their mark if society had been organized differently, we can get a sense of the interest that women of all sorts took in science by looking at the field of botany.

Unlike most of the sciences, botany was considered to be an acceptable field of study for middle-class girls, much like drawing or needlework. Botany – the collection and categorization of plants – was believed to prevent idleness and encourage spiritual growth. Many introductory books on botany were addressed to mothers to help them teach their children the science. Because botany was considered acceptable, women could cultivate the hobby as amateurs and professionals. English women corresponded with leading male botanists, sent reports to the *Journal of Botany* and contributed to compilations of local botanical observations. They collected and drew plants for publication, and earned a living writing about botany for both adults and children. Encouraged as a hobby, botany could provide financial support, intellectual recognition, and a sense of purpose. Mary Kirby (1817–93), an ardent amateur botanist, began writing about botany after the death of her father. Her *Flora of Leicestershire* (1848) became the definitive botanical reference on this region. Lydia Becker (1827–90) learned botany from an uncle. As an adult, she turned her hobby into a profession and a crusade, writing *Botany for Novices* in 1864 and arguing passionately for a scientific education for girls. The acceptability of botany demonstrates that given a chance, significant numbers of nineteenth-century girls and women developed interest and expertise in the sciences. Botany's ranking among the sciences fell by the late nineteenth century, when physics and chemistry were seen as increasingly important. It was not until the late twentieth century that most girls were able to contemplate careers in these sciences or in mathematics.

From popular to mass culture

The importance of amateurism in both the arts and sciences demonstrates how intellectual and creative activities were integrated into the everyday lives of middle- and upper-class girls and women. What about the women of the peasantry and working classes? While some women, like Rosa Bonheur, were born into a trade that led to a career in the arts, most women of the working classes and peasantry had to engage in hard manual labor to ensure their survival and that of their families. Yet the lives of the women of the working classes and peasantry were not bereft of cultural stimulation and entertainment.

The earliest forms of popular entertainment revolved around religious and agricultural cycles. Increasingly, as a result of efforts made by both Protestant and Catholic Churches, these festivals overlapped. Men and women celebrated with religious processions, singing and dancing, eating, storytelling, and competitive games, like races or bullfights. Such celebrations were community affairs, in which everyone actively participated. Whereas in earlier periods men and women of the upper classes had shared in these sorts of entertainments, by the nineteenth century such festivities were largely relegated to the lower classes. Middle- and upper-class critics cited the presence of women – dancing, laughing, talking loudly, and generally acting in a manner inconsistent with the norms of domesticity – as proof of the inferior nature of popular culture.

As criticism of "popular" entertainments grew, they became increasingly relegated to the small towns and villages of the countryside. In the early nineteenth century, however, one could still experience such festivities in the big cities at certain times of the year. In Paris, for example, during Carnival, the celebration that preceded the Catholic Lent, eating and drinking became the order of the day. Popular restaurants and cabarets were filled with seamstresses and shopkeepers whose eating and drinking was interrupted only by songs, jokes, and dancing. And although middle-class observers decried the wastefulness of such gatherings, where food was often thrown across the room and much drink ended up on the floor, workers often saved all year long in order to be able to indulge themselves at Carnival.

Carnival was associated with a reversal of the regular order of things, and this allowed middle- and upper-class individuals to participate in what at any other time would be criticized as a "popular" celebration. It was also associated with a relaxing of rules, including those that normally circumscribed the lives of women. For women of the upper and middle classes, the popularity of masked balls offered them a certain amount of anonymity. Under cover of a mask, they could speak more freely to men, flirting and joking provocatively in a way that would have been unacceptable at any other time. Love affairs forged during Carnival were considered to exist outside of normal life, and were abandoned once the festivities were over. Other traditions of Carnival, such as the practice of parading a "husband" sitting backwards on a donkey, aimed at reversing the usual gender hierarchy.

By the second half of the nineteenth century Carnival had been replaced by more commercial, and passive, activities. Whereas everyone participated in Carnival, men and women became spectators for other forms of popular entertainment. Small theaters that specialized in melodramas, street acts of singers or acrobats, seemingly magical demonstrations of new inventions such as the panorama, and – by the end of the century – the motion picture, captured the popular imagination and entertained the people on Sundays and holidays. More active forms of entertainment persisted as well. Bars, pubs and cafés offered individuals and families a place to gather where they could tell stories, joke, and sing. In London, laundresses regularly gathered at pubs on Mondays, where they drank and then often danced to relieve their fatigue from their hard, repetitive work.

As a general rule, middle- and upper-class women found their entertainment elsewhere. Socializing in private homes was a way for women to entertain without having to go out in public. Whereas middle-class men might eat in restaurants, middle-class women preferred the dinner party. However, both men and women attended plays and concerts, and found these forums conducive for socializing and entertainment. In cities like London, Paris, and Berlin, many in the theater-going public knew each other, and audiences spent the intermission and the period before and after performances renewing acquaintances, spreading gossip, and furthering love intrigues. Women wore their very best dresses on such occasions, for commenting on their appearance was as much a part of the entertainment as the play or concert in question.

Over the course of the nineteenth century, museums and exhibitions became increasingly popular with the middle classes. Men and women strolled through the museum galleries, contemplating the works of the great masters. One might often see young men and women standing at easels or with sketchpad in hand, attempting to imitate the works of their predecessors. The Crystal Palace Exhibition in London, held in 1851, set off a wave of national and international exhibitions designed to showcase advances in technological and artisanal production. These exhibitions were as popular with the working classes as they were with the middle classes. Working-class men and women, wearing their Sunday best, were admitted at a reduced rate, so that they could educate themselves and better appreciate the vast array of goods their nation produced.

Shopping was another favored pastime. Over the course of the nineteenth century, commerce became more recognizably modern. Shop owners began displaying goods in a way that would catch the eyes of a passer-by, and shops themselves became more inviting to browsers. This trend culminated, in mid-century, with the introduction of the department store. Department stores broke with retailing tradition by gathering a wide array of goods under one roof, emphasizing display and advertising, using fixed prices rather than bargaining, and attempting to lure female shoppers of all classes through their doors. Early in the nineteenth century, social commentators expressed concern over the dangers shopping posed for young women, especially women of the working classes. It was often feared that in passing by a shop on her way to work, a young woman's eye might be caught by the sight of a bonnet or shawl. Unable to afford such tempting goods, the woman might, critics warned, turn to prostitution to raise the funds. The department store heightened concern about shopping and expanded that concern to middle-class women; stories abounded of middle-class women who became shoplifters or nymphomaniacs after browsing the store's displays.

For all its supposed dangers, department store shopping became the center of a social and cultural life for many women, one that increasingly got them out of the house and into the world. London's West End became famous for its high quality shops and its department stores. To attract female shoppers department stores offered women not only goods to buy, but restaurants in which to eat and reading rooms where they might relax with a newspaper. As middle-class female shoppers became more numerous in the West End, more facilities were created for them, including tea rooms, restaurants, and Ladies' Clubs. The Clubs soon rivaled the stores for women's time; women came to the clubs to socialize, read books and newspapers, and also to attend lectures and meetings. They even offered women who had come into London by train from the surrounding countryside the option of renting a room for the night. Meant to be a "home away from home" where women could eat, rest, and find companionship, they were nonetheless "homes" based upon the premise that women were meant to be out in the world, not hidden away from it.

Shopping could also offer women a creative outlet. The emergence of department stores coincided with a significant growth of the fashion press. Women became active as fashion writers, helping other women navigate the ins and outs of shopping. They wrote articles that recommended specific shops, gave general fashion advice, and urged women to be confident in their ability to develop a sense of style. Women were urged to see themselves as "artists" who could use their talents to create a signature style for themselves. They were further encouraged to apply their styles to their homes, to create more aesthetically pleasing interiors. Although fashion writers believed that style was defined in part by class, they argued that all women could develop a sense of style appropriate to their socioeconomic status.

Department stores, like the motion pictures that became popular at the end of the century, were meant to appeal to men and women of all classes. They were part of a new "mass culture," that offered commercialized entertainment to individuals of both sexes and all socioeconomic ranks (excluding, of course, the poorest of society). Whereas institutions such as Ladies' Clubs maintained class exclusivity through membership fees and norms of conduct and dress, department stores, movie theaters, and the café-concerts where one could drink while watching singers and dancers, were patronized by members of all classes. Because of this, concern about improper mixing of the classes had outpaced concern over women's presence in public by the end of the century. Gender-based concerns did not disappear altogether, however. Critics of mass culture defined it as "feminine," arguing that it encouraged passivity and appealed to the emotions rather than reason. Yet some have argued that the emergence of mass culture was a key factor in forging bonds between the classes, thus enhancing nationalism.

From working as artists, composers, writers, and scientists to shopping at department stores or celebrating at the Carnivals, women of all classes spent a great deal of their time outside the bounds of domesticity. Indeed, whereas dominant cultural ideals prescribed a role for women within the confines of the private sphere, women's participation in nineteenth-century culture was significant. As writers, painters, and scientists, at a popular restaurant during Carnival or in the reading room of a Ladies' Club, women were central to the production and consumption of nineteenth-century intellectual life and culture. All of these activities brought women outside the private sphere of the home and into the public worlds of publishing, art expositions, scientific societies, or urban entertainments. Furthermore, although domesticity identified women with the family, achieving recognition in the arts and sciences forced others to recognize the individual accomplishments of certain women.

Examining the participation of women in the arts, sciences, and culture highlights the tension between the dominant ideals of domesticity and the real activities of European women. This tension is also present when we explore female mobility. Although according to the tenets of domesticity women were meant to prefer the calm of home life, many women experienced a desire for adventure outside the domestic realm. These women traveled throughout the world, often putting themselves at great risk. Other women may have indeed preferred to stay home, but economic or political necessity forced them to leave. Although often portrayed as sedentary creatures, nineteenth-century women participated in the great movements of people from countryside to city, nation to nation, and nation to empire that characterized the nineteenth century.

7

On the Move

In November 1862 an article appeared in the London *Times* whose headline, "Lady Travelers on the White Nile," must have sparked many an imagination. The travelers in question were Dutchwoman Alexandrine Tinné (1835–69), at 22 years of age one of the wealthiest heiresses in Europe, her mother, and her aunt. Their quest to find the source of the Nile was unsuccessful, but it inspired young women who were drawn by the same desire for adventure. As Matilda Betham-Edwards put it in her 1880 *Six Life Stories of Famous Women*, "Sedentariness is not a normal condition of things, and most young people possessed of high spirits and good health would choose an out-of-door, breezy, adventurous life, if choice were possible."[1]

European women had always been on the move, but for most, leaving one's home to venture elsewhere was driven more by necessity than by choice and the love of adventure. Until the nineteenth century women did not usually leave home for excitement or pleasure. And even then, although the lure of a new place, missionary zeal, or scientific inquiry may have drawn some away from their hometowns, the great majority of European women who left their homes did so to marry and to work. Throughout the long nineteenth century, half the population of the burgeoning cities came from the countryside, and of that mobile group, more than half were women.

The choice to pursue travel and adventure, and not just gainful employment or marriage, became increasingly possible over the course of the nineteenth century. Whereas in the eighteenth century such travel was largely the preserve of wealthy and aristocratic men, increasing numbers of both aristocratic and middle-class women traveled in the nineteenth century. Women traveled for new experiences, to broaden their education, and to find subjects to paint and write about. They traveled alone, with other women, and with their families. While many travelers returned home sooner or later, others left home permanently. Missionaries traveled at home and abroad to seek converts, while migrants looked for work opportunities in other cities and countries, often overseas. Political exiles were forced to leave their homes, sometimes never to return. And by the end of the century, even women who stayed at home were becoming more mobile than ever before, leaving their residences to walk the city streets unaccompanied, to shop, and even to ride bicycles. Women's growing mobility over the course of the century challenged the widespread belief that weak and passive females should spend most of their time inside the home. Women's travel, migration, and greater mobility in the cities forced Europeans to redefine what it meant to be female, pushing the door open even wider for a growing acceptance of women's activities outside the domestic realm. Yet even those, like Tinné, who breached convention in order to pursue adventure, followed many of the prescriptions and privileges that were part of being female and, in her case, wealthy, in the nineteenth century.

Women travelers

The English were by far the most numerous and intrepid travelers in Europe. Englishwomen did not face the sort of legal restrictions that limited the mobility of Russian women, for example, who were not allowed to travel – either in Russia or outside the country – without the permission of a father or husband. In Italy and Spain, a culture strongly influenced by Catholicism and a tradition of strong, patriarchal families made it difficult for women to travel alone without being at best criticized and at worst assaulted.

Englishwomen – especially those of the upper classes – also benefited from a national tradition of traveling. Wealthy parents in early modern England sent their sons to the Continent to polish their manners and learn French, the international language of the upper classes. By the eighteenth century, a young Englishman of any means at all left home to make the obligatory trip that always included France and Italy, with stops sometimes in Switzerland and the German states. This "Grand Tour," as it was known, had long been reserved exclusively for men, who were expected to use their knowledge gained abroad to better govern at home. Women, who played no political role, could not, it was believed, have any reason for visiting the Continent. This began to change in the late eighteenth century, when women such as Lady Elizabeth Webster and Lady Mary Coke decided to travel abroad. In both cases, these were wealthy women whose money allowed them to escape difficult domestic circumstances. Others, like Lady Anna Miller, wished to see the Italian ruins about which they had read so much. While the majority of female travelers by the turn of the century were aristocrats, literary middle-class women were also attracted to travel as a means to expand their education. Thus Mary Wollstonecraft and Maria Edgeworth (1767–1849) were attracted by the climate of intellectual excitement in Revolutionary Paris.

The increase in the number of English women visiting the Continent in the late eighteenth century was due in part to the publication of their letters and memoirs. By the end of the century, female travelers began to publish writings that previously had been destined for private consumption. Irish countess Marguerite Blessington wrote about her Grand Tour experiences, thereby providing a model for other women who wished to travel. English women who ventured abroad could also consult Anna Miller's *Letters from Italy* (1776) or Hester Piozzi's *Observations and Reflections made in the Course of a Journey through France, Italy and Germany* (1789) to gain both inspiration and practical information. If their language skills were sufficient, they could read travel books written by Continental women that were beginning to appear, such as Marianna Candidi Dionigi's *Viaggi in alcune città del Lazio* (Travels Through Cities in the Lazio Region, 1809).

The aristocratic and "literary" middle-class women travelers of the late eighteenth century gave way to a larger group of middle-class women travelers in the nineteenth century. Cultural and technological changes combined to make travel more desirable and possible for a larger group than ever before after 1800. As more women traveled, the range of their travels widened.

Like the growing number of books written by women about their travels, the best-selling novel by Germaine de Staël, *Corinne* (1807) encouraged women to see travel as a means to experience different societies and thus reflect upon their own place in the world. In her novel, Staël contrasted the smothering of female genius in France with its flowering in Italy through the tale of her heroine Corinne, a female poet widely admired by Italians. Corinne's tragic death following a doomed love affair reflected the ethos of Romanticism that Staël had done much to popularize. Romantic poets and painters looked to nature and to ruins of the past not only for inspiration, but also for an emotionally transcendent experience. Corinne's flights of poetic fancy when contemplating the ruins of the Roman Empire inspired many other travelers to venture south in search of strong emotional experiences. Corinne's reactions to the various sights of Italy, modeled largely upon Staël's own itinerary, indicated to potential travelers both what they might see and how they might see it.

The growth of the middle classes resulted in a growing number of individuals who, inspired by the books they read, desired to travel abroad. Technology facilitated the accomplishment of their desires. In 1816, the first steamboat passengers crossed the English Channel; by 1840, regular service was moving approximately 100,000 individuals between England and France each year. Steamers sailed down the Rhine River as early as 1828, and were navigating the Rhône and Danube by the 1830s. Steamers also allowed travelers to cross the Mediterranean, and in 1842, the passenger steamship Britannia traversed the Atlantic Ocean. Railroads also made travel less tiresome and more affordable. While as late as the 1840s, English visitors who debarked in Le Havre still had to make the trip to Paris by coach, a trip that could take over a day, within just ten years that trip was accomplished in a number of hours, and with much less jolting, by rail.

Responding to the increase in demand for and ease of traveling, publishers issued guidebooks in record numbers. William Murray in England and the Galignani Brothers on the Continent specialized in guidebooks that proposed itineraries for visitors who wished to see the greatest number of sights in a limited period of time. Unlike eighteenth-century aristocratic Grand Tourists whose travels might last one or two years and included extended stays in private homes, these new middle-class travelers took shorter trips and stayed in hotels. Lacking the personal contacts earlier aristocratic travelers had used to smooth their paths, these travelers relied upon an increasing number of travel professionals. Thus writer Mariana Stark (1762–1838) set the standard for later guidebooks when she wrote travel guides that were less personal memoirs and more standardized itineraries, full of practical information and slim enough to be carried with ease. While guidebooks helped the inexperienced traveler, those who were still wary of setting out on their own benefited, after 1855, from the tours arranged by the Thomas Cook Agency of London. Cook's tours provided transportation and accommodation, took care of currency exchanges, and suggested sightseeing itineraries. They were particularly popular with women, who came to be considered as the typical "Cook's tourist."

The growing ease of travel prompted many more women to venture out, alone or in pairs, than ever before. Reflecting this attitude, Englishwoman Mabel Sharman Crawford (*c.*1830–60) wrote in her posthumously published *Through Algeria* (1863), "In bygone days, the rule that no lady should travel without a gentleman by her side, was doubtless rational; but in a period of easy locomotion, and with abundant evidence to prove that ladies can travel by themselves in foreign countries with perfect safety, the maintenance of that rule certainly savours of injustice. For unquestionable as it is that women's sphere, as wife and mother, lies at home, it is surely unreasonable to doom many hundred English ladies, of independent means and without domestic ties, to crush every natural aspiration to see nature in its grandest forms, art in its finest works, and human life in its most interesting phases."[2] Yet while travel became more acceptable for women, especially in the second half of the century, not all women sought out the same destinations. As middle-class travelers increasingly voyaged throughout Europe, upper-class women went to Egypt and the Middle East. When middle-class women once again followed their example, upper-class women undertook more daring adventures, such as traveling around the world, or sought out travel venues, such as the luxury liner Titanic, where class boundaries were strictly maintained.

Some working-class women traveled on their own accord to seek jobs, husbands, or to join family members who had gone before; others voyaged to distant shores in the service of their employer. Tinné, for example, brought with her to Egypt a bevy of Dutch maids, who spent much of their time bemoaning the certain death that they believed awaited them as they ventured in search of the source of the Nile. Not all domestic servants complained about their fate, however. When the American Lorenza Stevens Berbineau accompanied her employer's family to Europe in 1851, she remarked repeatedly in her diary upon her pleasure at visiting sights such as the Champs Elysées in Paris where there, "were many places of refreshments and hundreds of People sitting there the streets thronged with carriages [sic] it looked like a City of lights."[3]

While all travel was a voyage of personal discovery, opening the woman traveler's eyes to new sights and making her see her own society in a new light, some women travelers sought to contribute to European knowledge about the world. Thus although Tinné never found the source of the Nile, she did collect valuable botanical specimens. Florence Baker (1841–1916) and her husband, Samuel White Baker, set out in 1864 with the same goal of discovering the Nile's headwaters, and were successful. In 1870, they undertook another expedition along the Nile to fight the slave trade. Amelia Edwards (1831–92) traveled the Nile in 1873 to sketch and measure the ruins. At the time of its publication, her *A Thousand Miles up the Nile* (1877) was the most complete account of Egyptian ruins to have been written by a man or a woman. Edwards also founded the Egyptian Exploration Fund in 1883 to further European knowledge of ancient Egyptian culture.

As these examples indicate, Egypt was a favored destination, but it was in no way the only one. Isabella Lucy Bird Bishop (1831–1904) traveled to the

United States, Canada, and Japan, writing travel books that included her own photographs. While Bishop traveled alone, other women were accompanied by their husbands. Lucy Atkinson (1820–63) traveled to Russia in 1848 to work as a governess, but instead married an Englishman. She and her husband voyaged east, becoming two of the first Europeans to describe the nomadic inhabitants of Russia's mountain ranges. When they returned to England in 1854, Atkinson's husband wrote about their travels without mentioning her or their son (who had been born in the Russian mountains). Two years after her husband died, Atkinson published her own account of the journey, including details about her family life on the trip. Frances Erskine Calderón de la Barca (1804–82), raised in Scotland and France, married a Spanish diplomat in 1838 and went with him to Mexico. The United States Army adopted her *Life in Mexico* (1843) in 1847 as the best existing guide to the country. On trips taken in 1869 and 1871 with her husband, Elizabeth Mazuchelli (1832–1914) became the first European woman to explore the Eastern Himalayas. Similarly, Isabel Burton (1831–96) traveled with her husband to Africa, South America, Syria, India, and Egypt.

Exploration of foreign lands drove many women to go overseas, but women had other motives as well. The Swedish nurse Frederika Bremer (1801–65) was invited to speak throughout Europe and in the United States after writing several popular novels. British women continued to be more numerous among the intrepid and adventurous female foreign travelers than those from other countries. Constance Cumming (1837–1924) traveled to India, Fiji, Ceylon, Tonga, Samoa, Tahiti, Japan, China, California, and the Pacific Northwest in order to find subjects to paint. Barbara Bodichon (1827–91) established in her home outside of Algiers a sort of central clearing house for women painters and writers who came to the French colony to pursue their artistic ambitions. By the end of the century, sporting activities were also drawing women overseas. In 1892, May French-Sheldon (1847–1936) published *Sultan to Sultan: Adventures among the Masai and Other Tribes of East Africa*, in which she recounted her experiences as the first woman to lead a safari. Traveling with over 100 porters and servants, French-Sheldon demonstrated that not all aspects of European civilization had to be left behind in order to venture into the wilds. Her work inspired other wealthy women to at least dream of, if not actually undertake, a safari. By contrast, Lady Florence Dixie (1855–1905) became an animal rights activist after accompanying her husband on a hunting trip in South America.

As Sheldon's many porters and servants reveal, women travelers often had to find ways to retain their femininity while traveling. A large number of servants, who carried changes of clothes, comfortable bedding and other furniture, and food could help to keep the trip within the boundaries of what was thought civilized for female travelers. Indeed, throughout the nineteenth century, many people believed that the degree of civilization reached by a given society was indicated by the condition and appearance of its women. Europeans, who felt themselves the most civilized of all, thus placed tremendous pressure on female travelers to maintain their femininity at all costs. When Mary Kingsley (1862–1900) traveled to West Africa in 1893, she crossed jungle and swampland wearing a long dress and hat, and carrying an umbrella. Her *Travels in West Africa* (1897) includes information on the uses of hairpins when traveling and the superiority of a long skirt with petticoats over trousers when walking in unknown territory. In attempting a shortcut through the underbrush, Kingsley fell into a hidden pit, on the bottom of which were spikes meant to trap game. In recounting this episode, she wrote:

> It is at these times you realize the blessing of a good thick skirt. Had I paid heed to the advice of many people in England, who ought to have known better, and did not do it themselves, and adopted masculine garments, I should have been spiked to the bone and done for. Whereas, save for a good many bruises, here I was with the fullness of my skirt tucked under me, sitting on nine ebony spikes some twelve inches long, in comparative comfort, howling lustily to be hauled out.[4]

While Kingsley extolled her feminine garb as eminently practical, others found that long skirts and elaborate hats impeded their progress, or even put them in danger. In 1859, Mrs H.W. Cole recommended to those who wished to follow her example in climbing the Alps that they leave their umbrellas behind and sew rings up the sides of their skirts. When a cord was strung through the rings, the skirts could be lifted up quickly if needed. Scotswoman Ménie Muriel Dowie (c.1860–?) dressed as a boy so that she could travel through Poland without being harassed. Lady Hester Stanhope (1776–1839) adopted men's clothes when she traveled through the Middle East because she found them more practical, although she did not try to hide her sex. While her behavior shocked many Britains, it was nothing compared to that of Isabelle Eberhardt (1877–1904). Eberhardt traveled to North Africa in the late nineteenth century, eventually settling in Tunis. She disguised herself as a nomad to wander the desert, then disguised herself as a man and converted to Islam. The necessities and opportunities of travel encouraged women to experiment with dress and lifestyle; although women adhered to some accepted notions of femininity, they called into question many others.

Travel also provided women an opportunity to reflect upon the organization of gender roles and family life at home. Faced with foreign customs and cultures, female travelers examined the situation of women in other societies. Their conclusions often led them to critique practices in their own society. In her *Memoirs of Egypt (1819–1828)* (1841), Amalia Nizzoli observed that the forced marriage of women of the harem mirrored her own marriage at age 14 to a man she had not yet met. Many female travelers to the Middle East viewed the supposed passivity and subservience of harem women as a metaphor for their own condition at home. Mary Kingsley, on the other hand, implicitly critiqued European domesticity in her discussion of polygamy among an African tribe. Polygamy occurred, she wrote, because "it is totally impossible for one woman to do the whole work of a house – look after the children, prepare and cook the food, prepare the rubber, carry the same to markets, fetch the daily supply of water from the stream, cultivate the plantation, etc. The more wives the less work, says the African lady."[5] Such an observation must have struck Kingsley, a woman who devoted most of her life to the care of her parents and brother, with particular force. As women travelers viewed different models of family life and gender roles in the areas they visited, their own assumptions concerning the "naturalness" of ideologies such as domesticity were called into question.

Women travelers such as Kingsley undertook voyages for both personal and intellectual reasons. Those like Tinné or Eberhardt who remained in the areas they visited were rare; most went home eventually, where they often wrote and lectured about their experiences. Although usually traveling under very different circumstances, many other women left home for good, migrating to another city or emigrating to another country, sometimes leaving Europe altogether for the colonies or the United States. Mostly from the peasantry and working classes, these women left home in search of employment.

Migrants and missionaries

Historians long attributed the tremendous increase in migration during the nineteenth century to the growth of cities. As cities such as London, Paris, and Berlin expanded their populations, the argument went, increased work opportunities attracted outlying rural populations to the city. While historians saw this movement as a new phenomenon, and thus a sign of modernity, recent scholarship has placed migration to cities within a long-term history of mobility. Agricultural workers, peddlers, and those seeking apprenticeships had traveled long distances even before the nineteenth century. It was this tradition of mobility that allowed men and women to take advantage of new opportunities in urban centers. The dramatic growth of cities in the nineteenth century shaped, rather than caused, migration. Furthermore, changes in the rural economy pushed people out as much as cities drew them in. The consolidation of landownership and the reduction of rural manufacturing increased poverty in the countryside, and made migration more appealing. This solution was only possible in certain areas and at certain times. In Russia, for example, the maintenance of serfdom until 1861 meant that impoverished peasants were forbidden to leave their homes in search of work. And, as with travel, advances in transportation occurred earlier in Western Europe, thus facilitating long-distance migration.

Before the nineteenth century, female migrants tended to travel shorter distances than their male counterparts, filling, for example, a position as a domestic servant in a nearby town or village. The number of female migrants increased during the nineteenth century, although migration patterns continued to be shaped by gender. Women were more likely to move to cities where they could work as domestic servants or in textiles, while men sought out work in mining towns and as agricultural laborers. Irish women migrants to Great Britain, for example, found work in the textile mills in Lancashire, Yorkshire, and Scotland; in one Scottish city, 44.3 per cent of the female workers were employed in textiles.

The perception that economic circumstances would be improved by migration often led women to leave home in search of work. Like the women travelers who consulted guidebooks, migrants tended to rely on information obtained from others in their community who had made the same or similar voyages. Because of this, migrants chose as their destination areas where others they knew or heard of had settled. Rebecca Burlend (1793–1872), for example, set off from England to the United States in 1831 with her husband and her five youngest children. Her account of their life as pioneers in Illinois, published in 1848, encouraged other English families to settle in the same county. Migrants could help other migrants in a number of ways. Throughout the second half of the nineteenth century, and until 1940, Jewish immigrants to the United States sent not only information, but money and boat tickets as well, to those left behind.

Migrants thus often preserved a strong sense of ethnic identity in their new locations. Very often, migrant women were charged with keeping this identity alive. Irish women in England, for example, were active in the Catholic Church, took in young Irish men and women as boarders, and spoke Gaelic to their children. The experience of migration could also alter cultural practices that were dominant at home. Jewish migrants from Eastern Europe settled in large numbers in the major Western European cities in the late nineteenth century. These men and women were fleeing the pogroms (violent attacks on Jewish individuals, homes, synagogues, and businesses) that were becoming more numerous in Russia and the growing anti-Semitism of Austria-Hungary. Nearly four million Jews left Eastern Europe in the years between 1830 and 1925; three quarters of those left between 1881 and 1914, when the persecution of Jews was at its height in Eastern Europe. By 1880, about 50,000–60,000 Jews lived in England alone, a number that would increase to 210,000 by 1925. Traditional gender roles in Eastern European Jewish families called for men to devote themselves to religious scholarship, while women focused on domestic life and economic activity. While many first-generation Jewish migrant women thus worked for wages or owned small businesses, the pressure on Jewish men to find paid labor combined with the influence of English models of domesticity to encourage the withdrawal of Jewish women from the workforce. As this change took place, religious and ethnic identity in Jewish families became more focused on women and the home.

Maintaining one's ethnic identity in a new city became a source of both pride and renewed persecution. Irish migrants in London's East End, mostly unskilled and living in poverty, were looked down upon by the English and by foreign visitors to London alike. French writer and labor activist Flora Tristan traveled to London several times in the 1820s and 1830s. In her 1840 *Promenades in London*, she remarked upon the incredible poverty and misery of the Irish. "I saw there children entirely naked; young girls and nursing mothers with *bare feet*, having only a chemise that fell in tatters, leaving almost their whole bodies bare."[6] Tristan argued that such poverty was the result of misguided government policies and insufficient wages, and that crime and prostitution were the result of hunger. Tristan was in a minority in this opinion; most considered the Irish to be immoral criminals, and other migrant communities took great pains to distinguish themselves from the Irish. Jewish migrants, for example, founded associations to help women who might be tempted by prostitution in an effort to prove that the virtue of Jewish women, unlike that of the Irish, could be preserved. Still, the large numbers of Jewish migrants to European cities in the late nineteenth century elicited negative reactions. Older migrants sought to socialize new arrivals, hastening their assimilation into the culture of the host country.

Facing increased anti-Semitism in France, a turn-of-the-century Jewish news-paper argued that it was necessary "to give this population … a very suitable Parisian demeanor, to 'wash away' that which is exotic and too shocking."[7] The pressure to assimilate thus further eroded cultural practices and beliefs brought from home.

Although women outnumbered men in migration to European cities during the nineteenth century, men usually predominated in international migration. Yet even here the number of women increased. Over half the Polish migrants in Germany were women who were sought after because they accepted low wages and were skilled at working root crops. Italian women worked in Southern France and in Switzerland, where they made up an important percentage of the embroidery industry. Women also increasingly traveled to overseas colonies in search of work.

Early in the nineteenth century, colonial conquest was largely seen as a male preserve. Indeed, one of the attractions of the colonies for many men was the opportunity it afforded them to escape the binds of domesticity. Colonial administrators were encouraged to take native women as mistresses, since it was believed that these women provided men with a valuable link to native society. More casual dress and manners, the company of other men, and opportunities for adventure and conquest also attracted men who felt constrained by polite society. As conquest gave way to administration in the latter part of the century, women were encouraged to travel to the colonies. Many argued that European women could "civilize" the colonies by domesticating husbands and acting as mothers to the natives. Colonial administrators were increasingly encouraged to bring their wives with them (or to marry women from home if they were still single) and to raise families overseas.

Some of the earliest European women to settle in the colonies were mis-sionaries. The religious revival that swept across Europe in the early nineteenth century increased missionary activity both in Europe and abroad. Before 1800, most missionaries to overseas territories had been men, but this began to change in the nineteenth century. Not only were more women active in religious organ-izations than men, but also the belief that women served as moral guardians of the family could be easily transposed into missionary work. Missionaries trav-eled to Asia and Africa to preach Christianity. Along the way, they often met with hostility and danger. Annie Royle Taylor (1855–c.1909) went to China under the sponsorship of the China Inland Mission in 1884. She decided to open a mission in a Tibetan city closed to foreigners. Arriving in the city dis-guised as a Tibetan nun, her identity was revealed by a servant and she was forced to leave the country. She established the Tibetan Pioneer Mission near the border. Fellow missionaries to China, Algerian-born sisters Evangeline (1869–1960) and Francesca (1871–1960) French were almost killed in 1900 during an attack on foreign missionaries.

In the French colonies in Africa, Catholic missionaries predominated. Anne-Marie Javouhey (1779–1851) established a religious order for women in Gorée, West Africa, in 1822. In 1828, Javouhey responded to a French government request for help in Guiana. Taking with her 36 nuns and 50 emigrants, she con-verted many to Christianity, facilitating conquest of the area. In Algiers, a female religious order, the White Sisters, founded by Cardinal Charles-Martial-Allemand Lavigerie (1825–92) pursued a policy of assimilation and conversion of Algerian Muslims, running orphan asylums, industrial schools, hospitals, and agricultural settlements.

Missionary work could be an attractive occupation for women who felt a strong religious faith, and who also wanted to venture overseas. In her novel, *Jane Eyre* (1847), Charlotte Brontë has her main character reflect on the attractions of missionary life, especially for those suffering a broken heart: "Is [the work of the missionary] not the most glorious man can adopt and God assign? Is it not, by its noble cares and sublime results, the one best calculated to fill the void left by uptorn affections and demolished hopes?"[8] Travelers, explorers, and settlers often admired the amount of power a missionary woman could acquire overseas. Scottish missionary Mary Slessor (1848–1915), who sailed from Liverpool to West Africa in 1876, acquired great influence among the Calabar people, whose chiefs regularly asked her to mediate disputes among them.

For those seeking work in the colonies, rather than the conversion of other peoples to Christianity, emigration societies facilitated their voyage overseas. In England, women were encouraged to emigrate to the colonies for a number of reasons. An 1835 report of the Legislative Council on emigration to Australia stated that, "The great object of importing young women is not merely to supply the demand for servants; it is to restore the equilibrium of the sexes; to raise the value of female character; and to provide virtuous homes for the labouring classes of the community ... none but women of pure and unexceptional character should be assisted in coming to the colony."[9] The issue of female emigration reached the awareness of the general public in mid-century, after a census revealed a greater number of women than men in the population. These "redundant" or "superfluous" women, women who did not marry by choice or due to a lack of men, were encouraged to go abroad. While feminists argued that the problem was not a lack of men, but a lack of job opportunities, they also advocated emigration. In 1862, English feminists founded the Female Middle-Class Emigration Society. Between its founding and 1914, it helped over 20,000 women to emigrate to the colonies by providing interest-free loans for their passage. Although the society aimed to employ governesses overseas, most of the women became either domestic servants or wives. Other emigration societies were founded in England and in France as well.

While in the colonies, European women adhered to strict standards of dress and conduct. They kept their skin pale by staying out of the sun, since brown skin would make them appear too similar to the populations over whom they ruled. They wore long, white dresses and elaborate hats in the dust and heat of India and the humid rubber plantations of Indochina. European social customs, such as drinking tea and dining with tablecloth and candles, were rigorously observed. As the guardians of European culture in the colonies, women served as the symbol of cultural and racial difference.

In certain circumstances, however, women breached the line between colonizer and colonized. Despite belief in their own cultural superiority, Europeans were also convinced that all peoples could eventually share, or at least aspire to, common cultural ideals. Domesticity was part of that culture, and one of the roles of European women in the colonies was to teach native women how to organize their families according to the principles of domesticity. To this end, women in the colonies visited native women in their homes and supported female education and health care, just as others did among the poor at home. In India, the wives of colonial administrators helped fund schools for Indian girls, while Indians and British women cooperated to provide scholarships to Indian girls and founded a hospital for women and children in Bombay. Such efforts increased during the twentieth century. By the end of the nineteenth century, the bond between women of different cultures came to be seen by many as the key to a successful "civilizing mission," a term Europeans used to indicate the adoption of European values and practices by those people they had conquered. Annie Besant (1847–1933), who moved to India in 1893, expressed a widely shared sentiment that the colonies would progress as women progressed: "What you [Indian men] want most in this country is that practical spirit of self-sacrifice, that public spirit which looks upon the interests of the country as greater than the interests of the individual. You can learn this from women. They sacrifice themselves every day and every night for the interests of the home. [...] Learn that from your women and then you will become great, and India will become great."[10] In the colonies, where native men had few rights and little autonomy, domesticity was a model that could be applied to both sexes.

While women were supposed to promote domesticity abroad, for some women in the colonies, as for some female travelers, their exposure to different ways of organizing family life and gender roles led them to question the tenets of domestic ideology. Hubertine Auclert (1848–1914) lived in Algeria for many years, traveling throughout the colony and taking stock of the situation of Algerian women. She concluded that French conquest had worsened, rather than improved the status of native Algerian women. The solution, she argued, was to give both French and Algerian women the vote. Auclert believed that French women, if they exercised political power, would never allow Algerian women to be treated badly.

Whereas these examples illustrate that European women in the colonies sometimes perceived themselves as sharing with native women a common lack of freedom, historians and literary critics have raised the issue of women's complicity in the conquest and control of overseas territories. Auclert's condemnation of the status of Algerian women, for example, was based on her hostility to practices that were part of Muslim tradition, such as arranged marriages. Furthermore, Auclert's recommendation that Algerian women be given the vote was not a call for withdrawal from the colony. Rather, she wished France to adopt a form of rule that would allow women greater autonomy. Similarly, English women who decried the Indian practice of widow-burning (suttee; outlawed by the British in 1829 although still practiced well into the twentieth century) as "barbaric" and "primitive" argued that only British colonial rule could eradicate such traditions. Many British feminists believed, as did Auclert, that the government would not turn its attention to such issues until and unless women got the vote.

Penal colonies, political exile, and pilgrimage

Most European women who went to the colonies did so willingly. However, some colonies were used as penal colonies. Some of the first settlers in Australia and Algeria, for example, were convicts and political exiles who were forcibly sent overseas. Many in government believed, especially in the first half of the nineteenth century, that both crime and revolutionary activity were a product of overcrowded urban environments, where "troublemakers" could develop an undue influence over their fellow citizens. The solution, some believed, was to deport such troublemakers to a more healthy, rural environment where they could focus on farming or other types of work rather than crime or politics.

British authorities transported 24,960 women to New South Wales and Van Diemen's Land in Australia between 1788 and 1868. Nearly half of these women were transported between 1830 and 1850, a period of intense economic crisis and revolutionary upheaval in Europe. Most were young, and about two-thirds were single. Some brought their children with them, while others left them behind. Women came from all trades in the working and artisanal classes, including domestic servants, seamstresses, wool-spinners, and midwives. They were convicted of a variety of crimes, including vagrancy and theft, mostly committed out of economic necessity. Contemporaries, however, believed that these women were unrepentant, hardened criminals, and prostitutes.

Upon arrival, convicts were either sent to a prison for incarceration, sent to work in factories, hospitals, or on farms, or ordered to work as servants for administrators, military officers, and free settlers. Employers and administrators in Australia hoped that the labor of convicts would help further their efforts at colonization; they also feared, however, that convicts would transfer to the new colony the disorder they had left behind at home. Beginning in the 1830s, authorities thus put great effort into convincing single women from England to immigrate to the colony so that they could replace the female convicts as domestic servants. Despite the widespread concern over female convicts, most women transported to the colony proved to be hard workers, and the colony grew tremendously over the course of the nineteenth century.

The French were inspired by the Australian example to set up similar penal colonies. In both the French and the British case, about 15 per cent of convicts sent to penal colonies were women. Transportation of women to French penal colonies began in 1852. Pauline Roland (1805–52) was among the 12,000 men and women sent to Algeria for opposition to the 1851 coup d'état of Napoleon III. Under his regime, penal colonies were opened in French Guiana, in South America, in 1852 and in New Caledonia, in the South Pacific, in 1863. Between 1852 and 1938, roughly 15,600 French women were transported to penal colonies. Many of the women who participated in the 1871 socialist uprising in Paris, the Commune, were sent to New Caledonia, including activist Louise Michel (1830–1905). Michel was transported to the penal colony in 1873; in 1878, she participated in an uprising organized by the native Kanuk people against French colonial administrators. Michel set sail on August 5 on the *Virginie* with 22 other women and many more men. All the women were kept in a single cell for the next 120 days. Many women faced problems of seasickness and other illnesses on the voyage, others were sexually assaulted by crewmembers, and a few became psychologically unbalanced.

Conditions in the penal colonies were harsh. In Australia, women assigned to work in the factories had their hair cut or heads shaved, and were subject to many different sorts of punishments for misbehavior, including the stockade, branding, and hard labor. Those who could avoid transportation did so, preferring exile if possible. Jeanne Deroin (1805–94) had worked with Pauline Roland to organize a workers' cooperative, and in 1850, both were imprisoned in Paris for this offense for six months. Following Napoleon III's coup d'état, Deroin fled to England, where she lived in exile until she died.

The political upheavals of the nineteenth century made exile a necessity for many women who became involved, voluntarily or not, in political struggles. The largest group of such exiles left France during the French Revolution. Since many left in secret, the total number of *émigrés*, as those who left during the Revolution are called, is hard to determine. Yet hundreds left, establishing themselves in cities such as London, Edinburgh, and Philadelphia. Before 1792, most *émigrés* were aristocrats who opposed the movement toward constitutional government begun by the revolutionaries in 1789. The Princesse de Conti (1731–1803) was among the 612 female exiles who made their way to Fribourg, Switzerland, during the Revolution. After arriving under a false name in 1791, her assets were seized in France. Although she was able to sell some diamonds she had brought with her, her income was greatly reduced, and she, like many aristocratic women in exile, had to find ways to save or make money. The Countess of Flahaut likewise arrived in London in 1792 with only a few jewels. She turned to writing to support herself and her infant son, publishing a dozen novels over the next 20 years. Madame de la Tour du Pin (1770–1853), who bought a farm near Troy, New York, with her husband, was forced, with the help of a single French cookbook, to do her own cooking. Talleyrand surprised her in the act one evening, declaring, "One could not put a leg of lamb on the spit with greater majesty."[11] As this anecdote illustrates, while women from all social classes emigrated, aristocratic women experienced the greatest change in lifestyle. Women accustomed to working, either in the home or for wages, faced problems of cultural adjustment in exile, but could transfer their skills to a new location. Aristocratic women, however, found themselves forced to live like the bourgeois or working women they had previously looked down upon, caring for home and family, and, in some cases, working for wages. Following the Revolution, many aristocratic women embraced the ideology of domesticity. Perhaps their experience abroad during the Revolution contributed to this changing vision of the role of women among the aristocracy.

Throughout the tumultuous nineteenth century, many other women went into exile for political reasons. Madame de Staël was exiled by Napoleon in 1803 because of her political views. Her salon united liberal intellectuals opposed to Napoleon's rule. Staël moved to Switzerland, but also spent her time traveling to Italy, England, and Germany. Despite her physical exile, her works continued to be widely read in France. Similarly, the exile of Christina Trivulzio di Belgiojoso, who fought to free Italy from Austrian control in 1830, did not end her influence in her home country. She fled to France, on the run from the

Austrian police. She returned to Italy in 1848, when revolution once again broke out, but after the fall of the Roman Republic in 1849 she was again forced to leave. She headed to the Middle East, and remained there until 1853. Her *Souvenirs dans l'exil* (Remembrances in Exile, 1850) and *La vie intime et la vie nomade en Orient* (Intimate and Nomadic Life in the Orient, 1855) were read by Italians and other Europeans. Upheaval in Russia also forced women into exile; the wives of the Decembrists – Russian officers who opposed the tsar's refusal of representative democracy in 1825 – gave up their titles, property, and children to follow their husbands into exile in Siberia, where they contributed to the development of public education. A revival of oppositional activity later in the century led to another wave of exiles. The most famous, Alexandra Kollontai (1873–1952) furthered the cause of socialism in Germany, England, Switzerland, Belgium, Italy, Sweden, Scandinavia, and the United States after she fled arrest for political activity in 1908.

Some women undertook a self-exile that was motivated less by political necessity than by belief. In 1834 Suzanne Volquin joined a number of her fellow Saint-Simonians on a spiritual quest in Egypt. The Saint-Simonians were a group of men and women of both the middle and working classes who came together in Paris beginning in the 1820s to preach a solution to the poverty, competition, and class conflict that resulted from industrialization. The leader, Père Enfantin, led a search for "The Woman," a sort of female messiah, and Volquin, a seamstress, was among those who left for Egypt on this quest.

Volquin's spiritual voyage is reminiscent of one of the earliest forms of female mobility in Europe, that of the pilgrimage. Migration for work and pilgrimage for purposes of devotion were practices that European women had been engaged in for centuries. Catholic women from all over Europe continued to make pilgrimages to sites such as Rome or Santiago de Compostela. By far the most famous new pilgrimage site in the nineteenth century was the village of Lourdes in Southern France. In 1858, 14-year-old Bernadette Soubirous (1844–79) saw a vision of the Virgin Mary in Lourdes. She saw her 18 more times before entering a convent in 1866. As word spread of her visions, crowds of people, many of them ill or suffering, accompanied her to the site where her visions occurred. Eventually, several chapels were built on the site, and in 1872 pilgrimages organized by the French Catholic Church began. These pilgrimages were made possible through the work of hundreds of women who gave their time to the cause. The laywomen of Notre Dame de Salut and the nuns of the Petites Soeurs de l'Assumption were especially important in helping pilgrims make their way to Lourdes.

On the move at home

Travel, colonization, deportation, migration, exile, and pilgrimage were the many ways in which women moved from place to place. Far from being sedentary and retiring creatures, many nineteenth-century women, willingly or not, left their homes and voyaged to distant places. Yet even a woman who never ventured outside her hometown's city limits would, in all likelihood, become increasingly mobile by the late nineteenth century. Changing attitudes concerning women's physical fitness combined with new cultural practices to allow women greater physical freedom in the decades approaching 1900.

Sports became increasingly important in European society during the nineteenth century. Young boys were encouraged to engage in sports as a means to becoming gentlemen, and to increase their physical fitness. Many believed that sports taught boys how to compete in a civilized manner, a skill they would need in the worlds of business and politics that awaited them after graduation. Sports also helped keep boys physically strong, a benefit in case of military service. Throughout most of the century, the upper classes were most likely to participate in organized sports. By the late nineteenth century, however, when European intellectuals began in great numbers to express concerns about the physical degeneration of their young men, sports were encouraged for boys of all classes.

Women were thought less able to play sports because of the association between sports and both competition and military service. Since women neither competed in the public realms of business and politics nor engaged in military service, they did not require regular physical exercise. This did not mean that women did not get physical exercise. Laundresses who washed heavy wet clothes, women in the mines who pushed carts full of coal, or rural women who worked in the fields all spent their days engaged in strenuous physical activity. The leisure activities of working women also often involved physical activity. On Sundays off, women strolled with their sweethearts or husbands, and often ended the day with a visit to an establishment where they could dine and dance the night away. Middle-class women also walked quite a bit. In the countryside, they were often able to leave their home and walk through the fields and forests on their own. In the cities, chaperones were required for young single women at the beginning of the century, but as the century progressed, more women went out alone. Walking in the countryside often included stops to sketch or collect botanical specimens, while walking in the city allowed women to window shop or visit friends.

Until the end of the century, upper-class women were the most likely to engage in sports as a leisure-time pursuit. Popular sports included horseback riding and tennis. Attitudes concerning women and sports began to change in the mid-nineteenth century, as doctors and intellectuals reversed earlier medical opinions and became increasingly convinced that limited exercise would help women have healthier babies. Those who advocated physical exercise recommended sports such as gymnastics and calisthenics that could, they believed, be practiced without encouraging competition. Instead of seeing who could do the most or the best, girls were encouraged to work together and focus on their own individual improvement. Some schools provided courses with titles such as "Posture, Figure, and Carriage." Private schools for wealthy girls were in general the first to adopt some sort of physical education curriculum. By the late nineteenth century, physical education was becoming more widespread in some countries. The London School Board, for example, adopted Swedish gymnastics, hockey, netball, and tennis.

The ability of girls and women to play sports varied from country to country. In Norway, women were active throughout the nineteenth century in ice skating, skiing, hiking, and swimming. In Spain, only a small segment of the population composed of wealthy women were engaging in golf, tennis, horseback riding, and skiing at the very end of the century. Real progress in women's sports did not come until the twentieth century; in the 1920s, women's athletic clubs were established and the Women's World Games were held in 1930. But even in the late nineteenth century, some countries were demonstrating that women's involvement in sports was on the rise. Norway established the first women's athletic team in gymnastics in the 1850s. In 1894, the British Ladies Football Club was established. The next year, matches began between various teams. Ladies football became a popular spectator sport; a match in Newcastle, for example, drew 8,000 fans. However, much of the attraction was due to the "oddity" of women playing sports.

While women playing European football (soccer) was considered an oddity, women riding bicycles was seen by many as a threat to civilization. The bicycle developed from a wheeled wooden horse invented in the 1790s in France. It did not become widespread until the 1880s, when a bicycle with two equal-sized pneumatic tires and a chain was introduced. Bicycles were now safer and more affordable than ever before, and women took to them in great numbers. Bicycle tours became more common, even to far-off locations. Americans William and Fanny (1859–1925) Workman, for example, wrote several books about their travels on bicycle to destinations such as Algeria and India. Some women also began participating in bicycling as a sport. Elizabeth Le Blond (1861–1934), a mountaineer and expert in snow photography, was one of the first, eventually specializing in alpine cycling.

Bicycles allowed women to move about more freely, and thus became a practical means of transportation. Although travelers such as Mary Kingsley considered traditional female dress no impediment to trekking through the jungle, long skirts did pose a problem for the female bicycle rider. Englishwoman Helena Swanwick (1864–1939) adopted trousers for bicycle riding after her first experience, about which she wrote, "It is an unpleasant experience to be hurled on to [the paving stones] and find that one's skirt has been so tightly wound around the pedal that one cannot even get up enough to unwind it."[12] While most women did not begin wearing trousers instead of skirts while playing sports until the 1920s, new types of skirts, along with bloomers and knicker-bockers (pants that fit tightly below the knee, or what American women in the 1950s aptly called "pedal pushers") were developed to allow women to cycle more comfortably. In 1893, 16-year-old Tessie Reynolds shocked many when she rode a bicycle from Brighton to London and back (a journey of 120 miles) wearing knickerbockers. In her *Bicycling for Ladies* (1896), Maria Ward recommended instead a simple skirt, uncorseted blouse, flat shoes, and walking hat. The emergence of new styles of clothing for bicycle riding was part of a general shift in fashion that occurred at the end of the nineteenth century. Tightly corseted waists, low necklines, and layer upon layer of crinoline petticoats gave way to more comfortable shirtwaists and straight long skirts that allowed women greater ease of movement.

The widespread adoption of the bicycle by women coincided with the rise of feminist organizations that were demanding the vote and, in countries like France and England, concerns about declining population health and numbers. Many critics of women's emancipation linked these issues, arguing that bicycle riding was another sign that the generation of women coming of age in the last two decades of the nineteenth century no longer cared about the home and family. A French cartoon showed a woman, dressed in bloomers and smoking a cigarette, getting ready to hop on her bicycle to attend a Feminist Congress. Her husband was left at home to deal with screaming children and a pile of dirty dishes. The chaos of the home indicated the husband's inability to run the household properly, and the viewer is left wondering, as the cartoonist intended, what would happen to the children who lacked a well-ordered home? Some medical authorities argued that not all exercise enhanced women's reproductive health, and declared that riding a bicycle was especially dangerous to a woman's reproductive organs, while others believed that bicycle riding might cause women to become overly stimulated sexually, leading them into promiscuity and possibly, prostitution. In either case, bicycle riding was linked to emancipation, a connection implied by male students at Oxford when they protested the admission of female students by ridiculing an effigy of a woman on a bicycle.

The bicycle became the flashpoint for many of the changes that women were experiencing in the late nineteenth century. The greater freedom of movement the bicycle allowed was often seen as a metaphor for greater freedom in general: freedom to postpone or eschew marriage as work opportunities increased, freedom to attain an education, and freedom to travel and explore. The female bicycle rider became, for many, emblematic of the "New Woman" of the nineteenth century who had more opportunities and greater independence than ever before. Critics argued that "New Women" were selfish, immoral, mannish, and aggressive. New Women themselves, however, often saw these changes in education, employment, and mobility as precursors to changes in the law. New Women thus embraced new social practices such as bicycle riding as symbols of their current and future emancipation. As Maria Ward wrote, "riding the wheel, our own powers are revealed to us ... you have conquered a new world, and exultingly you take possession of it ... you become alert, active, quick-sighted, and keenly alive as well to the rights of others as to what is due yourself ... to the many who earnestly wish to be actively at work in the world, the opportunity has come."[13]

Women on the move fractured many of the bounds of prescribed domesticity, especially during the decades leading up to the war in 1914. Leaving family and community behind, and proving accepted notions of female passivity wrong, they set out to forge new lives for themselves. Although female mobility – especially in search of work opportunities or for reasons of religious devotion – had long been common in European society, the dominance of the ideology of domesticity in the nineteenth century led contemporaries to associate women's mobility with modernity.

Other women, who did not break away in travel, stretched the boundaries of domesticity to include associational life. Often using the ideology of domesticity to justify their activities, women came together in charitable and philanthropic organizations, in order to abolish slavery or protect animals, or to advance socialist ideals. And just as women who traveled or migrated often set off in search of new experiences and better opportunities, women involved in associations worked to create a new and better world.

8

Associational Life

Although contemporary literature and social commentary prescribed women's activities as limited to their homes and families, women of all social and economic groups left those homes to go out into public arenas – to work, to travel, or to associate with other women in a wide variety of charitable, philanthropic, and social reform endeavors. Association and sociability had brought women into public life throughout the centuries, yet associations flourished in the nineteenth century. On the eve of the First World War, women in the German town of Wuppertal-Eberfield, for example, could belong to any of the town's 30 women's associations. Six of these were concerned with trades, four with welfare, and two with religion. The others included an association for legal protection, a female hiking group, a temperance organization, and an association to promote women's suffrage. By this time in Germany as a whole, it is estimated that about 500,000 women were active in women's associations.

The names of elite and noble women, countesses and baronesses, appear on the rosters of nineteenth-century philanthropic associations; but middle-class women from all propertied walks of life were also heavily involved. These women formed associations for sociability, religion, and good deeds. In France, they included members of prominent wine families and also politicians' wives. In Russia, before the 1861 emancipation of the serfs, elite women or wives of local officials were members of charitable associations; after the reforms of the 1860s, many were of the lesser gentry. Observers have estimated that thousands, if not hundreds of thousands, of women throughout Europe engaged in some kind of charitable or philanthropic work, with their numbers increasing during the century. Many of these women had a religiously based vision of justice and morality, while secular notions of human rights inspired others. They were self-confident and enjoyed participating in associations for the good that they did and also for their own sense of empowerment. Many served in multiple groups with a sense of mission, forming bonds of common interests and networks for civic activity, either at one time or over the course of their lifetime. For example, the Englishwoman Mary Lloyd (1795–1865) was a member of the Ladies' Bible Society, as well as the cofounder of the first women's antislavery society and of the Juvenile Deaf and Dumb Association. She established a Benevolent Society to aid poor mothers, a Provident Society to encourage the poor to save and a mother's meeting for wives of her husband's employees. She was also a temperance advocate and a traveling Quaker minister. It is hard to determine any commonality in the diverse backgrounds of the women who belonged to the vast variety of associations. In general, however, they came from relative prosperity and from families with political, moral, and religious interests in the social issues of the time.

Although the dominant culture prescribed women's place at home in the domestic sphere, it also suggested that wealthy women should go among the poor to help others. Aristocratic women had always considered it a duty of their rank to help the poor on their estates. In the early nineteenth century, middle-class women adopted and altered this ethic of helping others, an ethic bolstered by their religious belief, often expanding it beyond the poor to include slaves, alcoholics, and animals. Associations provided a means for middle-class women to care for others, especially in towns and cities, while also allowing aristocratic women a new, highly visible means of fulfilling their traditional duties toward the poor. Associations that included, or were dominated by working-class women were fewer in number. However, although philanthropic and charitable associations were directed at helping working-class women, and associations geared toward causes such as animal protection or peace discouraged working-class women from participating, working-class women were active in socialist organizations throughout the century.

The expansion of associational life for women occurred at the same time as the ideology of domesticity gained acceptance. Viewing charity and philanthropy as an extension of women's domestic sphere resolved the apparent conflict between the ideology of domesticity and women's desire to do good deeds in the world. Indeed, the ideology of domesticity provided women with an argument for moving outside the private sphere of the home and into the community. This was especially true of charity and philanthropy. Because much of this work was church related and focused on poor women and children, society smiled benevolently on these activities. In addition, at times of national crisis, women were often called to leave their homes to help others. Women who engaged in many types of associations provided a public service. From the state's perspective, associations mobilized women to remedy social problems for free.

Associational life also benefited the women who participated. Associations could function as social clubs for women, allowing them to make friends and acquaintances in a public, but all female and socially respectable organization. Associations brought women into contact with other women from a variety of religious and social backgrounds. The antislavery movement in England, for example, brought together women from the families of wealthy industrialists, bankers, prosperous farmers and merchants, and clergymen. Quakers, Baptists, Independents, Unitarians, and evangelical Anglicans were all active in the movement. The contacts women made in associations could benefit their other endeavors in philanthropy, aid their families in getting ahead in society, and form the basis of lifelong friendships. In some cases, such as early nineteenth-century England, the networks that middle-class women formed through their activities in associations laid the foundation for a unified class identity. In others, such as late nineteenth-century France, associations facilitated the forging of ties among different social classes.

Working for an association, especially in a leadership role, could provide women with a source of prestige and public acknowledgment that was difficult for them to attain any other way. For some women, philanthropy was performative, requiring an acting role and an audience to observe them. These women wanted to see their name and picture in the newspaper when they gave benefits or fundraising parties. Although their motives may have been to seek status, they raised large sums of money to benefit the poor. Prime examples of this type of activity were the annual, highly publicized, charity bazaars in Paris.

Women who were involved in more controversial causes, such as establishing worker's associations, were viewed with greater suspicion, yet they acquired the same sorts of skills as did women in philanthropy. Women learned to organize and run meetings, speak in public, write pamphlets, create and maintain budgets, raise money, recruit new members, work with other organizations, hold demonstrations, and even petition their governing bodies. This experience would be invaluable when women turned their attention to the vote in the second half of the nineteenth century.

Through associations, women gained a civil identity, establishing themselves as active members and even leaders of nongovernmental organizations aimed at improving society. To some women, especially after mid-century, activities in philanthropic associations were part of their quest for citizenship and self-identity. By their chosen activities, female philanthropists, for example, worked toward defining citizenship for themselves and others. For themselves, being a good citizen meant bringing about the betterment of others and taking an active role in social reform. Philanthropy conferred "social citizenship" on these women, allowing them to participate actively in a public national life, even without the vote, and shaping their identity outside their home. Philanthropic women also sought to create good citizens among the objects of their charity. This meant at best enabling, or at worst forcing, the poor to work, maintain good hygiene, practice sexual abstinence outside of marriage, and educate their children to be good workers. Creating citizenship through philanthropy, as through other types of associations, rarely meant equality between the donor and recipient; rather women in associations wanted to maintain a social and economic hierarchy between themselves and those they sought to help. Moreover, a hierarchy marked the associations themselves. Men held prominent positions in many associations, but women often dominated numerically and had active voices in the governance and activities of these societies. In the early nineteenth century women's auxiliaries of men's associations often took on leadership roles, whereas after 1848 women increasingly took control of their own associations.

As they attended meetings, organized projects, worked on legislative proposals, and went out among the poor, women not only shifted the boundaries between public and private, but also expanded the parameters of their social roles. Women's associational activities became essential to the shaping of a civil society that developed over the course of the nineteenth century in all countries of Europe. They empowered themselves outside their own homes as they molded their social and political culture.

Charity and philanthropy

The words "charity" and "philanthropy" can be used interchangeably, but generally charity was an arm of religion. It involved local initiative and was based on personal contact between donor and receiver. Philanthropy, on the other hand, could be secular or vaguely spiritual, and did not necessarily involve personal contact between the benefactor and beneficiary. By mid-century, an increase in the number of urban poor combined with urban renewal that concentrated the poor in specified areas of big cities produced a spatial separation of the classes. As a result, philanthropy tended to become more impersonal. Nevertheless, even with the spatial separation of the poor, many female philanthropists took a personal interest in the needy. Charity and philanthropy provided contact between women of different social classes, even though the poor did not always welcome this contact; philanthropic women stated that they provided the "social glue" holding the classes together.

Some historians have argued that women's maternalistic and philanthropic associations had more civic, social, and political influence in states with weak central governments, such as England and the United States than in states with strong central governments, such as France, Germany, and Russia.[1] Recent research, however, has shown that the influence of women's philanthropic associations was as great in the so-called strong states as in the so-called weak ones. Private associations acted on behalf of public policy, and also influenced that policy in all the states of Europe.

Religion inspired most women's charitable activities. For Catholic women, it was part of the tradition of *caritas*. During the first half of the century, in Ireland, France, and the Catholic portions of Germany, women had little opportunity for associational life outside the Catholic Church; therefore women's charities were church related. *Tsedakah*, which means both charity and justice in Hebrew, involved giving to the poor, usually in the form of money for the synagogue to distribute; although not part of women's associations, per se, this was part of the Jewish "sacred duty" of the rich providing for their poor brethren. Protestant women sought to deliver the word of God, through the Bible, to the poor.

Philanthropic and charitable women in Western Europe developed the category of "deserving poor" as part of their religious beliefs. They had strong views that "God helps those who help themselves" but those who could not help themselves, such as widows and orphans, deserved charity from those acting on God's behalf. Initially, religious charities wanted personally to redeem individual "sinners" rather than improve the slum housing in which they found poor women and children; or they urged the poor to work harder and save, rather than improve their employment opportunities, conditions of work, and wages. The idea of sexual respectability prevailed as the religious associations differentiated between the good mothers who were widows or married women with children, and the bad or "fallen" mothers, such as women who bore children outside of marriage. Russian Orthodoxy had a different view of poverty than the Western religions. To the Orthodox Russian, the poor were not immoral sinners, but rather suffered the results of unfortunate experiences and events. In Russia, as in the west, women, particularly holy women, were the best able to provide charity to the poor by personal contact. Toward the end of the century, throughout Europe, women's philanthropy became increasingly secularized and distant from strict adherence to a particular denominational group.

Philanthropists became more concerned with structural changes in the lives of the poor, such as improving housing and hygiene.

Although lay women constituted most of the membership of charitable associations, nuns in convents played an important role in caring for the poor in Catholic areas of Europe, such as Ireland, Italy, France, Spain, and parts of Germany. Sisters of Charity, one of the major religious orders of the nineteenth century, went where middle-class matrons feared to tread – to the worst slums and homes of the sick. The Sisters also worked in institutions for the elderly and taught manual tasks befitting a person's station in life. The prevailing concepts of deserving and undeserving poor influenced the type of charities the nuns supported, both materially and emotionally. In Ireland, especially, convents formed a major portion of associational life for women, and as such they were institutions where women held considerable power and where they could exercise that power in dealing with the poor, especially in running orphanages, schools, homes for the elderly, and Magdalene asylums supposedly to redeem prostitutes and "fallen women," as they believed that Christ had redeemed Mary Magdalene. A major component of the religious sisters' charity involved visiting the sick and nursing them, especially when their lay sisters feared that duty. The nuns concentrated their work on women and children, setting their own standards and often excluding never-married mothers and ex-nuptial children. Although the nuns favored their own denominational groups, they could also give to the truly deserving needy of other faiths, perhaps out of altruism, or perhaps with a wish to convert. Religious laywomen supported nuns in their work. In Ireland, all deeply religious women had ties with convents and friendships with nuns. One of their main forms of charity was to give donations to the convents for nuns to use in their work with the poor.

Some Protestant women joined lay religious institutions in order to carry out their charitable activities. Anglican and Protestant deaconesses began to appear in the 1830s in Germany and Great Britain. They also existed in France, Belgium, and Switzerland. Most deaconesses were subject to male supervision, but not all. When Mariane von Rantzau (1811–55) took charge of the Bethanien home for deaconesses in Berlin in 1847, she insisted on independence for the women involved. Like their Catholic counterparts, these Protestant "sisters" nursed the ill and cared for the elderly, and set up schools, orphanages, and hospitals.

Female philanthropists, whether in convents or as lay Catholics and Protestants, believed that their Christian mission involved bettering the lives of the disadvantaged, and they developed a civilizing mission toward the urban poor of their home country. They formed missionary societies, some as Protestant Church auxiliaries, which provided an important form of associational life throughout the entire nineteenth century. In England, these included the Baptist Missionary Society, the British and Foreign Bible Society, the Church Missionary Society, and the Wesleyan Methodist Missionary Society. The Irish Bible Society was emblematic of many Protestant missionary societies. Women in these organizations used words such as "dirty savages" and "dangerous natives" in referring to the poor in the industrial cities of Great Britain and Ireland. Imbued with the idea of saving bodies and souls, they practiced their Christian missionary zeal, seeking to colonize those "pitiable unfortunates" at home, as well as in India and Africa. They were trying to domesticate the local working poor, as others were trying to domesticate the empire, to middle-class family norms and forms. These domestic missionaries were convinced that their middle-class culture was superior to that of the poor. As a result, they took children away from their families to raise them in workhouses or boarding schools, much as the Australian government removed aboriginal children and authorities in the Western United States removed Native American children to put them in boarding schools run by the middle classes. Christian philanthropic societies, some as part of the English Evangelical movement, and countless others in different countries, saw part of their mission as creating national identities and concepts of citizenship. They attempted to normalize the working classes through privileging their own middle-class ideal of the domestic and hygienic woman, pitying and infantalizing poor women and maintaining a distance even as they tried to mold them.

Secular philanthropic women, by and large, believed in the Enlightenment's optimism in the perfectibility of men and women. After mid-century, some saw philanthropy as a means of social reform and a way to bring women into civil society at all levels. They realized the potential benefits of combining private philanthropy with public governmental programs. In some areas, mixed-gender philanthropic associations, such as the French Philanthropic Society and the Society for Maternal Charity, worked in the service of the state. A multiplicity of philanthropic associations developed, and the emerging picture varied with the particular locality. These different associations reflected the diverse characteristics of the women who formed them.

German women's philanthropic activities are well documented for Hamburg, where Protestants and Catholics worked together in Christian charity, although the women's associations were somewhat separated by social class. In the 1840s, Amalie Sieveking (1794–1859) founded the Female Association for the Care of the Poor and Sick with the goal of alleviating the suffering of the poor. But, to her "at least as important were the benefits which it seemed to promise my sisters who would join me in such work of charity. The highest interests of my sex were close to my heart."[2] Sieveking belonged to one of the most elite families of Hamburg; the daughter and granddaughter of senators, she was part of a mid-century religious awakening. But her "sisters" in charity could also exclude others of a less elite social milieu, as they did Charlotte Paulsen (1797–1862).

Humiliated and smarting upon her exclusion from Sieveking's association, yet undaunted, Paulsen formed her own group, the Women's Club of Hamburg, which included other women whose husbands were men of the commercial and manufacturing classes, without preference for religion. Since Catholics, Protestants, and Jews all owned businesses in the same neighborhood, Paulsen's Women's Club was more community-based than religious and included Protestant, Catholic, and Jewish women. These women subordinated organized religion to their ethical concerns for the poor. For Jewish women, the Women's Club, and other similar philanthropies, served as vehicles for their assimilation. Johanna Goldschmidt (1806–84), the wife of a Jewish businessman in Hamburg worked closely with Paulsen, a Catholic, united in their belief that furthering the cause of women in associational life and in education should also advance spiritual freedom and ecumenical relations. They saw associations as a way to structure their own lives and social world. Paulsen and Goldschmidt were also active in another Hamburg association, the non-denominational "Women's Association for the Support of Poor Relief." These two women, and others in their associations, made philanthropy for women and children their major concern.

In all their activities, regardless of background or country, charitable and philanthropic women focused their energies on poor women and children, which historians label as "maternalism." The philanthropic women regarded charity to poor women and children as a maternalist extension of their own domestic and religious duties. Moreover, women and children were attractive beneficiaries of charity. Poor children, especially orphans, invoked pity, and people tended to open their pocketbooks and hearts when seeing or reading about the plight of poor orphans. Publicly providing for orphans through fund-raising events constituted a performative act of charity for donors. Also, children represented virgin minds to be educated in religion, the work ethic, and the ideals of citizenship. Associations advised and supported poor mothers, desiring to reduce the high mortality rate of their children, as well as the likelihood that these mothers would abandon their children to baby farms or to foundling homes.

Philanthropic women donated time and money in a variety of ways, most frequently at the community level because the women knew about local conditions and could have a direct impact on them. Even national philanthropic associations, such as the Society for Maternal Charity in France, had local branches to deal with local concerns. To provide charity, however, they needed funds. Therefore, fund-raising to support their causes was always their most basic activity; and among fund-raising endeavors, charity bazaars were the most common in Protestant and Catholic areas alike. These took place at the local church, as part of the women's church auxiliaries' projects, as well as on a grand scale in major cities, such as in Paris.

Visiting the poor prevailed as the major charitable activity of women throughout Europe and throughout the century. They exposed themselves to the illness and misery of the poor, even as they donned their raincoats and boots over their better dresses and shoes before going out in the slums of London, Manchester, Lille, Lyon, and Hamburg, or among the peasants of the Russian villages. Face-to-face contact with the recipients of their charity allowed them to exercise some surveillance and promote their version of morality and domestic order. Visiting the poor was part of Catholic charity as well as integral to Protestant Bible societies. Volunteer visitors, usually in groups of two or three, brought the Bible, along with coal, blankets, clothing, and food to the deserving poor. Although at the end of the century women's associations became more secular, they continued visiting the poor as their duty, either to their religion or to the state. In France after 1870, as in the United States, they served as republican mothers in the public arena.

In all countries, visiting societies proliferated. Each one wanted to convert their recipients, leading to religious rivalry among the societies. Catholic nuns, some coming to England from across the water in France, vied with Evangelical and Anglican visitors to the poor. Jewish propertied women also formed visiting societies in England, such as the Jewish Ladies' Benevolent Loan Society, established by Constance Rothschild Battersea. In its visits to the Jews of the East End of London, it met with some resistance. As one of the mothers visited said, "We are not like the *goyem* (Gentiles), we do not want to be talked to or taught, we do not drink, and we know how to bring up our children religiously and soberly."[3]

In Hamburg, Sieveking's Association for the Care of the Poor and Sick visited the poor, distributing clothing and food, and also organizing work among the poor, such as sewing, knitting, and menial chores. Starting out with 12 members, this association expanded to 53 during its first decade of existence in the 1840s. Sieveking wanted the poor to acknowledge that their sinfulness played a part in their misery and destitution. As with other elite women who visited the poor, Sieveking's group believed in a hierarchy in which the wealthy wielded moral authority over the poor.

Sieveking's association of elite women and the nonconfessional Women's Association for the Support of Poor Relief organized by women of the commercial and business middle classes, such as Paulsen and Goldschmidt illustrate the differences between traditional religious poor relief and the more modern developments, even though both operated in the same city at the same time, both visited the poor, and both were concerned with the welfare of mothers. Sieveking's association distributed clothes so the poor could attend church. Paulsen and Goldschmidt wanted to ease women's transition from rural to urban areas and teach new skills. It also distributed clothes, but aimed to teach the poor to repair clothes. Paulson and Goldschmidt's association trained new arrivals in domestic service and established a daycare center and school for children of the poor. Paulsen's group also had an eye on Hamburg's requirements for poor relief and for citizenship, and tried to enable the poor to gain the legal residence required for free schooling and licenses to work.

In France, several different associations visited the poor. The Society of Maternal Charity, which existed throughout the nineteenth century, sent visitors to poor married mothers. Finding worthy women in need, they would pay for a midwife, bring food to the new mothers, and baby clothes for the newborn. They might also give food and financial assistance to women who promised to breastfeed their babies. Toward the end of the century, philanthropic and secular associations proliferated, some with many members, and some with fewer than 20. One group of women, believing that they and the state owed assistance to poor mothers, formed an association called The Duty to Mothers, with the motto: "To create is good, but to take care of someone is better." Other societies, such as the Society for Maternal Aid and the Society for Maternal Breastfeeding, founded by propertied women, often the wives of politicians, helped supply furniture, food, and even nursing assistance to new mothers. Philanthropic women in each of the societies knew each other and often worked together to save poor mothers from destitution and their children from abandonment or death. They had a network, and when one found a poor mother on the street, or when another came knocking on her door, she would bring her to the appropriate organization. These women also worked with politicians lobbying for legislation and welfare measures benefiting poor mothers.

Their associations often received subventions from the state. Over the course of the century, female philanthropists became an increasingly integral part of social welfare and civil society.

The number of charitable women who visited poor women increased in all countries during the century. There was a degree of intimacy between the visitors and the poor, and perhaps a degree of conflict. Visitors could help, but they could also be matronizing, thereby furthering class antagonism. This might especially be the case when the visitors were young, single, childless women in their twenties (as they sometimes were) telling mothers of the same age, or older, how to raise their children.

In addition to visiting the local poor, women's philanthropic associations established institutions, ranging from meeting rooms to schools and orphanages. In England, women of property brought their Bibles and set up rooms, sometimes called Mission houses, where they would meet with poor mothers in their communities for a few hours a week. They would give lessons in cooking, supply blankets, help with needlework, and provide a forum for Bible reading, spiritual messages, and a discussion of children's health. The donors and recipients knew each other, and the propertied women could address the needs of the poor in their own communities. Ellen Ranyard (1814–79), well known for organizing mothers' meetings, encouraging self-help, and fostering needlework and religion, established the successful Bible and Domestic Female Mission in London.

Philanthropic women founded other institutions to save the children. In Ireland, religious groups particularly focused on saving children, not only from sin and starvation, but also from other religious groups; the Protestants wanted to save them from the Catholics and the Catholics from the Protestants. Both denominations ran orphanages staffed by matrons who tried to instill middle-class values. Catholic and Protestant women's associations in all Western European countries established orphanages and charity schools, the latter sometimes called "Ragged Schools" or Sunday Schools. In some places women's associations could influence legislators to establish schools, as when the British Parliament authorized pauper schools as part of the 1862 Poor Law. Women's charities ran these government schools as a type of halfway house between prison or the workhouse and domestic service. Designed to keep children off the streets, and away from sin and begging, as well as to reinforce ideas of hard work and domesticity, the schools provided only a rudimentary education, including some religion. Volunteers would train the girls to become better domestic servants. Since middle-class women employed domestic servants, this gave a different meaning to their goal of "helping others to help themselves."

Women's philanthropic associations became well known for establishing women's shelters. The best known were the Young Women's Christian Associations founded in England in 1855. Committees of philanthropic women and clergymen ran these institutions to befriend young Protestant women, especially those newly arriving in the cities, to keep them from falling into prostitution, to train them to be domestic servants, and to save their souls for Christianity. In France, the secular Philanthropic Society established shelters for homeless women in Paris at the end of the century. One shelter, founded in 1890, had beds for over 250 women.

In Russia, as in the West, charitable women sought to shelter homeless and family-less women. Early in the century, the Russian Women's Patriotic Society first tried to deal with the effects of the Napoleonic wars, but soon established girls' schools. During the middle of the nineteenth century, institutions such as orphanages, infirmaries, and schools for young girls increased, partially as a result of the reforms emancipating the serfs. Women's religious communities, often consisting of women of the lower gentry, staffed these institutions since at that time many of the charitable women were members of religious communities.

In addition to saving the children, secular female philanthropists saw their mission as rescuing unwed mothers, fallen women, and prostitutes, often failing to distinguish among these categories. In France, philanthropic women provided shelters for needy parturient women through a variety of institutions working in tandem. One association established a shelter for unwed mothers at least seven months pregnant; another provided midwife services, and another established asylums for new mothers and infants. Charitable associations based on religion early in the century thought in terms of redeeming the unwed mothers through religion; the secular societies toward the end of the century wanted to rehabilitate the women through financial support, so that they could find socially acceptable work.

Rescuing supposedly "fallen women" formed part of the mission of philanthropic women all over Europe during the entire century. The Good Shepherd societies and the Catholic Sisters of Charity, along with lay associations, established asylums, sometimes called Magdalene houses, to redeem young women who were too overtly sexual for their family's liking; or who were seduced, generally pregnant, and abandoned; or who were young prostitutes. According to religious authorities, these women needed redemption. In many ways, these institutions were intended to control girls' sexuality. But the institutions excluded women who had been sex workers for a long time or who had been convicted of other crimes. Many of these Magdalene institutions and other institutions for "wayward girls" resembled prison workhouses, where the inmates engaged in laundry and needlework, generally exploited for their labor. Nevertheless, some women entered voluntarily, and some chose to stay. Others were imprisoned when family members or judges wanted to keep them there. Still others escaped or were expelled for bad behavior.

An influential group of female philanthropists consisted of women pioneers committed to social service whose numbers increased after mid-century as men and women redefined the social question to address structural issues. Women such as Octavia Hill (1838–1912), Florence Nightingale, and the Fabian socialist, Beatrice Potter Webb (1858–1943) believed that society's structures, and not women's immorality, led to social evils and destitution. Octavia Hill is emblematic of female philanthropists in the second half of the nineteenth century. She was one of the founders of the English Charity Organization Society (COS) in 1866, which was to coordinate the disparate charities in order for them to be more efficient in responding to the increased numbers of poor. The COS also established more stringent criteria for the "deserving poor." Hill, a professional philanthropist, made her activities for reform a full-time occupation, advocating and helping to establish decent and affordable housing for the poor. Hill served as a liaison between private visitors to the poor and public Poor-Law officials, becoming one of the key women in moving charity and philanthropy from women's volunteer associations to social reform. Her career illustrates change from the tradition of volunteer charity and philanthropy (usually religious) to modern social work and social reform.

Annie Wood Besant represents another woman engaged in social reform, one without a denominationally religious tie. Born a Catholic in 1847, when her father died five years later she went to live with a fervently Evangelical family who raised her in their religion. Looking for a life of service, she married Frank Besant, a clergyman, hoping that this partnership would provide her an avenue for social service. The marriage failed, however, and in 1874 she joined the Secular Society. She established a friendship with Charles Bradlaugh and together they republished a pamphlet that provided information on birth control, which authorities deemed pornographic. In 1877 they were tried and found guilty of publishing pornography, but won their appeal. In her book, *The Laws of Population*, she outraged society by advocating birth control. As a result of the notoriety of the trial and book, Besant lost custody of her children. She then joined the Fabian socialists, a group committed to a gradual reform of society along socialist principles of improving the lives of workers. In 1888 she turned her attention to the health of young women workers and wrote of the dangers of phosphorous fumes in match making and the low wages paid to match makers. She helped the young women form the Matchgirls Union and led them on a successful three-week strike in 1889, which ended with the company granting concessions. Following her 1889 conversion to Theosophy (a religious philosophy incorporating mysticism and Eastern religions such as Buddhism and Hinduism), in 1893 she went to work in India to establish schools for girls and work for Indian Home Rule in the 1920s. She died in 1933.

Russian women also committed themselves to social change, starting with the reforms of the 1860s. Numerous women's associations established schools, maternity hospitals, training for midwives, housing for poor families, day care, and sewing workshops. Some of their names clearly indicate their mission, such as the "Society for Inexpensive Lodgings for the Poor Population of Petersburg."

Reforming society

While the great majority of female voluntary associations were concerned with helping women and children, some women realized the ability of associations to reshape other elements of society. Many women moved from charitable and philanthropic concerns into new areas of social reform, often bringing with them the same techniques and approaches. Whereas, especially in the early part of the century, religion formed the basis for charitable work, it could also serve as the foundation for a variety of activities besides helping the poor. In Germany, for example, male and female Catholics were active in campaigning against the dominance of the Pope, while male and female Protestants in the Friends of Light and Free Communities organized to promote a liberal and rational form of their religion. In England, the Quaker church produced many of the most active members of the antislavery and prison reform movements.

Like women in charity and philanthropy, women in a variety of social reform movements believed that their actions could make a difference in the world. Their activities shaped public opinion on a variety of issues. Prison reform moved women to act throughout the nineteenth century, and resulted in improved conditions for female prisoners. Elizabeth Fry (1780–1845) began visiting English female prisoners in 1813. She was shocked at the crowded and unsanitary conditions in Newgate Prison, where she found 300 women and their children sleeping on the floor without bedding or nightclothes. She worked for better accommodations for prisoners, and also established a school and chapel. In addition, after witnessing the vulnerability of female prisoners to male guards and fellow inmates, she came to believe that male and female prisoners should be held separately and that female guards should supervise female prisoners. She founded the local Newgate Association in 1817 and the national British Ladies Society in 1836 to push for reform. Her writings on prison reform were translated into several languages, and influenced women such as Concepción Arenal (1820–93) in Spain and Josephine Mallet and Madame d'Abbadie d'Arrast in France.

Temperance also became a popular cause for women throughout Europe. Temperance advocates argued that alcohol destroyed family life. They believed that men who abandoned their wives and children for the local pub and women whose addiction to drink caused them to neglect household duties were fundamental causes of poverty, crime, and prostitution. Women temperance activists arranged alternate activities for families, such as tea parties, and distributed pamphlets. In England, a national Ladies' Temperance Association was established to coordinate local activities. Temperance societies existed in many countries. In Germany and Italy, women acted as helpers to male members. In Norway and Finland, however, women's missions and temperance clubs became an important venue for women activists around mid-century. In France, temperance activists had little success, even though they focused on alcohol rather than wine, a necessary daily beverage for most French men and women. Some women who were involved in the temperance cause also became active in promoting abstention from tobacco, sex, and animal products. Many also supported the cause of dress reform, which advocated the creation of more practical and comfortable clothing for men and women. Some women active in the temperance movement had been influenced by the writings of utopian socialist Charles Fourier. Others moved from temperance into transcendental spiritualism. All believed that women had the moral power to change the world.

The peace movement and animal rights also attracted many women. Both were originally areas of exclusive male concern. Women, however, quickly made both causes their own. In the 1820s, several ladies' auxiliaries of the London Peace Society were established. Although women were not allowed to attend the National Peace Congress held in 1851, they were important to the movement because they worked hard to establish contacts with other activists both at home and abroad, such as Swedish novelist Frederika Bremer and the Swiss Marie Goegg-Pouchoulin (1826–99), founder of the International Association of Women, a group dedicated to the advance of pacifism. In France, Eugénie Niboyet (1799–1883) became a leading peace activist when she founded the

Peace Society and the *Journal de la paix des deux mondes* in 1844. Her society, comprised 32 men and 20 women, and sponsored monthly public lectures. By far the most well-known peace activist of the nineteenth century was Baronness Bertha von Suttner (1843–1914), who won the Nobel Peace Prize in 1905. Her novel *Lay Down Your Arms* (1896) opened the eyes of many Europeans to the sufferings caused by war. Her presence and speeches at the First Hague Convention of 1899 contributed to the establishment of rules of warfare and a permanent Court of Arbitration. Another sort of suffering inspired animal rights activists. In the 1870s, women in France brought the activities of the Society for the Protection of Animals, established in 1845, to the attention of the public by shifting the debate away from the scientific merits of vivisection toward the emotional and physical suffering of animals. Antivivisection societies gained in popularity among wealthy women in the 1880s, and some women began to establish private refuges for abandoned and abused animals. Women also campaigned to end violent public sports involving animals, such as cock fighting and bull-baiting.

The wide variety of associations open to women in the nineteenth century allowed each individual woman to chart her own path through the maze of social reform causes and organizations. Whatever the cause, women tended to employ different techniques and justifications in their work than did men. The antislavery movement provides a good example of this process. Inspired both by Enlightenment thought that emphasized the natural rights of all individuals and by the growing slave trade, men in France and England began discussing abolitionism and organized the antislavery movement in the late eighteenth century. In England, a 1787 article in the *Manchester Mercury* called for women to support the abolitionist cause. It focused on the victimization of female slaves and the destruction of the family under slavery, themes that would be widely used by female antislavery activists. As women became involved in the movement, they examined the topic of slavery in the London debating societies for women that became popular in the late eighteenth century and urged women not to consume sugar grown on slave plantations with their tea. Following the 1807 act abolishing the slave trade, the focus of the movement shifted to colonial slavery in 1823 when the National Antislavery Society was formed. In 1825, Lucy Townsend (d.1847) and Mary Lloyd founded the first women's antislavery society. Despite the reluctance of women active in the first wave of abolitionism to abandon their role as helpers to the men's associations, a network of women's groups was quickly formed. By 1831, 39 associations and 78 auxiliaries existed.

The women's antislavery movement differed from that of the men in a variety of ways, many of which demonstrate the influence of other forms of philanthropy on its members. Women abolitionists, for example, adopted a maternalist perspective in their writings and speeches, focusing on the need to help the mothers and children victimized by slavery. Their goal was to permit the female slave "to occupy her proper station as a Daughter, a Wife and a Mother."[4] At the same time, they maintained a distance between themselves and the women they wished to help. When Mary Prince (*c.*1788–?), a slave from the West Indies brought to London by her owners, ran away and sought her freedom, women abolitionists helped her by employing her as a domestic servant. Although they wished to publish her story for propaganda purposes, they edited her tale and revised her writing to make her appear less independent and more of a victim, and assured their potential readers that they had verified the details of her story, assuming that many might suspect Prince of lying.

The techniques women used to further their cause also reveal strong ties to other forms of philanthropy. Whereas men tended to distribute propaganda and petitions at public meetings, women preferred to go door to door, just as charitable house visitors did, selling pamphlets that women activists had written or lending these pamphlets to the poor. These techniques often allowed women to gather more signatures on petitions than men did; in Nottingham, for example, three times as many women as men signed the 1833 petition, while in Edinburgh about 162,000 women, close to a quarter of the city's adult female population, were signatories. Men were far more likely to insert articles and notices in the press, often choosing the major political periodicals. Women rarely used the press, but when they did, tended to choose religious periodicals. Many attended public meetings, but few were likely to speak at them. The approaches taken by male and female societies concerning the sugar question also differed. Men focused on petitioning Parliament to make sugar grown by free people in the East Indies as affordable as that grown by slaves in the West Indies. Women instead organized an abstention campaign, again going house to house to urge women not to buy or consume sugar from the West Indies. Elizabeth Heyrick (1769–1831), a leading abolitionist pamphleteer, argued that women must be targeted in this campaign because, "in the domestic department, they are the chief controllers; they, for the most part, provide the articles of family consumption."[5] Finally, while men focused exclusively on legislative reform, women also spent some of the money they raised on relief and education for slaves in the West Indies. Activities of abolitionist missionaries, funded by women's antislavery societies, often aided slave resistance. For example, the establishment of churches that combined Christian and African beliefs provided meeting places where resistance could be organized.

While women appealed to the ideals of domesticity and drew upon practices developed for charitable and philanthropic work, they did not see themselves as subordinate to male activists. Furthermore, their involvement in the antislavery movement brought them into the political realm. Women and men were divided over the timetable for the abolition of slavery. Men, citing the economic consequences of ending slavery, argued for gradual abolition, while women, arguing on moral terms, insisted it must be immediate. Members of women's associations, convinced that the men's associations did not represent their views, campaigned for immediate abolition, eventually winning over the men to their position. In this case, women relied heavily on moral and religious arguments, but some activists did frame the case for abolition in terms of individual rights. These women were fewer in number, and tended to be drawn more toward radical social reform movements. Heyrick, who argued that slavery was a human rights issue, also supported workers' rights to strike and form unions. Similarly, Anne Knight (1781–1862) supported utopian socialism, Chartism, and women's rights.

Whatever their position on the justification for abolition, whether based on morality and religion or human rights, women active in the antislavery movement found themselves being drawn into the political sphere. The antislavery petitions circulated in the early 1830s were signed by hundreds of thousands of women. Previously, petitioning had largely been a male preserve; petitioning by women thus constituted their first large-scale involvement in Parliamentary politics. The petitioning campaign, combined with women's efforts to write pamphlets, go door to door in the name of their cause, and organize public meetings, contributed enormously to shaping public opinion. After the abolition of slavery in 1833, women who supported other causes continued to influence both Parliament and public opinion through their activism.

Despite the discourse of domesticity that enveloped women's volunteer work, the fact that women were working to create a better society made their actions inherently political. Indeed, governments did not hesitate to call on women volunteers in times of national crisis. During the German wars of liberation against Napoleon, women's clubs were established to nurse the wounded and care for widows and orphans. Similar women's clubs were set up in Russian-controlled Polish territories following the 1832 uprising and in Germany during the 1848 Revolution. The best known, the Humania Association, founded by Kathinka Zitz-Halein (1801–77), provided support for political prisoners and refugees and their families. The 1832 cholera epidemic in France prompted many women to begin welfare work, while in that same year English women of the artisanal classes founded the Friends of the Oppressed to help the families of men who were arrested for advocating freedom of the press.

This last example indicates that associational activity was not the exclusive preserve of upper- and middle-class women. While fewer women of the artisanal and working classes were active in associations, they still supported many of the same causes that wealthier women did. In the antislavery movement, for example, artisanal women did not join associations, but they did sign petitions, attend public meetings, and abstain from consuming sugar grown in the West Indies. Women of the popular classes also organized on their own behalf. Friendly, or Mutual Aid, Societies provided women with a safety net in case of illness or accident. These societies collected dues that could then be distributed to members in need; they also served as a social network. In France, 41,736 women were members of such societies in 1855.

Women were also active in the Owenite and Saint-Simonian movements, which advocated social reform measures meant to render industrial capitalism less damaging to workers. These movements flourished in England and France in the first half of the nineteenth century, where industrialization was most advanced, and advocated men and women joining together in association, rather than competing with each other and thereby driving down wages. While many activists understood the concept of association to apply only to manufacturing, those involved in the Owenite and Saint-Simonian movements believed that household chores should also be shared, and joined communities of like-minded individuals to reshape both work and family life.

The principle of association that underlay the Owenite and Saint-Simonian movements of the first half of the nineteenth century reappeared in the late

nineteenth century. The Women's Co-operative Guild, founded in 1883, established cooperative laundries and bakeries and worked to improve working-class
housing. It also offered public lectures that included advice on budgeting and
domestic economy. Several of the leading members had parents who had been
active in the Owenite movement. Working- and middle-class women were also
drawn to socialism through organizations such as the Fabian Society in England,
cofounded by Beatrice Potter Webb, and the German Socialist Party, established
in 1875. Although women were not admitted to the party as equal members
until 1908, from 1889 on they established informal women's campaigning committees, organized meetings, and sponsored public lectures on topics such as
childcare, religion, prostitution, and divorce. August Bebel's *Women under
Socialism* (1879) was instrumental in attracting working- and middle-class
women to socialism. It touched upon the conviction held by many women active
in voluntary associations that they could, through their own actions, change the
world. In this case, Bebel argued that the establishment of socialism would lead
to the betterment not only of the working classes, but also of women.

The growth of socialist organizations in the late nineteenth century
prompted conservatives to organize women as well. The Ladies' Grand Council
of the Primrose League, established in 1884, was responsible for planning activities designed to gain working-class support for the Conservative Party. By
1900, nearly half of the 1.5 million members of the League were women.
Similar conservative and nationalist organizations proliferated in Austria, where
concern among ethnic Germans over the growing influence of ethnic minori-
ties led to the mobilization of women. The most important of these groups was
the German School Association. In 1883, Nina Kienzl led a group of women
in Graz in organizing the first women's branch of this organization; by 1885,
83 branches for women had been established and 10,000 women were members.
The association encouraged women to prohibit intermarriage with members of
other ethnic groups, to hire German servants so that their children did not
become bilingual, and to dress their children in traditional German clothes.
Nationalist causes became a growing source of women's mobilization throughout Europe in the late nineteenth century. The Patriotic Women's Association,
founded by Queen Augusta of Prussia in 1866 had almost 800 branches by
1891. The Ladies Land League was founded in Ireland by Anna Parnell
(1852–1911) to coordinate active resistance against landlords in the 1880s, and
quickly grew to 500 branches. Through their membership in these and other
associations, women claimed their right to shape and defend the nation.
Women's involvement in nationalist organizations was justified on the basis of
their natural role as mothers. As an Austrian activist argued in 1884, "Men alone
fight for issues of freedom; these questions are too distant from the concerns of
women. But when the enemy threatens our most precious of national possessions, the holiest legacy of our ancestors, our mother tongue, then the mother's
heart is also affected."[6] Despite such reassuring claims about the distinction
between male and female activism, women's associational activities blurred the
boundaries between public and private life.

Women experienced this blurring of public and private on a daily basis, as the
wide variety of associations they were involved in challenged their abilities to

meet their domestic responsibilities. Ann Taylor Gilbert (1782–1866), a woman active in the antislavery movement, wrote to a friend in 1838, "This generally, is my great practical difficulty – the drawing of the line correctly between *in door* and *out of doors* business."[7] Of course, servants helped make this balancing act possible for middle- and upper-class women; it is doubtful that Mary Lloyd could have continued her involvement in the many societies she founded and joined without servants, given that she also had ten children. In fact, single and widowed women, often seen as "redundant" women in the larger society, played an invaluable role in female associations. Single women tended to take on the most time-consuming jobs, such as that of secretary, while widows could devote not only their time but also their fortunes to their favorite causes. Associational activity was also made easier by the fact that it was often a family affair. In many cases, three or more generations of women might be involved in the same cause, and husbands and fathers were often members of complementary men's associations. Family involvement helped husbands and sons understand a woman's involvement in a cause, and, as Clare Midgley has argued in her study of the antislavery movement in England, brought public concerns into the private sphere of the home.[8]

Although women often justified their involvement in associational life using the language of domesticity and maternalism, they believed that by joining together, they could respond to the problems of modern society and reshape society for the better. Through their work in associations, they made claims to move their nations in what they considered to be a more positive direction. As such, they acted as social citizens, while also laying the groundwork for the feminist movement and for women's demands for the political rights of a citizen, particularly suffrage. This movement from philanthropy and other types of associational activity to feminism was so common that writers adopted it as a stereotype. For example, the fictional Mrs. Jellyby, the "Lady Bountiful" of Charles Dickens' novel, *Bleak House* (1853), went from philanthropy to female suffrage, just as so many actual female philanthropists did, not only in England, but also in all of Europe. In Spain, where the historical record of women's associations is scant, one woman stands out. Concepción Arenal was a philanthropist, prison reformer, and lawyer who engaged in activities advocating women's rights in the public sphere of government.

Women's voluntary associations were also a key force in the development of the modern welfare state. The relatively uncontroversial idea of saving babies' lives became the linchpin of the social welfare programs developed in the late nineteenth century. Over the course of the century, traditional faith-based charitable initiatives declined in number and influence, in part because they were unable to meet a continually growing need and in part because they arbitrarily focused only on the groups they considered deserving. As the century drew to a close, modern forms of philanthropy tended to dominate, often working with local and national governments. In turn, state and national programs resembled those pioneered by philanthropic organizations. The idea that not only individuals, or a community of women, but the state as a whole should care for its less fortunate members became a key component of political thought by the late nineteenth century. As states adopted programs pioneered by women volunteers, these programs risked becoming less personal and more bureaucratized. Nonetheless, the movement of the state into social welfare did not eliminate the need for women's philanthropic associations and many continued well into the twentieth century. Moreover, women formed new philanthropic associations that worked directly with state agencies. Many other women found employment with the state in schools, hospitals, day care centers, and orphanages. Employment in such areas was considered acceptable for women in part because women had been doing such unpaid work throughout the century. Associations designed to help others thus ended up helping middle-class women as well, who found new avenues for employment by the end of the century.

Associational life highlights the ambiguities and flexibility of contemporary ideas about women's nature and women's function in society. The ideology of domesticity appeared to limit women to the private sphere of the home, and yet men and women used it to justify women's involvement in public life. Associations brought women out of their own homes and into the homes of others, but also into a variety of social and political arenas. Similarly, the assumption that individualism did not apply to women was called into question through associations. In associations, women acted as individuals in a community of women, interacting with others and often receiving individual recognition for their actions. Even without public recognition, being active in an association could provide a woman with a sense of accomplishment. Finally, although women were considered to be the guardians of tradition, women in associations both faced the problems of modern life head on, and believed in the possibility of change. Through associational activity, women learned how to redefine the terms of domesticity so that it became an ideology that justified, and at times demanded, their involvement in the public sphere. These experiences would serve them well when they turned their attention to the question of women's rights.

9
Feminism and Politics

Few concepts in European women's history have generated as much discussion and disagreement as the term "feminism." On a general level, feminism can be defined as the belief that men and women should have equal rights and opportunities. A feminist could then be understood as someone who articulated and fought for this belief. Some would argue that both those individuals who fought for women as a group and those who struggled for themselves could be called feminists. While individual women may not have seen their efforts to become painters or scientists, to learn to read, to earn a decent wage, or to participate in associational life as part of a feminist struggle, their accomplishments often inspired others by proving that women could excel in areas formally reserved for men. This chapter focuses on individuals who fought for the rights and opportunities of women as a group. These individuals worked alone and with others, to explore and articulate the way in which sex and gender shaped personal interactions, social and economic life, politics, science, philosophy, and culture. During the nineteenth century, their goal was to end the secondary gender status of women in all areas. In her encyclopedic work on *European Feminisms*, the historian Karen Offen has defined feminism as "the name given to a comprehensive critical response to the deliberate and systematic subordination of women as a group by men as a group within a given cultural setting."[1]

To have been a feminist in the nineteenth century did not mean that a person was primarily interested in women's suffrage; only a minority made getting the vote their priority. Others were more interested in achieving women's rights within a family or in expanding women's access to work and education. Individuals of all classes, both men and women, became feminists in the nineteenth century. Although all believed that women should have equal rights and opportunities, not all believed that men and women were the same. To make sense of these different views, Offen has distinguished two varieties of feminism: relational and individual. Relational feminists claimed rights for women as women; they essentialized women, arguing that the qualities that distinguished women from men justified their access to work, education, and politics. Individual feminists, on the other hand, argued that in the debate over rights and opportunities, sex was irrelevant; women should have independence, autonomy and rights because they were human individuals. While the first position relied heavily on the language of domesticity, the second drew upon the Enlightenment concept of individual rights. Relational and individual feminisms can best be conceptualized as variations of broad feminist goals, and not as dichotomies. In some ways all feminists sought women's equality and independence, so the labels may distort as well as help explain the variety of feminisms.

Even those who argued from a position of individual rights argued that all women deserved rights, a paradox identified and discussed by historian Joan W. Scott. According to Scott, "Feminism was a protest against women's political exclusion; its goal was to eliminate 'sexual difference' in politics, but it had to make its claims on behalf of 'women' (who were discursively produced through 'sexual difference'). To the extent that it acted for 'women,' feminism produced the 'sexual difference' it sought to eliminate. This paradox – the need both to accept *and* refuse 'sexual difference' – was the constitutive condition of feminism as a political movement throughout its long history."[2] Adopting the language of domesticity to justify their demands outside the political sphere made this paradox less obvious. Thus, by the end of the century, terms such as "social motherhood" and "social housekeeping" were being successfully used to argue that women's ability to nurture and maintain order justified their greater involvement in education and social welfare. The use of the language of domesticity was less successful in helping women gain the vote.

Although some historians attribute the use of the word "feminism" to the utopian socialist Charles Fourier's coinage in the 1830s, its actual origins are obscure, and most historians find the term in general use starting in the late 1870s. By the 1890s, the words *feminism, feminismo, feminismus,* or *féminisme,* appeared in a proliferation of publications, although sometimes pejoratively. We maintain that the word "feminism" has meaning for gender equality and the rights of women even before that word may have actually been coined, and we use it to define women's political, social, cultural, legal, and economic search for rights as early as the late eighteenth century.

The French Revolution planted the seeds of feminism. The discussion and expansion of rights in France made it possible for individuals such as the Marquis de Condorcet, Olympe de Gouges, Etta Palm d'Aelders, Pauline Léon, and Mary Wollstonecraft to advocate greater rights for women. While these individuals were not the first to argue that women deserved greater opportunities, they were the first to argue the case for all women. The democratic nature of the French Revolution meant that individuals began to see all women as a group that deserved equal rights and opportunities with men. Even during the period of the Revolution, these ideas were contested. In 1793, Jean-Baptiste-André Amar, deputy to the Convention, justified the closing of women's political clubs by arguing that women could best serve their nation by staying home and raising their children to be Republican citizens. As reaction against the Revolution grew in the beginning of the nineteenth century, feminist arguments became even fainter. They did not disappear altogether, however. Indeed, the entire nineteenth century is marked by a continual discussion of women's rights. Although limited to certain groups and places at the beginning of the century, by century's end it was a loud and boisterous debate, one that focused on all aspects of women's relationships to family and society.

The foundations of feminism, 1800–48

By raising the issue of women's rights, the French Revolution incited debate throughout Europe. The decision to limit active citizenship to men in 1791, the execution of the Queen on the basis of her supposed failure as a mother, the outlawing of women's clubs in 1793, and the reorganization of sister and satellite republics beginning in 1795 prompted individuals throughout Europe to reflect on the position that women should occupy in society. Whereas some protested the growing exclusion of women in the French Republic, others attempted to develop a rationale for this exclusion. Arguments that women were weaker physically, less able to reason, prone to overexcitement and emotion, and driven by self-interest were made with increasing fervor in the years following the Revolution. Even when couched in the flattering language of domesticity, such attempts to denigrate women's abilities drew the ire of a small number of men and women that we can classify as feminists. In the early part of the century in particular, these individuals drew upon arguments concerning natural human rights – arguments that underlay much of the revolutionary legislation – to argue for women's inclusion in society. They also drew on the concepts of motherhood and domesticity to demand greater rights for women. With every step toward the expansion of democracy, these arguments were made with renewed vigor.

By breaking with centuries of tradition, the French demonstrated that in all areas – including women's status – changes could be made. The possibility of change was made further apparent due to the continued spread of industrialization. As family businesses and workshops gave way to larger concerns from which wives and daughters were absent, as production moved from the home to the factory, and as members of a family were no longer paid as a unit, but as individuals, the question of women's relation to the workforce was increasingly discussed. The development of domestic ideology along with gendered arguments used to protest innovations such as mechanization, made men and women more aware of how a person's sex could affect her job opportunities and her wages. As industrialization disrupted more and more of Europe, a feminist critique of the economy spread from marginalized groups of idealists to a larger segment of the population.

While antifeminists harkened back to tradition to justify women's inequality, feminists demonstrated that their arguments were possible because things had already changed. The continued development of democracy meant that the question of citizenship for women was repeatedly brought before the public. The spread of industrialization meant that women's working lives were often in flux. Perhaps because modern feminism arose in this time of great change, its proponents couched their arguments in terms of creating a better world. Although some looked to the past for role models and precedents, most feminists looked toward what they believed would be a better future. And for most, this better future depended upon women gaining their rights. As Charles Fourier wrote in 1808, "the extension of women's privileges is the general principle for all social progress."[3] This sentiment of optimism and possibility was especially strong in the years preceding the revolutions of 1848.

The first part of the century – especially the period before 1840 – was also marked by the strong involvement of women of all classes in politics. These women did not have the vote; nor, however, did most men. Their involvement in politics was rooted in earlier forms of protest and patronage. Women of the popular classes, for example, engaged in food riots in France as late as 1857. In Great Britain, women attacked Poor Law Officials, protested enclosure and fought tenant evictions. Women's role in such protest, which often turned violent and in some cases led to their arrest and even execution, was justified by their role as guardians of the family. In protesting practices that hurt their families, women were fighting for change. Aristocratic women also engaged in politics based on family ties. Throughout Europe, noble women sought positions and power for members of their families, petitioning those that could help and maintaining extensive networks of contacts. Although these practices survived the French Revolution, the equation of women and politics with chaos and terror made many question their appropriateness. Under assault from public opinion, traditional forms of women's political activism declined from mid-century, as parliamentary democracy took firmer hold in Western Europe. As this occurred, women of all classes became increasingly aware of the way in which their sex influenced their life chances and experiences. It was out of such awareness that feminism was born.

A good example of this phenomenon can be found among British radical women who began in the late eighteenth century to write books and pamphlets, form book clubs and debating societies, and attend political meetings. Their goal was the repeal of the Test and Corporation Acts, which denied noncon-formists (Protestants who were not members of the Anglican Church), along with Catholics and Jews, the right to attend or teach in Oxford and Cambridge, practice law or hold public office. Radical women were further galvanized in the 1820s by the Queen Caroline Affair. King George IV's attempt to divorce his wife, Caroline of Brunswick, ignited a tremendous public discussion. Women of all classes wrote pamphlets and petitions and demonstrated in favor of the Queen, whom they portrayed as a virtuous wife and mother wronged by her husband. This scandal brought the language of domesticity to the forefront of radical politics. Radical women increasingly turned away from the language of individual rights toward one of female (and especially maternal) purity and honor. Yet they did not use this language to call for the retirement of women to the private sphere of the family, but rather to justify their actions by "claiming their right to engage in public politics as wives and mothers."[4]

Radical organizing against the Test and Corporation Acts was successful; they were repealed in 1829. Trade unionism was also legalized, and women began to organize. Sixty London women founded the Society of Industrious Females in 1832; the following year another group formed the Practical Moral Union of the Women of Great Britain and Ireland. The repeal of the Test and Corporation Acts also initiated a discussion on the expansion of the suffrage. Some argued that women, as well as men, should have the vote. The 1832 Reform Act, however, included – for the first time in British law – specific use of the word "male" when describing voter qualifications. Many radical women, accustomed to seeing themselves as part of a group in which men and women were equally oppressed, became uncomfortably aware that the fight for reform had led to their formal exclusion from parliamentary politics. This awareness was crystallized by their exclusion, despite their extensive involvement in the cause, from speaking at the 1840 London Anti-Slavery Convention. As a result, women like Marion Kirkland Reid realized the necessity of organizing for the cause of women's rights, and looked to the antislavery movement as a model. Her *Plea for Women* (1843) published under the motto "can man be free, if woman be a slave," a quote from the romantic poet Percy Shelley, was a call to arms for middle-class English women.

The experience of radical women in the early part of the century was common to many women who became feminists. In fighting for a common cause, they became aware of the new importance of sexual difference in modernizing and democratizing states. This experience led them to fight for the rights of women as a group. The slow and irregular, and yet continuous move toward modern industrial and democratic states meant that the "woman question," as it came to be called, was on the agenda throughout the century.

In the years before 1848, many women who became feminists were drawn to alternative social and religious movements. Leaders of these movements identified women as both victims and saviors. The utopian socialists, in particular, linked the improvement of women's status with the betterment of society. In England, the most important of these movements was the Owenite movement.

The Owenite movement emerged around Scottish mill owner Robert Owen (1771–1858) in the 1820s. Owen created a model worker's community that included shorter work hours for children, schools, and good housing. He also advocated retail cooperatives. While many criticized the Owenites for their belief that women should be independent of their husbands, women were attracted to his vision of a society in which community, cooperation, and mutual respect were privileged. Significant numbers of the middle and working classes became members of the Rational Society, the organization created to promote Owenism; they participated in the establishment of cooperative workshops and stores, and joined his model communities, including those in New Lanarck, Scotland and New Harmony, Indiana.

While some women explored new ways to organize housework and childcare in Owenite model communities, thousands of others joined local branches of the Owenite Grand National Consolidated Trade Union during its short existence (it was founded and outlawed in 1834). Women also wrote for and read the Owenite paper, *The Pioneer*, which equated husbands and employers, and criticized them both for exploiting others. Anna Doyle Wheeler (1785–1848), prominent in the movement, wrote for another Owenite paper, *The Crisis*. She gave public lectures on women's issues, translated articles on women written by French socialists, and served as a liaison between French and British socialist movements. With landowner William Thompson, she published *Appeal of One Half of the Human Race, Women, Against the Pretensions of the Other Half, Men* (1825). Widely distributed and translated into French, this pamphlet argued that cooperation and association in the economic realm were necessary for women's independence.

In France, the Saint-Simonian movement offered many women an alternative community and worldview. Based on the ideas of the Count Henri de

Saint-Simon, who advocated industrial and technological progress through cooperation rather than competition, the movement of the early 1830s was led by Prosper Enfantin. Enfantin gave the increasingly accepted idealized notion of female virtue a different spin when he argued that women's love was the key to social harmony. Enfantin encouraged his male disciples to develop their feminine side by doing housework, and urged his female disciples to take an active role in the movement. The revolution of 1830, which resulted in a change of regime but only a slightly expanded suffrage was key in bringing significant numbers of working-class men and women into the movement. In 1830, approximately 200 women regularly attended lectures given by Saint-Simonians, and in 1831, 110 women identified themselves as "faithful adherents."[5]

As the movement evolved, Enfantin sought to consolidate his authority by declaring his mystic quest for "The Woman," who, with Enfantin, would regenerate society. While this development caused some to leave the movement, others found themselves energized by the idea that a woman could change the world. Inspired by Enfantin's praise of the feminine, some female Saint-Simonians realized that they had the right to live independently. As a result, they began to question the inequality of laws that defined them as legal minors, subservient to their husbands. They challenged assumptions that women did not need well-paid work because men would care for them. They also questioned the sexual politics of the Saint-Simonian movement itself. Motivated by the conviction that marriage was primarily an economic arrangement that degraded women and made men tyrants, the Saint-Simonians advocated free unions based on love and companionship. Women such as Pauline Roland, who had several ex-nuptial children with two different lovers, embraced the freedom and passion that this lifestyle brought them. However, women soon came to realize that without well-paid employment, and lacking any legal recourse against the fathers of their children, they faced dire straits. Ostracized socially and impoverished economically, Saint-Simonian women who adopted these new ideas concerning love and relationships found that they came with a high price.

The primary vehicle for these critiques of both society and the movement was a newspaper founded by several working-class women. Published intermittently from 1832 to 1834, and taking a number of different titles over this time, this newspaper celebrated, *La Femme libre* (The Free Woman), one of its more notorious titles due to the sexual connotations that many contemporaries saw in it. Echoing Anna Wheeler and William Thompson's brochure, the first issue proclaimed, "Women, through to the present, have been exploited, tyrannized. This tyranny, this exploitation must end. We are born free like men; and half of the human race may not, without injustice, enslave the other half."[6] Contributors to the paper referred repeatedly to the same set of demands: equality in marriage, education, and employment. True to their Saint-Simonian convictions, they called for rich and poor women to unite behind the banner of motherhood. Saint-Simonianism, and especially its feminist branch, strongly influenced many women both in France and in other countries.

Although these movements received a great deal of negative attention for promoting a lifestyle in which men and women were more equal than in society as a whole, they were both short-lived and ultimately involved a relatively small number of men and women. Chartism, on the other hand, was a major political movement that involved hundreds of thousands of English men and women. The Great Charter was a document drawn up by radical artisans in response to the 1832 Reform Bill that extended the vote to a portion of the upper middle class, and to the New Poor Law of 1834 that gave the government the authority to separate and intern indigent families in workhouses. The Great Charter demanded, among other items, the vote for all men and regular meetings of Parliament. Women were active in the Chartist movement. They wrote pamphlets, made banners and formed organizations designed to further the passage of the Great Charter. Women constituted one-third of the signatories of the 1839 and 1841 petitions. They participated in demonstrations, set up schools for their children, and organized campaigns to shop only from merchants who supported the Charter. And although the Charter demanded the vote for men alone, some in the movement argued that women should also receive the vote. In addition, there is evidence that many women considered the vote of the male head of household to be a family vote that would represent their views as well. Chartism also spurred women on to other efforts. Anne Knight, a middle-class Chartist who was also active in the antislavery movement, founded a women's suffrage society in Sheffield in 1851.

Later middle-class campaigns for women's rights were shaped by both the arguments made by those involved in Owenism, Saint-Simonianism, and Chartism, and the reactions to them. Even in the first half of the century, these movements raised awareness of both gender inequality and different means that could be used to combat it. Flora Tristan, although not a Saint-Simonian herself, was influenced by many branches of the utopian socialist movement. Inspired by the Owenites, she toured France trying to organize a Worker's Union, but died before she could accomplish it. She shared the utopian socialists' conviction that society could only advance through cooperation and that the status of women was key to that advancement. "I demand rights for women," she wrote in 1843, "because I am convinced that *all the ills of the world come from this forgetfulness and scorn that until now have been inflicted on the natural and imprescriptible rights of the female*. I demand rights for women because that is the *only way that their education will be attended to* and because on the education of women depends that of men in general, and *particularly of the men of the people.*"[7]

While Tristan traveled through France, preaching her idea of a national workers' union, utopian socialist ideas were also making inroads among German intellectuals. While those who had the financial resources and cared little for public opinion found the idea of romantic relationships without marriage liberating, others took these ideas in a new direction. The German Catholic Sect, established in 1844, for example, advocated a religious practice based on love, which was held to be the special domain of women. In practical terms, this meant engaging in charitable activities. This doctrine can be linked to feminism, however, because members of the sect believed that such activities were part of a move toward the emancipation of women, which would eventually eradicate egoism and privilege.

In each of these instances, radicals and utopian socialists developed a concept that Ann Taylor Allen has called "maternal feminism," referring to the idea that the duties and character of a mother enabled her to take action in a wider sphere than that of the household.[8] Also called "civic motherhood" or "republican motherhood," this ideology provided women with a place in the nation, but a place different from men's and based on their essential difference as women and mothers. While present-day historians have debated whether arguments furthering women's rights and responsibilities as mothers could be considered feminist, we contend that they are because they sought to increase women's status, albeit as mothers, but respected and remunerated mothers. Early nineteenth-century feminist ideology defined woman as mother just as did other ideologies of the time, but feminist ideals and goals differed from those of traditional social analysts in stressing equality within relationships and equal opportunity in education and work.

Feminists spread their ideas through written works as well as through organizations. What Gisela Bock referred to as "literary and journalistic feminism" flourished in the 1830s and 1840s.[9] Throughout Europe, female novelists and journalists took pen to paper and wrote about women's role in society. By far the most famous – and infamous – was the French novelist George Sand, the pseudonym of Aurore Dupin. Sand was the author of novels that decried women's restricted position in society and celebrated those who broke free from convention to lead a life of their own design. Brought up to be independent, Sand found the marriage she made at the age of 18 unbearable, and left her husband after eight years. Her involvement in socialist politics, her series of romantic relationships, as well her habit of wearing men's clothing and smoking cigarettes earned her a scandalous reputation. Her early novels, such as *Indiana* (1832), contained a strong critique of marriage as an institution that oppressed women. Translated and published throughout Europe, her novels set off a wave of what was referred to as "George-Sandism," as young women became enamored of the ideas and lifestyle of the French author. Although few were able or willing to emulate her daring lifestyle, many began to question the limitations they experienced as women after reading her works. Others, however, felt that George Sand served as a negative symbol for female emancipation. In Germany, Louise Otto-Peters responded to the vogue for George Sand by advocating "true womanliness." According to Otto-Peters, this distinctly German form of womanhood needed rights and opportunities to be fully realized. Otto-Peters' vision would be more fully articulated in the newspaper, *Frauenzeitung* (Woman's Newspaper) that she founded in 1849. Otto-Peters' "true womanliness," along with the Saint-Simonians "free woman," the vogue of George-Sandism and the rise of maternal feminism all indicate that during the 1830s and 1840s, interest in the question of women's status in society was on the rise.

Activism and the woman question, 1848–70

Women's involvement in a variety of political and philanthropic causes was key in laying the foundation for the organized feminist movement that would come in the second half of the century. Women's increased awareness of their status, their frustration with their exclusion, and their continued desire for a better world created an explosive situation when revolutions broke out throughout Europe in 1848. For almost two years, upheaval throughout the Continent provided women an opening for speaking and organizing. In those countries that experienced a revolution – France, the German states, and the Austrian Empire – the reaction to the events and ideas of 1848 slowed the development of women's organizing. By the 1860s, however, the "woman question" was once more at the forefront throughout Europe.

In France, the Provisional Republican Government established following the revolution of February 1848 declared, "the election belongs to everyone without exception." Unlike the 1832 Reform Act in England, which had explicitly limited the suffrage to men, this declaration presented the possibility that women would be granted the vote. The committee for the rights of women sent a delegation requesting clarification, but the Mayor of Paris declared that the National Assembly, which was yet to be elected, would settle the issue. Women would not, therefore, be voting in the new republic's first election.

In spite of the fact that they did not have the suffrage, women organized to make their voices heard. Former Saint-Simonians Désirée Gay, Adèle Esquiros, Eugénie Niboyet, and Jeanne Deroin founded the Société de la Voix des Femmes, and a newspaper, *La Voix des femmes* (The Voice of Women), dedicated to women's issues. The writers focused in particular on the conditions working women faced in their various trades, arguing that they deserved higher wages, more diverse work opportunities, and control over their earnings.

The editors and readers of the newspaper also met at the Club des femmes (Women's Club) to discuss republican politics and the place of women within them. This club became a necessary meeting ground for women activists. Unfortunately, many men saw the club as little more than a source of entertainment, going to its meetings to jeer and heckle the speakers rather than participate in debate. This was part of a general shift in attitudes toward women's involvement in revolutionary politics. Whereas many women participated in the revolutions of both 1830 and 1848, women in the first instance were celebrated by both men and women as heroes, whereas in 1848 they were all too often portrayed as "furies" out to destroy the family, private property, and civilization. The satirical newspaper *Le Charivari* waged a full-front war on women activists, likening them alternately to prostitutes or masculinized old maids. Furthermore, working-class organizers portrayed male workers as protectors of women in an attempt to justify higher wages and the vote. Because of this hostility, women activists recognized that their role would be circumscribed in the new regime. As a contributor to *La Voix des femmes* wrote, echoing Flora Tristan, "In the Republic of 1848, which has for its mission the abolition of privilege, there still exist pariahs, and these pariahs will be you [women]!"[10]

Women were also active in the German states during the 1848 revolution. Women rallied to the cause of the revolution in large numbers, yet although the Mainz Democratic Association invited radical feminist Louise Dittmar to speak, the newly formed Frankfurt Parliament not only did not discuss women's suffrage, but also did not admit women to watch its proceedings. In Austria, where the question of women's suffrage was raised, it was rejected on the grounds that giving the vote to women would be like giving it to children or the insane. In Hungary, the petition presented by the group "Radical Hungarian Women," did not demand the vote, but did prompt the new government to discuss the question of women's education.

Frustrated with slow or no government response on women's issues, women organized themselves. As in France, newspapers and clubs helped women communicate with each other. Louise Otto-Peters began her *Frauenzeitung* (Women's Newspaper) out of frustration, when male journalists refused to publish her articles. She called for professional opportunities, and full equality in marriage and citizenship. Throughout Central Europe, women's clubs were formed as well; over 300 members belonged to one Viennese club. In the less oppressive climate of the revolutionary period, women also experimented with new forms of education. The kindergarten movement started by educator Friedrich Froebel in 1839 gained ground in the months following the revolutions of 1848. Froebel designed a system for early childhood education based on play that was meant to allow children both to develop as individuals and to learn to cooperate with others. At a time when almost all teachers were men in the German states, his insistence that women leave the home to teach in kindergartens was revolutionary. In the reaction that followed the revolution, German authorities banned the kindergarten movement.

Even in England, which did not experience a revolution, the question of women's votes was raised in Parliament. Conservative M.P. Benjamin Disraeli argued, "In a country governed by a woman, where [...] women are peeresses in their own right – where women possess manors and hold law courts [...] I don't see [why women] should not also have the right to vote."[11] Although women were not granted the vote, such sentiments encouraged the passage of a Parliamentary Act in 1850 that specified that all masculine pronouns in existing acts should be understood to include women unless specifically stated otherwise. This opened the door for activists to begin, in the 1850s, chipping away at the system of coverture that limited women's legal and financial rights. The women who would form the central nucleus of this new wave of activism were coming together during this period through philanthropic work, religious networks, and attendance at newly founded women's educational institutions such as Queens College (est. 1848) and Bedford College (est. 1849).

The efforts of these women to bring about change in women's status were facilitated by the fact that England did not experience the extreme repression that spread throughout the Continent as the revolutions were put down. In June 1848, women's clubs were closed in France and shortly thereafter women were banned from political activity. Leading activists Jeanne Deroin and Pauline Roland were arrested. Significantly, these women were punished as much for their politics as for their lifestyle. Thus the charges against Pauline Roland read: "As an unmarried mother, she is the enemy of marriage, maintaining that subjecting the woman to the control of the husband sanctifies inequality."[12] In Austria-Hungary, women's political activity was banned in March 1849, and in Prussia women were forbidden to become members of political organizations or attend meetings after 1850, a law written into the protocols of the German Federation in 1854.

Such restrictions meant that until the 1860s, England was the only country that saw any significant organizing for women's rights. Women throughout

Europe did, however, continue to write novels and articles that kept "the woman question," as it was coming to be called, in public view. In Norway, Camilla Collet's (1813–95) *Amtmandens Døttre* (The District Governer's Daughter; 1855) revealed the humiliation experienced by women married to men they were completely dependent on, and yet didn't love. Frederika Bremer's *Hertha* (1856) was seen as immoral when published for its portrayal of marriage as a financial transaction, but it convinced many that unmarried women should be allowed to have control over their own destiny. The discussion elicited by the novel led to the overturning in 1858 of Sweden's Paternal Statutes, which gave fathers complete control over their daughters. By 1872, unmarried adult women were fully emancipated. Denmark granted unmarried women full legal standing even earlier, in 1857.

The question of married women's dependence on their husbands prompted a group of women to take action. The central figures of what came to be known as the Langham Place Circle, Bessie Rayner Parkes, and Barbara Smith Bodichon, were both Unitarians raised in families shaped by the radical politics of the beginning of the century. The women who were drawn to Parkes and Bodichon undertook a series of initiatives to better the condition of women. They founded the all-female Victoria Press to publish their newspaper, *The Englishwoman's Journal* (est. 1858), which would be instrumental in keeping readers aware of their activities. These included the creation, in 1859, of the Society for the Promotion and Employment of Women and the Ladies' Institute, which included a club, reading room, and classrooms.

On the political front, their efforts in the 1850s were directed toward the reform of laws governing married women's property. Inspired by Parliament's 1850 decision that the masculine pronoun should be taken to include women unless stipulated otherwise, Bodichon and others took on the issue of coverture. In 1854, both Bodichon and novelist Caroline Norton (1808–77) published critiques of married women's legal status. The next year, Bodichon, along with Parkes, Anna Jameson, Eliza Fox, and Mary Howitt organized a petition campaign that resulted in 26,000 signatures. Although the petition failed to convince Parliament to grant married women control over their property, the group kept the idea in the public mind with newspaper articles, public lectures and published works such as Bodichon's *Women and Work* (1857). As a result, married women were granted control over their earnings in 1878 and their property in 1882.

Although the Langham Place group did not focus on suffrage in the 1850s, others did. The Female Reform Association of Sheffield founded by Quaker Anne Knight petitioned the House of Lords without success in 1851 to grant women the vote. That same year, Harriet Taylor Mill (1807–58) published an essay calling for woman's suffrage in a radical journal. Comparing women to slaves, she demanded better education, legal reform, protection against male violence, and the vote. The radical nature of her ideas can be seen from the fact that when *The Englishwoman's Journal* decided to publish an abstract of her essay in 1864, they worried that it would offend too many readers and hurt the cause of women's rights. However, as Jane Rendall has argued, by the 1860s the cause of women's rights was gaining acceptance in liberal political circles.[13]

This helps to explain why John Stuart Mill's *The Subjection of Women* (1869) received a warm welcome among liberal reformers upon its publication. Heavily influenced by the thinking of his then late wife, Harriet Taylor Mill, the work shed new light on the question of whether women were "naturally" subservient or "naturally" independent by arguing that no one could state with any assurance what woman's true nature was until artificial constraints imposed by society were removed. Mill's work was translated into nearly every European language and did much to energize the women's movement in the last third of the century.

Even before *The Subjection of Women* appeared, however, the 1860s saw an increase in feminist organizing and debate. The Langham Place group continued its campaign for the reform of married women's property laws, while organizing in favor of women's access to higher education. Successful in these areas, they also began to work for the vote. In 1865, they organized the Woman's Suffrage Committee, later called the National Society for Women's Suffrage. These individuals shared the conviction expressed by one activist later in the century, when she wrote, "I want to see the womanly and domestic side of things weigh more and count for more in all public concerns."[14]

They also supported the candidacy of John Stuart Mill for M.P. in 1865. In return, Mill presented a petition for women's suffrage the following year, bearing 1,499 names. Although the petition was unsuccessful, and the 1867 Reform Act extending the suffrage still only included men, activists considered the 73 votes for the inclusion of women (as opposed to 196 against) a great victory. Their feeling that this vote represented a shift in attitudes was borne out when in 1869 women ratepayers (therefore unmarried or widowed women) were allowed to vote in local elections. Shortly thereafter, women gained the right to be elected to school and Poor Law boards (1870 and 1875, respectively).

Although the greatest progress toward women's legal and political equality with men was made in Great Britain, women in other countries continued to keep the debate over women's status alive. In several countries, state-building and reform created an opening for this discussion. During the turbulent reign of Queen Maria Christina of Spain (1833–68) reformers demanded women's political rights, as did those who participated in debates in Switzerland during the 1860s over Constitutional reform in German-speaking cantons. In Italy, the process of unification raised the issue of women's rights. As the disparate territories of the Italian peninsula came together to form one state, activists such as Anna Maria Mozzoni argued that women should be fully emancipated, and a group of women petitioned for the vote. In all these cases women's demands had minimal, if any influence.

Internal reforms also prompted an expansion of the woman question in Russia. Following Russia's defeat in the 1853–56 Crimean War, intellectuals began to question all aspects of Russian society, including the status of women. Numerous women contributed to journals, raising the issues of inadequate education and economic dependency. Whereas during the 1840s, a wave of George-Sandism had led to a discussion of the merits of freely chosen romantic partners, in the 1850s and 1860s practical questions related to employment gained ground. Central to this discussion was the work of economist

Mariya Vernadskaya (1831–60), who urged gentry women to enter the labor force as a way to find happiness and independence. The emancipation of the serfs made this a necessity for many women. Leaving their families to journey to St. Petersburg in search of education and employment, many of these women were attracted to the burgeoning nihilist movement. Nikolai Chernyshevsky's novel *What is to be done?* (1862) was inspired by these young women, as well as by the ideas of the utopian socialists. The novel, which urged women to live independently through collective organization and work, became a handbook for young nihilist women, who with their short hair and plain clothes rejected outward signs of traditional femininity. Their insistence on the equality of the sexes in both personal and social relationships horrified an older generation of women who were nonetheless sympathetic to feminist issues. These women gathered in the St. Petersburg salon of Maria Trubnikova (1835–97), engaged in philanthropic work, founded a woman's publishing cooperative, and campaigned heavily for women's access to higher education.

In France and Germany during the 1860s, a slight easing of the government censorship and surveillance that had been established after the 1848 revolutions allowed women to once again argue for their rights. Louise Otto-Peters established the Allgemeiner Deutscher Frauenverein (General Association of German Women) in the 1860s to further employment and education opportunities for women. A similar society, Revendication des Droits de la Femme, was founded by André Léo (Léodile Bera Champceix). It championed educational and legal reform. Legal reform was also at the forefront of the paper founded by Léon Richer in 1868, *Le Droit des Femmes* (1868). Like many of their contemporaries, contributors to *Le Droit des Femmes* argued that women's qualities as women made them qualified for political life. As one wrote, "A good housewife would be the best Finance Minister, and what is lacking in France [...] is that our ministers are not generally distinguished by any of the virtues that are the honor of the good housewife."[15] By 1870, it appeared to many as if real progress was being made in women's struggle for legal and political rights.

Feminism flowers – 1870–1914

By the 1870s the European political world had changed. Italy and Germany had unified and France was a Republic. In 1878 the French feminists, Léon Richer and Maria Deraismes (1828–94) convened the first women's rights congress, attracting men and women from around the globe, including participants from most countries in Western Europe as well as from Russia. They disagreed over the importance of suffrage, but proclaimed equality in civil and political rights. By the 1890s a broad variety of feminist ideologies and activities marked the European scene. Women across all political, ideological, and national boundaries increasingly came together in international congresses, sometimes held annually, that addressed women's issues and proposed reforms. In addition, national forms of feminism grew in numbers and strength.

In places where the concept of citizenship was important, women sought to obtain those rights of citizenship. With the growth and development of republican democracies, women wanted a share in decision making, usually in the form of achieving the right to vote. The right to vote, however, was not the hallmark of feminism all over Europe as voting rights had greater importance in republics where men also had a meaningful right to vote, such as England, France, and the United States. Only Finland in 1906 and Norway in 1913 had given women the right to vote in their national governments before 1914, although in some places women could vote on the local level.

Although the rights of women to citizenship and suffrage first appeared in France during the revolutions of 1789–93, the ensuing governments in France as well as the rest of Europe strongly resisted allowing women into the male public sphere, and especially resisted giving them the right to vote. They found this denial easier since women had already been denied property rights, and property rights were a criterion for voting. However, by the first decade of the twentieth century, after having achieved property rights in Western European countries, feminists agreed that women should be full citizens in their nations. Their agitation for the right to vote grew out of their civic activities as philanthropists and in associations in the public sphere. In keeping within their social context, some argued for the right to vote as a means of improving the social and economic situation of mothers and for giving motherhood new support.

The movement for suffrage in England has gathered the most attention, in part owing to the widely publicized activities of many proponents and opponents, and in part because the English suffrage movement was the largest and most active in Europe. But even English women were far from united on the ways and means of getting the right to vote. In 1890 the many English suffrage societies that had formed united in the National Union of Women's Suffrage Societies (NUWSS), headed by Millicent Garrett Fawcett (1847–1929). This association involved thousands of women in their campaigns to obtain the vote. Primarily a middle-class movement, it had some representation from workingwomen, in a minuscule cross-class alliance. Women working in textiles and in sweated labor, and even women miners had an interest in suffrage and sent delegates to the NUWSS. These working-class representatives took the message of the benefits of the right to vote back home, especially to the textile workers, pointing out that the vote would help them feed their children.

After the men in the British Parliament voted in 1892 to exclude women from the right to vote, feminist activities for suffrage became more militant and violent. The Women's Social and Political Union (WSPU) founded by Emmeline Pankhurst (1858–1928) held parades and engaged in violence against property, such as breaking windows, in order to defeat candidates that refused to grant women the right to vote. This became the "Suffragette" campaign led by Pankhurst and her daughters Christabel (1880–1958) and Sylvia (1882–1960). They argued that organizing techniques appropriate to their gender had failed. Therefore, in order to be "law-makers" they had to become "law-breakers." They disrupted political rallies by heckling speakers, and chained themselves to the gates of Parliament when the lawmakers debated women's suffrage. The British government jailed many of the suffragettes, at which point the women staged hunger strikes. The suffragettes' campaign became great media fodder, and they received public sympathy, in part as a result of the British government's harsh repression. Treating the women as animals, the women's opponents would drag the demonstrators by their hair or by their breasts, with one suffragette, Emily Wilding Davison (1872–1913) becoming a martyr by throwing herself before the King's horses in 1913. With the outbreak of war in 1914, the suffragettes supported the British war effort, for which the government rewarded women with the right to vote as soon as the war was over.

The British Parliament related women's suffrage to Irish Home Rule, and in some ways had colonized both women and the Irish who were now asking for rights of self-determination and citizenship. In Ireland, both men and women gained the right to vote in local elections in 1898, but sought Home Rule and the right to vote in national parliamentary elections. Irish Party leaders, all men, opposed the idea of enfranchising women, because they thought it would compromise their movement for Home Rule. This led to the formation of militant Irish suffragettes and the Irish Women's Franchise League, modeled after the British women's organizations. They argued that Irish Home Rule should provide equal voting rights for men and women to the Irish Parliament and they engaged in window smashing. Their imprisonment followed. As in other nationalist movements for emancipation, however, although political activists associated national self-determination with suffrage for both men and women they ultimately subordinated women's claims for equal rights to men's rights of national Home Rule. Irish women obtained the right to vote in 1918, which the Irish Free State confirmed in 1922.

French feminists arguing for suffrage behaved less violently and dramatically than their British and Irish sisters. They did not stage their first public demonstration until July 1914. Yet, politically active women held numerous congresses where they discussed suffrage along with issues relating to children and the family. Maria Deraismes and Léon Richer formed the French League for Women's Rights in the 1870s. Hubertine Auclert and Marguerite Durand soon assumed their mantel. Auclert, more than other feminists, led the movement for women's right to vote in France, inviting suffragists from the United States, such as Susan B. Anthony, to work with her. She also worked with socialists who sought women's suffrage, which in part weakened her credibility.

French feminists wrote and argued for suffrage up to the war in 1914, but met resistance. In 1909 they organized the French Union for Women's Suffrage (*Union Française pour le Suffrage des Femmes*, UFSF), which worked with the International Woman Suffrage Alliance leading the drive for the right to vote. Women also formed networks among themselves and united with sympathetic male colleagues. Throughout the Third Republic (1871–1940) French republican parliamentary leaders refused women the right to vote. They believed that their republican government was fragile and could be overthrown or voted out. Furthermore, they argued that women tended to be religious, and would vote as their priests (and not their husbands) advised them, thereby voting to oust republican members of parliament in favor of conservative Catholics who abhorred republicanism. With the outbreak of war, the French feminists stilled their demands for suffrage, as their British sisters had also done, to support their nation in the war. Unlike the British, Irish, Dutch, Danish, German, Austrian, and Russian women who obtained the right to vote either during the war or immediately after, French women had to wait until 1945.

Arguments for women's suffrage did not have deep roots in Germany. Although Louise Otto-Peters founded the German Woman's Association (*Allgemeiner Deutscher Frauenverein*, ADF) in 1865, this was devoted to women's education and working conditions rather than to suffrage. The conservative Federation of Women's Organizations (*Bund Deutscher Frauenverein*, BDF) established in 1894 had limited goals, similar to the ADF, and confined its activities mostly to charity and welfare for women and children. Initially, it regarded women's suffrage as anathema, and instead emphasized education and the advancement of women as teachers. Other groups, however, did advocate suffrage. Lily Braun (1865–1916) and Minna Cauer (1841–1922) met at a women's congress in Germany in 1896 and protested the new German Civil Code. From this meeting, a group of radical women organized the League of Progressive Women's Organizations (*Verband Fortschrittlicher Frauenvereine*), which worked with the German Association for Woman's Suffrage in demanding the vote. The BDF and the VFF members also belonged to other women's organizations, such as the League for the Protection of Mothers (*Bund für Mutterschutz*) that wanted to reform marriage and divorce laws and improve the legal conditions of motherhood. By 1907 the BDF expanded its interests to include greater rights for women of all social classes within the family, in education, in economic life, and in politics at the community and state level. This organization, although viewing women primarily as mothers, nevertheless advocated paid work, equal pay for equal work, equality in marriage, and inclusion of women in all aspects of the public sphere, including the right to vote.

Demanding suffrage, however, was only one of many feminist goals during the last decades of the century. Feminists formed alliances for the abolition of the white slave trade (traffic in women for sex work) and agitated against governmental regulation of prostitution. This conversation about prostitution was revolutionary since women were discussing the topic of sex, something they were not supposed to know much about. Spearheaded by a politically active middle-class feminist, Josephine Butler (1828–1906), the repeal of the British Contagious Diseases Acts became one of their prime concerns. Butler's crusade of the 1870s and 1880s to repeal those acts was not successful until 1886, and not without help from an international alliance. Butler was among the first to regard prostitutes as sex workers, trying to support themselves and their families. She removed prostitution from questions of women's morality and spoke about men's sexual immorality in frequenting prostitutes.

Similar feminist alliances developed to rescind government regulation of prostitution and eliminate the power of the vice squads in France, Italy, and Germany. The governments of France and Italy had been licensing brothels, demonstrating the legality of prostitution. But licensing also opened prostitution to government inspection and regulation. Feminists had less success in France and Italy than they had in England. Much of the feminist activity evolved from women's philanthropic endeavors in rescue work, such as finding housing and paid legitimate work for prostitutes when they left prison, or protecting young girls newly arrived in the cities from falling into the grasp of pimps or madams who would coerce the girls into prostitution. Feminists sought to end the double standard that allowed sexual freedom for men and not for women, while subjugating women to men. Yet, sex workers were not the only women workers who had become objects of middle-class feminists concerns.

Throughout the nineteenth century, some feminists bridged the social-class divide and expressed concern for their working-class sisters, arguing for their equal right to work for fair wages in conditions that were not ruinous to their health. Feminists disagreed, however, about whether labor legislation would benefit women or whether it might interfere with one of their basic rights – the right to work. Debate centered over whether women took away men's jobs, whether there should be a male breadwinner, whether women had a right to work, and how maternity should be protected. Women worked in dangerous conditions for abysmal wages, and one of the major arguments to alleviate the dire work-related conditions focused on how those working conditions impinged on women's morality and motherhood. Legislation to "protect" women workers in the interest of protecting first their wombs and then their motherhood increased in the 1890s when legislators limited women's hours at work and banned nighttime work. Switzerland was the first European nation to ban women's nighttime work. Then, Germany banned nighttime and Sunday work for women over 16. During the 1890s, Austria and the Netherlands enacted similar legislation limiting women's hours.

The French legislation of 1892 limited the number of hours per day women could work in factories and forbad women's work at night, arguing that such work was morally dangerous, and also dangerous for their reproductive health. Officials also argued that women's work in "men's jobs" should be limited. Feminists insisted that women had the right to earn their living, and such legislation deprived women of needed income and of better-paying jobs. In England, the Factory Act of 1895 intended to make it harder for employers to hire women, leaving more jobs to men who would be the family breadwinner with stay-at-home wives. English feminists, such as the well-known Edith Ellis (who was married to the sexologist Havelock Ellis) and Rebecca West, disagreed with the "male breadwinner" model, arguing that women should not live dependent on men; they should be neither "a parasite or a slave and be economically free."

Although arguing for the right to work and equal pay for equal work, feminists also called for the protection of pregnant women. Their support for the protection of motherhood came at a time when many nations, but especially France, feared national depopulation as a result of women's sterility, spontaneous abortions, or having small, weak infants who soon died. Women working in the fabrication of matches became one of the first groups protected from deleterious conditions because they worked with phosphorus. Doctors had discovered that women working with phosphorus had a significantly higher rate of miscarriages and sterility than the norm. Women in the tobacco industry faced similar protection. To protect mothers and babies in other industries, feminists argued that protective labor legislation should eliminate some of the most egregious horrors of paid work, especially for pregnant women and new mothers, economically forced to earn a wage. Feminists called for paid maternity leaves, rather than the unpaid ones that employers and the state stipulated, and asked for direct financial assistance to new mothers so they could stay home and not depend on the male breadwinner. The majority of feminists, however, stressed women's right to work and opposed legislation restricting women's jobs and hours.

Working-class women usually did not write in opposition to labor legislation nor call themselves feminists. However, their actions spoke loudly as they found ways around gender-specific labor legislation so they could continue to work and earn enough to feed their children. Toward the end of the century hundreds of thousands of working women participated in unions. For example, the Women's Protective and Provident League in England argued for better working conditions and equal pay with equal access to jobs. Yet, by most accounts, only about 10 percent of the female labor force participated in unions, with heavier participation in the textile industry. In part, this was owing to men's refusal to allow women to join them in unions, and husbands pressuring their wives not to join. In addition, union activity took time and money that women did not have. Moreover, women's work tended to be isolated, which inhibited joining or forming a union; some worked several jobs, and others did homework.

Feminists in all European countries strove to strengthen married women's rights. In mid-century, organized feminist activity resulted in a series of measures allowing married women to control their own wages and the property they brought into the marriage. This ensued primarily in the 1860s and 1880s in England and as late as 1914 in France and Germany. German property laws differed by region, even after unification in 1871. With the new Civil Code of 1900, however, women were no longer legally subjugated to "paternal power." Although property remained under their husbands' control, they had the right to control their own wages.

In general, many feminists at least tacitly supported the dominant political agenda that envisioned women as mothers in the service of the nation. Concern about depopulation and degeneration contributed to the politicians' desire to protect mothers for the good of reproducing children for the nation. France was the first to experience the fertility decline and to cry depopulation, but other nations, including England, Germany, and Spain picked up the cry. Feminists, however, argued that if motherhood were a social function, then the state should support it by paid maternity leaves. Switzerland was the first country to enact laws permitting unpaid maternity leaves for women workers, and Germany followed suit in the 1880s by medicalizing childbirth so it would fall within their social insurance scheme, enabling women to take maternity benefits. Sweden had unpaid maternity leaves in 1900, and France had minimal paid maternity leaves in 1913.

Feminists debated how parturient women should support themselves, or be supported, during the last weeks of pregnancies and the months following childbirth. Some more conservative women argued for the male breadwinner's support and the father's responsibility. Less conservative feminists argued that support of parturient women and new mothers was the duty of the state. If the state wanted more babies, then motherhood was a social function, they argued, and as such it should be subsidized by the state; but they debated how the state should do that. Most agreed that there should be a tax on wage earners; some favored a national savings plan for maternity. In Germany, for example, by 1907 the *Bund für Mutterschutz* wanted the state to recognize maternity as a national service for which all mothers should be compensated. They wanted to protect the mother who was creating future soldiers, by enabling her to take a paid maternity leave and return to her job without penalty. The conservative BDF acknowledged that work was a necessity, and wanted fathers, including fathers of illegitimate children, to pay for rearing those children.

More radical feminists wanted motherhood to be a choice, and wanted women to have a choice in how they would raise their children and provide for them. The 1896 International Feminist Congress debated the obligations of the state to mothers and children. Some opposed any movement by the state into women's reproductive rights, and called for contraception and abortion. French feminists were particularly outspoken about the rights of motherhood and the state's responsibility. Nelly Roussel (1878–1922) argued in speeches and in writing that women should have the right to control their own fertility. She supported the "Strike of the Wombs" and the idea that women should refuse to give the nation cannon fodder, work fodder, and "fodder for suffering."

Very few feminists made abortion an issue in the nineteenth century. It was illegal everywhere. In France, the feminist, doctor, and political activist Madeleine Pelletier (1876–1939) was one of at least three feminists who thought women should have a right to abort. In a widely publicized printed pamphlet, she presented the case for a first-trimester abortion as a woman's right to choose. Feminists tended to view abortion and infanticide as acts of desperation for women victimized by men. Feminists sponsored sex education and contraception more than abortion. In 1897 the Swiss feminist, Emma Pieczynska-Reichenbach published a sex education manual for girls, which was reprinted in many languages. It included physiological information as well as lessons in moral purity. The feminist movement disseminated information that encouraged women to take control of their own fertility, whether that meant just saying no, or the use of barrier contraception.

The Swedish feminist, Ellen Key (1849–1926), is emblematic of the sometimes ambiguous attitudes feminists held toward motherhood, and how their ideas changed with the cultural context of the times. Key's ideas relate back to the mid-century ideas of "social motherhood," agreeing that women's energies should be devoted to rearing their children. Nevertheless, she also wanted women to achieve their maximum potential, and she envisioned this through a newly restructured and revalued motherhood. As mothers in service of the state, she argued, they should have increased status as well as economic and political support, including state-subsidized childcare. She transposed the idea of "social motherhood" to one of "civic motherhood" for which women should be trained and rewarded in doing their service for the state just as soldiers were trained and rewarded for their military service. But, Key also recognized women's sexual side. She envisioned the new woman as rejecting the prevailing concepts of home and domesticity, and thought a woman could find happiness without a man, living with a friend, and even being a mother without a husband.

Feminists came in all varieties, including those who ignored or shunned the label. The New Woman, for example, who appeared at the turn of the century, was a feminist for all practical purposes. She did not necessarily advocate feminism, or belong to any group, yet she lived her life as an emancipated woman and others certainly perceived her as a feminist. Not only did she not see motherhood in the service of the nation, she did not see motherhood in the service of anything that concerned her. The New Woman rejected marriage in which the patriarch would control her both legally and culturally. Novelists in England and on the continent wrote about the New Woman, with a mixture of admiration and condemnation. The protagonists of George Gissing's novel, *Odd Women* (1893), refused marriage, preferring lives as independent women. Others left their husbands, sometimes slamming the door behind them, as did Nora in Henrik Ibsen's *A Doll's House* (1879). Art imitated life and lived experiences paralleled literature.

A different kind of feminist, more in the tradition of motherhood than espousing modern ideas of the New Woman, appear within the Catholic women's movement. Most, like the German Catholic women's activist, Elisabeth Gnauck-Kuehne (1850–1917), preferred to think of themselves as part of the "women's movement" and not as feminists. Marie Maugeret (1844–1928) in France was one woman who tried to reconcile her feminism with the Catholic Church. In her journal, *Le Féminisme chrétien* (*Christian Feminism*), she argued for women's right to work and to control her own property; but she considered the right of girls to an education and the right of women to participate in politics even more important. Catholic women's groups sprung up in other nominally Catholic European countries, such as Austria, Ireland, Italy, and Spain. Although some called themselves Christian feminists and took up the cause of women's rights, especially in advocating women's education and benevolent societies, they were more Catholic than feminist. Those who were more feminist than Catholic found themselves at odds with more conservative members of the Church.

In France and Germany, a plethora of Protestant women held prominent positions in the secular feminist movement. Sarah Monod (1836–1912) and Julie Siegfried (1848–1922), Protestant activists and members of important political families, were staunchly republican feminists – republicans first, and feminists second, but always advocating the rights of women to their own wages and the duty of the state to support motherhood. They thought in terms of the Rights of Man, extending those rights to women. Protestants dominated the German bourgeois women's movement, in which Helene Lange (1848–1930) and Gertrud Bäumer (1873–1954) featured significantly.

The Marxist and socialist feminist agenda differed markedly from that of the bourgeois feminists associated with a confession. The socialists called for women's suffrage as well as state support for mothers. Seemingly paradoxically, they campaigned for complete equality of women but also for labor legislation that could eliminate women from certain dangerous occupations. The more radical among them advocated the overthrow of the capitalist industries and governments in order to end the exploitation of both women and men. Capitalism, they argued, with its exploitation of all workers, its emphasis on private property, and the exultation of the patriarchal family, was at the base of women's subordination. Because of the fundamental nature of private property under capitalism, and men's desire to accumulate and control that property, men positioned women's sexuality and reproduction in their own interest of protecting the sanctity of men's property. As a result, men insisted on women's fidelity (men's fidelity was inconsequential because in most countries they could not be forced to support their out-of-wedlock children) and in keeping the women home and "protected."

Many socialist or Marxist feminists believed that if the economic order were overthrown, then women's emancipation would follow. Clara Zetkin (1857–1933) joined Karl Marx and Friedrich Engels in viewing capitalism as the wrong that they should right, rather than focusing on women's rights within the capitalist and patriarchal structure of society. Until the Revolution, however, Zetkin, who regarded herself as the spokesperson for the workingwomen of Berlin, believed in women's right to work and maintained that only pregnant women should be protected. Although some men saw women competing for men's jobs, she blamed capitalism for exploiting women's labor. When push came to shove, however, socialist feminists were socialists before they were feminists, creating tensions and conflict within groups of feminists. Zetkin formed the German Social Democratic Women's movement, and separated herself from the bourgeois liberal feminists. In the Social Democratic Party of Germany (SPD) Zetkin closely associated with Ottilie Baader (1847–1925), a politically active seamstress who represented working women's political activism.

By the time of the Second International in 1907, the German Social Democratic Party (SPD), led by Zetkin, advocated universal suffrage for men and women but envisioned women's suffrage as part of the general struggle of the working class against bourgeois capitalism. Zetkin, and her branch of socialists, did not want to cooperate with "bourgeois" feminism. In response, Madeleine Pelletier who edited the suffrage journal *La Suffragiste* said that "The proletarian woman is twice a slave; the slave of her husband and the slave of her boss; the success of feminist claims would assure that she would only be once a slave; that would already be progress." Hubertine Auclert retorted, "There cannot be both a bourgeois feminism and a socialist feminism because there are not two female sexes."[16]

Russia presented a unique situation, remaining staunchly patriarchal. Slow to industrialize, and dominated by an autocratic Tsar, Russia had no significant public sphere, but after the reforms of the 1860s, women actively engaged in forming a civil society; some became quite radical, seeking to overthrow the Tsar after 1881. Most radical feminist activity in Russia occurred in the first decade of the twentieth century prior to 1914, primarily after the Revolution and reforms of 1905. Radical feminists linked the liberation of Russia with the liberation of women, advocating suffrage for both men and women. The government's October 1905 Manifesto, however, paid no attention to civil rights for women. Nevertheless, women successfully pressured the newly elected Duma (Parliament) to discuss women's suffrage. Even though women could vote in the Duma in 1905, a man had to cast their ballot. Alexandra Kollontai, in a voice similar to that of Zetkin, opposed what she called bourgeois feminism because it disrupted the working-class movement; yet in another type of paradox, she also wanted the emancipation of women. In an essay on the New Woman ("Novaya Zhenshchina") in 1913, she described the New Women as heroines who fight for the rights of women. The Russian Revolution of 1917 gave women the right to vote by and for themselves.

In countries with strong socialist tendencies for revolution, feminists tied women's emancipation and rights to socialism, willing to wait for women's rights until the Revolution secured rights for all workers. Yet, even these groups extolled both the New Woman as well as motherhood as a social function. The key was to allow women a choice.

Nineteenth-century feminist politics covered a broad spectrum of individuals and groups who advocated women's rights, opportunities, and increased status in the family and in society. Just as female philanthropists belonged to several organizations and formed networks, so did feminists. Feminism included inter-national movements, but also allowed particular national differences. The Anglo-Saxon model, emphasizing suffrage, could not serve as the model for all countries. Feminism existed as part of the intellectual life and culture of the country, often times reacting against anti-feminist actions and male subjugation, both in deeds and words. Nineteenth-century feminism redefined the bound-aries of public and private, bringing the most private aspects of women's lives (sexuality, marriage, reproduction) clearly into the public debate. The community, in the form of the feminist congresses and meetings, and then the state and legislation, were discussing individual lives. And in tying the question of women's rights to progress and change, feminism positioned itself at the forefront of modernity.

Conclusion

This book has covered European women's history during what historians refer to as the long nineteenth century; the major demarcations of that century are neither 1800 nor 1900, but rather c.1780 and 1914. The periodization of modern European women's history begins in the 1780s because in this decade a series of ideological and structural changes ushered in a new era in European women's lives. Shifts in the ideology about what constituted women's proper place was part of this change. In the second half of the eighteenth century, writers articulated new ways of thinking about women, while scientists and philosophers began to portray the female sex as distinct from the male. These new perceptions of what it meant to be female had gained broad acceptance by the 1780s and began to shape changes in the legal and political systems of Europe. At the same time, women's lived experiences underwent fundamental changes, not always matching their prescribed roles. The prescriptive ideology of domesticity and separate spheres became more fully developed in the nineteenth century and was linked to questions of nationalism and citizenship. Some women willingly followed the prescription that placed them in the private sphere of the home. Others thought it a bitter pill and took pens in hand to write treatises on women's rights. Still others found it irrelevant and took to the streets actively to voice their demands, or were driven out to work by economic necessity. Throughout the nineteenth century, women continued working and writing about or acting out their goals, despite restrictions resulting from a gender imbalance of power.

During the first half of the nineteenth century, a series of revolutions influenced ideologies about women and also shaped women's actual lives. The industrial revolution (that began in some countries at the end of the eighteenth century) altered the nature of the work experience for many, not usually for the better. It closed off some work opportunities while opening others, sometimes shifting the locus of work from the home to the factory, contributing to new waves of migration. Although historians continue to debate the cause and effect of industrial change and population growth, there is little doubt that the population explosion, which accompanied the industrial revolution, affected women's most private sexual and reproductive lives. The political revolutions of 1830, 1848, and 1871 removed the lid from the fermenting ideas and hidden problems in society, enabling women to play active and transforming roles, if only temporarily.

At the end of the century, the first decade of the twentieth century is barely distinguishable from that of the 1890s. But the 1880s constitute another era when women's lives, broadly writ, became more modern. Political, social, cultural, and economic changes of the 1880s, many of which had begun decades earlier, led to different opportunities, and restrictions, for women of all social classes. The advent of free, compulsory primary education for boys and girls enlarged women's possible work experiences and took young children out of the full-time workforce. Increasing secondary and university education for women further expanded avenues of women's lives especially for the upper and middle classes. Women's enhanced experiences and knowledge contributed to advancements in science and medicine. Women had always managed to engage in scientific and cultural activities, but now more had some recognizable success. They taught school, practiced medicine and nursing, and entered the expanding tertiary sector of the economy. New technologies of scale modified labor force participation, to some extent resulting in greater separation of home and workplace and requiring different work skills. The depression, which was primarily agricultural, hit much of Western Europe during the 1880s and led to changes in women's lives as many migrated, the cities swelled, and poverty became more visible. On the political level, newly consolidated governments enacted reforms to buttress their hold on power. Sometimes those reforms appealed to women, and sometimes women influenced the reforms – both by their writings and by their actions. The reforms affected women of all classes and ages. Finally, the fertility decline of the late nineteenth century coincided with a reinforced ideology of motherhood for women of all social classes. Women's lived experiences did not always mesh with the ideology.

In a path-breaking article, historian Joan W. Scott argued that gender is a main category of historical analysis and "a primary way of signifying relationships of power."[1] In this book, gender has been an overriding organizing principle, and a lens through which we have explored women's history and power relationships. However, in nineteenth-century European history, class remains an essential category as well. Working women's experiences, wishes, and goals were not always the same as those of elite women. Moreover, the ideological prescriptions for women's behavior varied according to class. Similarly, race shaped the way in which women were perceived by others and the opportunities available to them. Despite European women's claims that they wished to help their colonized sisters, power imbalances between the two groups were always evident. Yet, certain aspects of women's history transcended class in particular and applied to all European women. Our three overarching themes pertain to all nineteenth-century women, regardless of class.

Nineteenth-century women broke the boundaries between public and private. They began during the years of the French Revolution, and continued throughout the century, in fits and starts, to become the modern women of the twentieth century, despite attempts to keep them confined to the private realm of the home and hearth. When historians broaden their angle of vision, women can be found all over the public arena during the entire nineteenth century: at work, in associations, as part of civil society, in shaping a vast variety of cultural opportunities, in agitating for social change, and in living their daily lives. By the end of the century, in some countries women could even vote and hold local office – in the parish, the municipality, and the workplace. However, men denied them equal rights of citizenship, and by 1914 they could still not vote or hold office on a national level (except in Finland and Norway). They did not generally enter the political public sphere of decision making; yet they influenced it through their activities – ranging from the personal to the political. Moreover, the expanding public sphere influenced women's innermost private lives through the impact of ideology on their sense of identity and through laws affecting sexuality, reproduction, family life and motherhood.

The First World War, which lasted from 1914 to 1918, and which some historians view as a decisive break between tradition and modernity, may have been only a strong catalyst in women's lives, speeding up changes that had been taking place throughout the nineteenth century. Throughout this century a tension existed between modern practices and traditional behaviors. As women defined their families by their particular experiences, others wanted to keep women tied to an idealized conjugal home. As women sought modern intellectual and work experiences, laws and a powerful culture inhibited, if not prohibited, their formal entry into schools, professions, and the arts. As women sought to move about, whether by bicycle, steamship, or train, their voyages often met with objections and ridicule from men. As working women sought security and better pay, employers realized that women remained an inexpensive labor source. Even women on the farms and in traditional occupations such as domestic service faced modern changes during the century.

In forging modern identities, individual women created new communities – whether in associations, nonconjugal families, or as independent women. Historians have oft noted that the French Revolution ushered in an emphasis on the individual. Individual rights, however, pertained more to men than to women. Women only slowly, and with great difficulty, were able to appropriate the language and laws of individual rights for themselves. Women continued to play an important role in communities such as in their rural villages, their social milieu, their workplace, in associations they formed, and in utopian socialist, revolutionary, and feminist societies.

Women's activities in work, in experiencing their sexuality, and in forming cultural and social life, forced Europeans to redefine what it meant to be female, pushing the door open even wider for a growing acceptance of women's activities outside the domestic realm. Although the ideology of domesticity called for women to remain confined to their homes and families, women of all social and economic classes left those homes to go out into public arenas, to work, to travel, or to associate with other women in a wide variety of charitable, philanthropic, and political endeavors.

Strong and courageous women refused to live within the discursive bonds of domesticity and poor women could ill afford to do so. The history of women in the nineteenth century is not one of unmitigated progress. Throughout the century, many middle-class women married and stayed home, tending their house, garden, husbands, and children, perhaps with pleasure and perhaps in silent suffering. Industrialization did not initially improve women's lives, and in fact it worsened many. Likewise, the vast majority of women were without power and without property in their own name until late in the century. They could not control their own fertility and their sexuality was open to public scrutiny and repression. Some historians believe that the emphasis on motherhood and the consolidation of men's power in the nineteenth century led women to lead more restricted and restrictive lives. Others acknowledge the restrictions on what has been called "the second sex" yet recognize that women struggled and broke through those restrictions. As we have attempted to demonstrate, both interpretations can be correct, depending on which individual or group of women one is studying. As the history of half the human race, women's history cannot be fit into neat interpretive boxes.

The writing of women's history has changed over the past half century. Initially, women's history was seen as one in which women were the victims of patriarchy. To overcome this general feeling of victimization, women's history focused on the history of "women worthies" – great and notable individual women. More recently, in an effort to show that many women had individual power, and that the power was local and dispersed, women's history has stressed women's agency. Women were neither victims nor agents of their own destinies; they were both. They lived complex lives in a changing world – lives that are continually being reinvestigated and reinterpreted as historians look more deeply as well as more widely.

Notes

1 The Era of the French Revolution

1. Marie-Jeanne Roland, *The Memoirs of Madame Roland: A Heroine of the French Revolution*, ed. and trans. Evelyn Shuckburgh, London: Moyer Bell Ltd, (reprint edition) 1992, pp. 138–40, 58. Upon hearing of her beheading, her husband threw himself on his sword, committing suicide.
2. Michel Foucault, *History of Sexuality, vol. 1: An Introduction*, trans. Robert Hurley, New York: Random House/Vintage, 1990, pp. 37–50.
3. "Aux Républicaines," *Moniteur*, XVIII, 450, 21Brumaire Year II. Quoted in Dominique Godineau, *The Women of Paris and their French Revolution*, trans. Katherine Streip, Berkeley: University of California Press, 1998, p. 275.
4. *The Frederician Code*, part 1, book 1, Title VIII, Edinburgh, 1761, pp. 37–9. Originally published in German, Berlin, 1750. Reprinted in Susan Groag Bell and Karen Offen, eds. *Women, the Family, and Freedom: The Debate in Documents*, Stanford: Stanford University Press, 1983, vol. 1, pp. 31–3.

2 Reproduction and Sexuality

1. John Hajnal, "European marriage patterns in perspective," in D. V. Glass and D. E. C. Eversley, eds. *Population in History*, London: Edward Arnold, 1965, pp. 101–43.
2. Franklin Mendels, "Proto-industrialization: the first phase of the industrialization process," *Journal of Economic History*, vol. 32, 1972, pp. 241–61.
3. David Levine, *Reproducing Families: The Political Economy of English Population History*, Cambridge: Cambridge University Press, 1987. Gay Gullickson, *Spinners and Weavers of Aufay: Rural Industry and the Sexual Division of Labor in a French Village, 1750–1850*, New York: Cambridge University Press, 1986.
4. Hans Medick, "The proto-industrial family economy," in P. Kriedtke, H. Medick, and J. Schlumbohn, eds. *Industrialization before Industrialization*, Cambridge: Cambridge University Press, 1981.
5. Cissie Fairchilds, "Female sexual attitudes and the rise of illegitimacy: A case study," *Journal of Interdisciplinary History*, vol. 8, 1978, pp. 627–67; Joan W. Scott and Louise Tilly, "Women's work and the family in nineteenth-century Europe," *Comparative Studies in Society and History*, vol. 17, 1975, pp. 36–64; Rachel G. Fuchs, *Poor and Pregnant in Paris: Strategies for Survival in the Nineteenth Century*, New Brunswick, NJ: Rutgers University Press, 1992.
6. Karl Ittmann, *Work, Gender and Family in Victorian England*, Basingstoke: Palgrave Macmillan, 1995.

7. J. A. Banks, *Prosperity and Parenthood*, London: Routledge & Kegan Paul, 1954.

8. Michel Foucault, *History of Sexuality: Volume I: An Introduction*, trans. Robert Hurley, New York: Random House/Vintage, 1990, p. 124. Originally published as *La Volonté de savoir*, Paris: Gallimard, 1976.

9. J. Compton Burnett, *Delicate, Backward, Puny, and Stunted Children*, Philadelphia, 1896, pp. 89–92. Originally published in London in 1895. Reprinted in Erna Olafson Hellerstein, Leslie Parker Hume, and Karen M. Offen, eds. *Victorian Women: A Documentary Account of Women's Lives in Nineteenth-Century England, France, and the United States*, Stanford, CA: Stanford University Press, 1981, p. 94.

10. Marc Colombat, *A Treatise on the Diseases and Special Hygiene of Females*, trans. Charles Meigs, Philadelphia, 1850, pp. 544–7. First published in Paris in 1838. Reprinted in Hellerstein, Hume, and Offen, eds. *Victorian Women:* pp. 92–3. For same-sex relationships in England, see Martha Vicinus, *Independent Women: Work and Community for Single Women, 1850–1920*, Chicago: University of Chicago Press, 1985.

3   Family Life

1. These words were spoken by the Reverend W. J. Butler, the founder of the community in 1861 as quoted by Martha Vicinus, *Independent Women: Work and Community for Single Women, 1850–1920*, Chicago: University of Chicago Press, 1985, pp. 71 and 314, taking the quotation from Peter F. Anson and Allan Walter Campbell, *The Call of the Cloister*, rev. ed. London: SPCK, 1964, p. 243.

2. Edward Garrett [Isabella Fyview Mayo], *By Still Waters*, quoted in *The Englishwoman's Year Book*, p. xxxix, and quoted by Vicinus, *Independent Women*, pp. 39, 308.

3. Barbara Alpern Engel, *Mothers and Daughters: Women of the Intelligentsia in Nineteenth-Century Russia*, Cambridge: Cambridge University Press, 1983, pp. 88–90.

4. *Marthe*, trans. Donald M. Frame, New York: Harcourt Brace Jovanovich, 1984.

5. Quoted by Jo Manton, *Mary Carpenter and the Children of the Streets*, London: Heinemann, 1976, p. 147 as quoted by Vicinus, *Independent Women*, p. 43. Italics in the original.

4   Working for Wages

1. Florence Nightingale, "Cassandra," (unpublished, 1852), quoted in Raymond G. Herbet, ed. *Florence Nightingale: Saint, Reformer or Rebel?* Malabar, FL: Robert E. Krieger Publishing Company, 1981, p. 37.

2. Mme Jules Michelet, *The Story of My Childhood*, trans. Mary Frazier Curtis, Boston, 1867, pp. 1–4, 9–11, 13–14, 16–18, 20–2. Quoted in Erna Olafson Hellerstein, Leslie Parker Hume, and Karen M. Offen, eds. *Victorian Women: A Documentary Account of Women's Lives in Nineteenth-Century*

England, France, and the United States, Stanford, CA: Stanford University Press, 1981, p. 25.

3. Quoted in Ute Gerhard, *Verhältnisse und Verhinderungen.Frauen arbeit, Familie und Rechte der Frauen ins 19. Jahrhundert. Mit Dokumenten*, Frankfurt am Main: Suhrkamp, 1978, pp. 282–3 as quoted in Deborah Simonton, *A History of European Women's Work, 1700 to the Present*, London and New York: Routledge, 1998, p. 95.

4. Serge Grafteaux, *Mémé Santerre: A French Woman of the People*, trans. Louise A. Tilly and Kathryn L. Tilly, ed. Louise A. Tilly, New York: Schocken Books, 1985.

5. Great Britain, *Parliamentary Papers*, 1888, XX, Select Committee of the House of Lords on the Sweating System, pp. 149–51. Quoted in Hellerstein, Hume, and Offen, eds. *Victorian Women*, pp. 328–29.

6. Leonore Davidoff and Catherine Hall, *Family Fortunes: Men and Women of the English Middle Class, 1780–1850*, Chicago: The University of Chicago Press, 1987.

7. Gwendolyn Stephenson, *Edward Stuart Talbot, 1844–1934*, London: Society for the Propagation of Christian Knowledge, 1936, p. 17. Quoted in M. Jeanne Peterson, *Family, Love and Work in the Lives of Victorian Gentlewomen*, Bloomington: Indiana University Press, 1989, p. 164.

8. Margaret Oliphant, "The laws concerning women," *Blackwood's Edinburgh Magazine*, April 1856, vol. 79, p. 486. Quoted in Bell and Offen, *Women, the Family, and Freedom*, vol. 1, p. 306.

9. Reprinted in M. Twellmann, *Die Deutsche Frauenbewegung: Ihre Anfänge und erste Entwicklung, Quellen, 1843–89*, Meisenheim: 1972, p. 14. Quoted in Ute Frevert, *Women in German History: From Bourgeois Emancipation to Sexual Liberation*, trans. Stuart McKinnon-Evans with Terry Bond and Barbara Norden, Oxford: Berg, 1988, p. 76.

10. F. H. Low, *Press Work for Women: A Textbook for the Young Woman Journalist*, London: L. Upcott Gill, 1904, p. 83. Quoted in Barbara Onslow, *Women of the Press in Nineteenth-Century Britain*, Basingstoke: Palgrave Macmillan, 2000, p. 18.

11. Mary Louise Roberts, *Disruptive Acts: The New Woman in Fin-de-Siècle France*, Chicago: University of Chicago Press, 2002, p. 14.

12. Anna Volkova, "Zametki i vpechatleniia," in *Vospominaniia, dnevnik i stat'i*, Nizhnii Novgorod, 1913, p. 49. Quoted in Adele Lindenmeyer, "Anna Volkova: From merchant wife to feminist journalist," in Barbara T. Norton and Jehanne M. Gheith, eds. *An Improper Profession: Women, Gender and Journalism in Late Imperial Russia*, Durham, NC: Duke University Press, 2001, p. 127.

13. Nightingale, "Cassandra," quoted in Hebert, ed. *Florence Nightingale*, p. 38.

5 Education

1. Marie-Jean-Antoine-Nicolas Caritat, Marquis de Condorcet, "Sur l'Admission des femmes au droit de cité," *Journal de la Société de 1789*,

July 3, 1790. Quoted in Susan Groag Bell and Karen M. Offen, eds. *Women, the Family, and Freedom: The Debate in Documents*, Stanford: Stanford University Press, 1983, vol. 1, p. 101.

2. Jean-Jacques Rousseau, *Emile*, trans. Barbara Foxley, London: J. M. Dent, 1993, p. 393.

3. Sarah Bernhardt, *My Double Life: The Memoirs of Sarah Bernhardt*, trans. Victoria Tietze Larson, Albany: State University of New York Press, 1999, p. 9.

4. Private Correspondence. Quoted in Barbara Alpern Engel, *Mothers and Daughters: Women of the Intelligentsia in Nineteenth-Century Russia*, Cambridge: Cambridge University Press, 1983, p. 88.

5. Quoted in Françoise Mayeur, *L'Education des filles en France au XIXe siècle*, Paris: Hachette, 1979, p. 46.

6. Ministry of Education, *Règlements organiques de l'enseignement primaire*, Paris: 1887, p. 344. Quoted in Linda L. Clark, *Schooling the Daughters of Marianne: Textbooks and the Socialization of Girls in Modern French Primary Schools*, Albany: State University of New York Press, 1984, p. 16.

7. Ute Frevert, *Women in German History: From Bourgeois Emancipation to Sexual Liberation*, trans. Stuart McKinnon-Evans with Terry Bond and Barbara Norden, Oxford: Berg, 1988, p. 10.

8. Sofia Kovalevskaia, *Vospominaniia i pis'ma*, Moscow, 1951, pp. 70–2. Quoted in Engel, *Mothers and Daughters*, p. 66.

9. Louise Michel, *The Red Virgin: The Memoirs of Louise Michel*, ed. and trans. Bullitt Lowry and Elizabeth Ellington Gunter, University, Al: University of Alabama Press, 1981, p. 140.

10. Gary B. Cohen, *Education and Middle-Class Society in Imperial Austria, 1848–1918*, West Lafayette, IN: Purdue University Press, 1996, pp. 189–90.

6   Culture, the Arts, and Sciences

1. Quoted in Francine Prose, *The Lives of the Muses: Nine Women & the Artists they Inspired*, New York: Harper Collins, 2002, p. 111.

2. John Lockhart to Elizabeth Rigby, cited by Pamela Gerrish Nunn, "Critically speaking," in Clarissa Campbell Orr, ed. *Women in the Victorian Art World*, Manchester: Manchester University Press, 1995, p. 112.

3. *Art Journal*, June 1869, p. 184. Quoted by Sara M. Dodd, "Art education for women in the 1860s: A decade of debate," in Orr, ed. *Women in the Victorian Art World*, p. 187.

4. From the preface of her 1806 novel *Emiliya ili pechal'nye sledstviya lyubvi*. Quoted by Joe Andrew, " 'A Crocodile in Flannel or a Dancing Monkey': The image of the Russian woman writer, 1790–1850," in Linda Edmonson, ed. *Gender in Russian History and Culture*, Basingstoke: Palgrave Macmillan, 2001, pp. 57–8.

5. Pnina G. Abir-Am and Dorinda Outram, "Introduction," to Abir-Am and Outram, eds. *Uneasy Careers and Intimate Lives: Women in Science 1789–1979*, New Brunswick, NJ: Rutgers University Press, 1987, p. 5.

6. Charitas Bischoff, *The Hard Road: The Life Story of Amalie Dietrich, Naturalist, 1821–1891*, London: 1931, p. 47. Quoted by Marilyn Bailey Ogilve, "Marital collaboration: An approach to science," in Abir-Am and Outram, eds. *Uneasy Careers and Intimate Lives*, p. 109.

7 On the Move

1. Matilda Betham-Edwards, *Six Life Studies of Famous Women* (1880: reprint) Freeport, NY: Books for Libraries Press, 1972, p. 44.
2. Mabel Sharman Crawford, *Through Algeria* (1863). Quoted in Mary Morris, *Maiden Voyages: Writings of Women Travelers*, New York: Vintage, 1993, pp. 43–4.
3. Lorenza Stevens Berbineau, *From Beacon Hill to the Crystal Palace: The 1851 Travel Diary of a Working-Class Woman*, ed. Karen L. Kilcup, Iowa City: University of Iowa Press, 2002, p. 76.
4. Mary Kingsley, *Travels in West Africa: The Classic Account of One Woman's Epic and Eccentric Journey in the 1890s*, ed. Elspeth Huxley, London: Phoenix Press, 1976, p. 113.
5. Kingsley, *Travels in West Africa*, pp. 80–1.
6. Flora Tristan, "Promenades in London," in *Flora Tristan, Utopian Feminist: Her Travel Diaries and Personal Crusade*, ed. Doris and Paul Beik, Bloomington: Indiana University Press, 1993, p. 83.
7. *L'Univers israélite*, February 15, 1907. Quoted in Nancy L. Green, "The modern Jewish diaspora: Eastern European Jews in New York, London and Paris," in Dirk Hoerder and Leslie Page Moch, eds. *European Migrants: Global and Local Perspectives*, Boston: Northeastern University Press, 1996, p. 271.
8. Charlotte Brontë, *Jane Eyre*, Oxford: Oxford University Press, 1975, p. 409.
9. "New South Wales final report of the committee of the Legislative Council on emigration … ," British Parliamentary Papers, 1837 (358) XLIII, p. 11. Quoted in Deborah Oxley, *Convict Maids: The Forced Migration of Women to Australia*, Cambridge: Cambridge University Press, 1996, p. 180.
10. Annie Besant, "The education of Indian girls" (1913). Quoted in Jane Slaughter and Melissa K. Bokovoy, eds. *Sharing the Stage: Biography and Gender in Western Civilization*, Boston: Houghton Mifflin Company, 2003, pp. 210–11.
11. Marquise de la Tour du Pin, *Journal d'une femme de cinquante ans, 1778–1815*, Paris: Librairie Chapelot, 1914, vol. II, pp. 31–2. Quoted in Thomas C. Sosnowski, "French Émigrés in the United States," in Kirsty Carpenter and Philip Mansel, eds. *The French Émigrés in Europe and the Struggle against Revolution, 1789–1814*, Basingstoke: Palgrave Macmillan, 1999, p. 139.
12. Quoted in Bonnie S. Anderson and Judith P. Zinsser, *A History of Their Own: Women in Europe from Prehistory to the Present*, 2 volumes, New York: Harper & Row, 1988, vol. 1, p. 202.

13. Maria E. Ward, *The Common Sense of Bicycling: Bicycling for Ladies, with Hints as to the Art of Wheeling, Advice to Beginners, Dress, Care of the Bicycle, Mechanics, Training, Exercise, etc.*, New York and Paris: Brentano, 1896, pp. 12–13.

8 Associational Life

1. Sonya Michel and Seth Koven, "Womanly duties: Maternalist politics and the origins of welfare states in France, Germany, Great Britain, and the United States, 1880–1920," *American Historical Review*, vol. 95, October 1990, pp. 1076–108.
2. Amalie Sieveking, "Vortrag in Bremen, gehalten am 25 Oktober 1841," *WVAK, 10. Bericht*, p. 73. Quoted in Catherine Prelinger, *Charity, Challenge, and Change: Religious Dimensions of the Mid-Nineteenth-Century Women's Movement in Germany*, New York and Westport, CT: Greenwood Press, 1987, p. 29.
3. Constance Battersea, *Reminiscences*, London, 1922, pp. 414–17. Quoted in F. K. Prochaska, *Women and Philanthropy in Nineteenth-Century England*, Oxford: Clarendon Press, 1980, p. 103.
4. Petition of the women of Spilsby, Lincolnshire, to the House of Lords, March 28, 1833. Quoted in Clare Midgley, *Women Against Slavery: The British Campaigns, 1780–1870*, London: Routledge, 1992, p. 68.
5. Elizabeth Heyrick, *Appeal to the Hearts and Consciences of British Women*, Leicester: A. Cockshaw, 1828, p. 6. Quoted in Midgley, *Women Against Slavery*, p. 61.
6. *Schulvereinskalender für 1884*, pp. 6–7. Quoted in Pieter M. Judson, "The gendered politics of German nationalism in Austria, 1880–1900," in David F. Good, Margarete Grandner and Mary Jo Maynes, eds. *Austrian Women in the Nineteenth and Twentieth Centuries: Cross-Disciplinary Perspectives*, Providence, RI: Berghahn Books, 1996, p. 6.
7. Letter from Ann Gilbert to Mary Ann Rawson, April 9, 1838. Quoted in Midgley, *Women Against Slavery*, p. 75.
8. Midgley, *Women Against Slavery*, p. 60.

9 Feminism and Politics

1. Karen Offen, *European Feminisms, 1700–1950: A Political History*, Stanford, CA: Stanford University Press, 2000, p. 20. We owe a debt to Karen Offen for her work that has laid the groundwork for this chapter. She has provided a framework for scholars to think about feminism across cultures. Portions of this chapter are based on this book.
2. Joan Wallach Scott, *Only Paradoxes to Offer: French Feminists and the Rights of Man*, Cambridge, MA: Harvard University Press, 1996, pp. 3–4.
3. Charles Fourier, *Théorie des quatre mouvements et des destinées générales* (1808). Quoted in Susan Groag Bell and Karen M. Offen, eds. *Women, the Family, and Freedom: The Debate in Documents*, 2 volumes, Stanford: Stanford University Press, 1983, vol. 1, p. 41.

4. Kathryn Gleadle, *British Women in the Nineteenth-Century*, Basingstoke: Palgrave Macmillan, 2001, p. 29.

5. Bonnie S. Anderson and Judith P. Zinsser, *A History of their Own: Women in Europe from Prehistory to the Present*, 2 volumes, New York: Harper & Row, 1988, vol. 2, p. 377.

6. *La Femme libre. L'Apostolat des femmes*, vol. 1, 1832, p. 1.

7. Flora Tristan, *Workers Union*, 1843. Quoted in Doris and Paul Beik, eds. *Flora Tristan, Utopian Feminist: Her Travel Diaries and Personal Crusade*, Bloomington: Indiana University Press, 1993, p. 119.

8. Ann Taylor Allen, *Feminism and Motherhood in Germany, 1800–1914*, New Brunswick: Rutgers University Press, 1991, p. 41.

9. Gisela Bock, *Women in European History*, trans. Allison Brown, Oxford: Blackwell Publications, 2002, p. 108.

10. Jeanne-Marie, *La Voix des femmes*, vol. 26, April 18, 1848, p. 3.

11. Benjamin Disraeli, speech during the June 20, 1848 debate in the House of Commons on the reform of representation: *Hansard's Parliamentary Debates*, 11 and 12 Vic., 1847–48, vol. 99, May 29–June 30, 1848, p. 950. Quoted in Offen, *European Feminisms*, pp. 111, 435.

12. Quoted in Claire Goldberg Moses, *French Feminism in the Nineteenth Century*, Albany: State University of New York Press, 1984, pp. 147–8.

13. Jane Rendall, "John Stuart Mill, liberal politics, and the movements for women's suffrage, 1865–1873," in Amanda Dickery, ed. *Women, Privilege, and Power: British Politics, 1750 to the Present*, Stanford: Stanford University Press, 2001, p. 178.

14. H. Fawcett, *Home and Politics*, 1898, p. 8. Quoted in F. K. Prochaska, *Women and Philanthropy in Nineteenth-Century England*, Oxford: Clarendon Press, 1980, p. 228.

15. Arthur Arnould, "Causerie politique," *Le Droit des femmes*, vol. 3, April 1869, p. 1.

16. Hubertine Auclert, "Socialistes et bourgeoises," *Le Radical*, September 3, 1907. Quoted in Steven C. Hause with Anne R. Kenney, *Woman's Suffrage and Social Politics in the French Third Republic*, Princeton: Princeton University Press, 1984, p. 70.

Conclusion

1. Joan W. Scott, "Gender: A useful category of historical analysis" in *Gender and the Politics of History*, New York: Columbia University Press, 1988, pp. 28–50.

Suggested Readings

Chapter 1

Books on women and salons and during the Enlightenment provide different views on the debate concerning the extent of women's activities in the public sphere.

Goodman, Dena, *The Republic of Letters: A Cultural History of the French Enlightenment*, Ithaca, NY: Cornell University Press, 1994.

Hertz, Deborah, *Jewish High Society in Old Regime Berlin*, New Haven: Yale University Press, 1988.

Hesse, Carla, *The Other Enlightenment: How French Women Became Modern*, Princeton: Princeton University Press, 2001.

Landes, Joan B., *Women and the Public Sphere in the Age of the French Revolution*, Ithaca, NY: Cornell University Press, 1988.

Pekacz, Jolanta, *Conservative Tradition in Pre-Revolutionary France: Parisian Salon Women*, New York: Peter Lang, 1999.

Among the many authors who have considered the role of women in the French Revolution are:

Godineau, Dominique, *The Women of the French Revolution*, trans. Katherine Streip, Berkeley: University of California Press, 1988, provides a very useful narrative of women's behavior as activists and militants.

Gutwirth, Madelyn, *The Twilight of the Goddesses: Women and Representation in the French Revolutionary Era*, New Brunswick, NJ: Rutgers University Press, 1992.

Hunt, Lynn, ed. *The French Revolution and Human Rights: A Brief Documentary History*, Boston/New York: St. Martins Press, 1996, contains important documents on women with commentary from one of the pre-eminent historians of the French Revolution.

Levy, Darline Gay, Harriet Branson Applewhite, and Mary Durham Johnson, eds. *Women in Revolutionary Paris, 1789–1795*, Urbana, IL: University of Illinois Press, 1979. This edited collection of documents is useful not just for the documents, but also for the introductions the editors provide.

Chapter 2

For the history of sexuality, contraception and abortion as well as other reproductive strategies the following books are most relevant.

Engelstein, Laura, *The Keys to Happiness: Sex and the Search for Modernity in Fin-de-Siècle Russia*, Ithaca, NY: Cornell University Press, 1992.

Foucault, Michel, *History of Sexuality: Volume I: An Introduction*, trans. Robert Hurley, New York: Pantheon/Random House, 1978. Originally published as *La Volonté de savoir*, Paris: Gallimard, 1976. This theoretical account has changed the way historians view sexuality in nineteenth-century Europe.

Fuchs, Rachel G., *Abandoned Children: Foundlings and Child Welfare in Nineteenth-Century France*, Albany, NY: State University of New York Press, 1984; *Poor and Pregnant in Paris: Strategies for Survival in the Nineteenth Century*, New Brunswick, NJ: Rutgers University Press, 1992.

Gallagher, Catherine and Thomas Laqueur, eds. *The Making of the Modern Body: Sexuality and Society in the Nineteenth Century*, Berkeley: University of California Press, 1987. Chapters examine representations and meanings of the body.

Kertzer, David I., *Sacrificed for Honor: Italian Infant Abandonment and the Politics of Reproductive Control*, Boston: Beacon Press, 1993. Sexuality, honor, and society in Italy.

Mason, Michael, *The Making of Victorian Sexuality*, New York: Oxford University Press, 1994.

McLaren, Angus, *Birth Control in Nineteenth-Century England*, New York: Holmes & Meier, 1978; *Sexuality and Social Order: The Debate over the Fertility of Women and Workers in France, 1770–1920*, New York: Holmes & Meier, 1983; and *A History of Contraception from Antiquity to the Present Day*, Oxford: Blackwell, 1990. Basic general works on contraception and sexuality.

Nye, Robert A. ed. *Sexuality*, New York: Oxford University Press, 1999. Introduction and selections represent new research.

Stewart, Mary Lynn, *For Health and Beauty: Physical Culture for Frenchwomen 1880s–1930s*, Baltimore, MD: The Johns Hopkins University Press, 2001.

Vicinus, Martha, *Independent Women: Work and Community for Single Women, 1850–1920*, Chicago: University of Chicago Press, 1985. Provides an excellent discussion of women's communities.

Weeks, Jeffrey, *Sex, Politics and Society: The Regulation of Sexuality since 1800*, London: Longman, 1989. A basic overview of 200 years in Britain.

For the debate on the causes for the population explosion and the fertility decline, the works cited in the notes have informed this chapter. For additional reading, see:

Banks, J.A. and Olive Banks, *Feminism and Family Planning*, New York: Schocken Books, 1964. One of the earliest and still useful interpretations of the economic motives for birth control.

Gillis, John R., *For Better, For Worse: British Marriages 1600 to the Present*, Oxford: Oxford University Press, 1985.

Gillis, John, Louise Tilly and David Levine, eds. *The European Experience of Declining Fertility, 1850–1970: The Quiet Revolution*, Oxford: Basil Blackwell, 1992.

Chapter 3

The history of the family constitutes an entire subfield of history, comparable to the history of women. This list represents only a few of the works in the area. Two major edited volumes provide overviews of aspects of family life.

Kertzer, David, I. and Marzio Barbagli, *Family Life in the Long Nineteenth Century, 1789–1913. The History of the European Family: vol. 2*, New Haven: Yale University Press, 2002. This is one of the best general introductions that pays attention to issues of women's history.

Perrot, Michelle, ed. *A History of Private Life, vol. 4. From the Fires of the Revolution to the Great War*, trans. Arthur Goldhammer, Cambridge, MA: Harvard University Press, 1990.

Important additional reading includes:

Accampo, Elinor, *Industrialization, Family Life, and Class Relations, Saint Chamond, 1814–1914*, Berkeley: University of California Press, 1989. A local study with broad ramifications.

Davidoff, Leonore and Catherine Hall, *Family Fortunes: Men and Women of the English Middle Class, 1780–1850*, Chicago: University of Chicago Press, 1987. One of the most influential and complete analyses of the English middle classes that speaks not only to the issue of family, but also to the roles of middle-class married women and work.

Gillis, John R., *For Better, For Worse: British Marriages 1600 to the Present*, Oxford: Oxford University Press, 1985.

Engel, Barbara Alpern, *Between the Fields and the City: Women, Work, and the Family in Russia, 1861–1914*, Cambridge: Cambridge University Press, 1994.

Kaplan, Marion A., *The Making of the Jewish Middle Class: Women, Family and Identity in Imperial Germany*, New York: Oxford University Press, 1991.

Laslett, Peter, *The World We Have Lost*, New York: Charles Scribner, 1965.

Medick, Hans and David Warren Sabean, eds. *Interest and Emotion: Essays on the Study of Family and Kinship*, Cambridge: Cambridge University Press, 1984. Fundamentally addresses the issues of material interests and emotions in family formation and life.

Seccomb, Wally, *Weathering the Storm. Working-Class Families from the Industrial Revolution to the Fertility Decline*, London: Verso, 1993. Excellent survey.

Segalen, Martine, *Love and Power in Peasant Society*, trans. Sarah Matthews, Oxford: Basil Blackwell, 1983. Disputes the notion of a rigid rural patriarchy and argues for cooperation between men and women in rural France.

Vicinus, Martha, *Independent Women: Work and Community for Single Women, 1850–1920*, Chicago: University of Chicago Press, 1985. The best discussion of female same-sex families and households.

Chapter 4

Berlanstein, Lenard, *Daughters of Eve: A Cultural History of French Theater Women from the Old Regime to the Fin-de-Siècle*, Cambridge, MA: Harvard University Press, 2001.

Canning, Kathleen, *Languages of Labor and Gender: Female Factory Work in Germany, 1850–1914*, Ithaca, NY: Cornell University Press, 1996.

Clark, Anna, *The Struggle for the Breeches: Gender and the Making of the British Working Class*, London: Rivers Oram Press, 1995.

Engel, Barbara Alpern, *Between the Fields & the City: Women, Work, and Family in Russia, 1861–1914*, Cambridge: Cambridge University Press, 1995.

Frader, Laura L. and Sonya O. Rose, eds. *Gender and Class in Modern Europe*, Ithaca, NY: Cornell University Press, 1996.

Gibson, Mary, *Prostituton and the State in Italy, 1860–1915*, New Brunswick: Rutgers University Press, 1986.

Rendall, Jane, *Women in an Industrializing Society: England, 1750–1800*, Oxford: Basil Blackwell, 1990.

Rose, Sonya, *Limited Livelihoods: Gender and Class in Nineteenth-Century England*, Berkeley: University of California Press, 1992.

Simonton, Deborah, *A History of European Women's Work 1700 to the Present*, London and New York: Routledge, 1998.

Tilly, Louise A., and Joan W. Scott, *Women, Work and Family*, New York and London: Routledge, 1989 reprint; first published 1978.

Thompson, Victoria E., *The Virtuous Marketplace: Women and Men, Money and Politics in Paris, 1830–1870*, Baltimore: The Johns Hopkins University Press, 2000.

Valenze, Deborah, *The First Industrial Woman*, Oxford: Oxford University Press, 1991.

Walkowitz, Judith R., *Prostitution and Victorian Society: Women, Class and the State*, Cambridge: Cambridge University Press, 1980.

On the middle-class women's work see:

Clark, Linda L., *The Rise of Professional Women in France: Gender and Public Administration since 1830*, Cambridge: Cambridge University Press, 2000.

Margadant, Jo Burr, *Madame le Professeur: Women Educators in the Third Republic*, Princeton: Princeton University Press, 1990.

Norton, Barbara T. and Gheith, Jehanne M. eds. *An Improper Profession: Women, Gender and Journalism in Late Imperial Russia*, Durham: Duke University Press, 2001.

Onslow, Barbara, *Women of the Press in Nineteenth-Century Britain*, Basingstoke: Palgrave Macmillan, 2000.

Peterson, M. Jeanne, *Family, Love and Work in the Lives of Victorian Gentlewomen*, Bloomington: Indiana University Press, 1989.

Schultheiss, Katrin, *Bodies and Souls: Politics and the Professionalization of Nursing in France, 1880–1922*, Cambridge, MA: Harvard University Press, 2001.

Smith, Bonnie, *Ladies of the Leisure Class: The Bourgeoises of Northern France in the Nineteenth Century*, Princeton: Princeton University Press, 1981.

Chapter 5

Albisetti, James C., *Schooling German Girls and Women: Secondary and Higher Education in the Nineteenth Century*, Princeton: Princeton University Press, 1988. A thorough study of the movement to expand women's education in the German states.

Clark, Linda C., *Schooling the Daughters of Marianne: Textbooks and the Socialization of Girls in Modern French Primary Schools*, Albany: State

University of New York Press, 1984. An examination of curricula in girls' schools beginning with the Third Republic.

Cohen, Gary B., *Education and Middle-Class Society in Imperial Austria, 1848–1918*. West Lafayette, IN: Purdue University Press, 1996. A detailed social history of secondary education in the Austrian Empire.

Engel, Barbara Alpern, *Mothers and Daughters: Women of the Intelligentsia in Nineteenth-Century Russia*, Cambridge: Cambridge University Press, 1983. A study of the socialization and education of upper-class girls based on correspondence and diaries.

Hunt, Felicity, ed. *Lessons for Life: The Schooling of Girls and Women, 1850–1950*, Oxford: Basil Blackwell, 1987. A collection of essays on women's education in Britain.

Kelly, Catriona, *Refining Russia: Advice Literature, Polite Culture and Gender from Catherine to Yeltsin*, Oxford: Oxford University Press, 2001. A wide-ranging history of etiquette books and female socialization.

Strumingher, Laura S., *What were Little Girls and Boys Made Of?: Primary Education in Rural France, 1830–1880*, Albany: State University of New York Press, 1983. A discussion of schools and curricula for boys and girls of the popular classes that includes extracts from children's textbooks.

Chapter 6

Pnina G. Abir-Am and Dorinda Outram, eds. *Uneasy Careers and Intimate Lives: Women in Science 1789–1979*, New Brunswick: Rutgers University Press, 1987. This series of essays explores the possibilities and problems for women in scientific careers in both Europe and the United States.

Bergman-Carton, Janis, *The Woman of Ideas in French Art, 1830–1848*, New Haven: Yale University Press, 1995. A discussion of how French artists, writers, and cartoonists depicted women intellectuals.

Heldt, Barbara, *Terrible Perfection: Women and Russian Literature*, Bloomington, IN: Indiana University Press, 1987.

Helland, Janice, *Professional Women Painters in Nineteenth-Century Scotland: Commitment, Friendship, Pleasure*, Aldershot: Ashgate, 2000. A study of Scottish women painters that highlights both individual careers and the institutional and social milieu in which they worked.

Kirkpatrick, Susan, *Las Romanticas: Women Writers and Subjectivity in Spain, 1835–1850*, Berkeley: University of California Press, 1989.

Orr, Clarissa Campbell, ed. *Women in the Victorian Art World*, Manchester: Manchester University Press, 1995.

Panizza, Letizia and Sharon Wood, eds. *A History of Women's Writing in Italy*, Cambridge: Cambridge University Press, 2000.

Rappaport, Erika, *Shopping for Pleasure: Women in the Making of London's West End*, Princeton: Princeton University Press, 2000.

Shteir, Ann B., *Cultivating Women, Cultivating Science: Flora's Daughters and Botany in England, 1760–1860*, Baltimore: The Johns Hopkins University Press, 1996.

Tiersten, Lisa, *Marianne in the Market: Envisioning Consumer Society in Fin-de-Siècle France*, Berkeley: University of California Press, 2001. A discussion of the evolution of the notion of female style.

Waller, Margaret, *The Male Malady: Fictions of Impotence in the French Romantic Novel*, New Brunswick, NJ: Rutgers University Press, 1993. A study of the feminine in male-authored romantic fiction.

Chapter 7

On women's travel see:

Dolan, Brian, *The Ladies of the Grand Tour*, London: Harper Collins, 2001.

Frawley, Maria, *A Wider Range: Travel Writing by Women in Victorian England*, Rutherford, N.J: Fairleigh Dickinson University Press, 1994.

Netzley, Patricia D., *The Encyclopedia of Women's Travel and Exploration*, Westport, CT: Oryx Press, 2001. As its title indicates, a useful reference concerning female travelers.

Robinson, Jane, *Unsuitable for Ladies: An Anthology of Women Travellers*, Oxford: Oxford University Press, 1995.

On European women and imperialism:

Burton, Antoinette, *Burdens of History: British Feminists, Indian Women, and Imperial Culture, 1865–1915*, Chapel Hill: University of North Carolina Press, 1994.

Chaudhuri, Nupur and Margaret Strobel, *Western Women and Imperialism: Complicity and Resistance*, Bloomington: Indiana University Press, 1992.

Clancy-Smith, Julia and Frances Gouda, eds. *Domesticating the Empire: Race, Gender, and Family Life in French and Dutch Colonialism*, Charlottesville: University Press of Virginia, 1998. A path-breaking series of essays on women in French and Dutch colonialism.

Wildenthal, Lora, *German Women for Empire, 1884–1945*, Durham: Duke University Press, 2001. A discussion of both gendered discourse in German imperialism and women's involvement in the empire.

On migration, exile and pilgrimage, see:

Carpenter, Kristy and Philip Mansel, eds. *The French Emigrés in Europe and the Struggle against Revolution, 1789–1814*, Basingstoke: Palgrave Macmillan, 1999.

Daniels, Kay, *Convict Women*, St. Leonards, Australia: Allen & Unwin, 1998. A study of British women convicts in Australia.

Harris, Ruth, *Lourdes: Body and Spirit in the Secular Age*, London: Penguin, 1999.

Hoerder, Dirk and Leslie Page Moch, eds. *European Migrants: Global and Local Perspectives*, Boston: Northeastern University Press, 1996.

Moch, Leslie Page, *Moving Europeans: Migration in Western Europe since 1650*, Bloomington, IN: Indiana University Press, 1992.

Oxley, Deborah, *Convict Maids: The Forced Migration of Women to Australia*, Cambridge: Cambridge University Press, 1996.

On the New Woman and urban mobility:

Rappaport, Erika, *Shopping for Pleasure: Women in the Making of London's West End*, Princeton: Princeton University Press, 2000. A discussion of the emergence of a female public realm of shopping and sociability in London.

Richardson, Angelique and Chris Willis, eds. *The New Woman in Fiction and in Fact: Fin-de-Siècle Feminisms*, Basingstoke: Palgrave Macmillan, 2001. A discussion of the New Woman and how she was depicted by her contemporaries.

Walkowitz, Judith, *City of Dreadful Delight: Narratives of Sexual Danger in Late-Victorian London*, London: Virago Press, 1992. An exploration of urban life from the point of view of sexual danger.

Chapter 8

On women and philanthropy see:
Koven, Seth and Sonya Michel, eds. *Mothers of a New World: Maternalist Politics and the Origins of Welfare States*, New York and London: Routledge, 1993. The articles by Koven, Christoph Sachsse, Jean Quataert, Susan Pedersen, and Pat Thane are particularly relevant.

Lindemann, Mary, *Patriots and Paupers: Hamburg, 1712–1830*, New York and Oxford: Oxford University Press, 1990. Especially good for the early nineteenth century.

Lindenmeyr, Adele, *Poverty is Not a Vice: Charity, Society, and the State in Imperial Russia*, Princeton, NJ: Princeton University Press, 1996. One of the best books on women, philanthropy, and the civil society in Russia.

Luddy, Maria, *Women and Philanthropy in Nineteenth-Century Ireland*, Cambridge: Cambridge University Press, 1995. Skillful analysis of women in Ireland with implications for other countries.

McCarthy, Kathleen D. ed. *Lady Bountiful Revisited: Women, Philanthropy and Power*, New Brunswick, NJ: Rutgers University Press, 1990. The chapters by Brenda Meehan-Waters on Russia and Ellen Ross on England are particularly relevant.

Prelinger, Catherine M., *Charity, Challenge, and Change: Religious Dimensions of the Mid-Nineteenth-Century Women's Movement in Germany*, New York: Greenwood Press, 1987. Especially good on Protestant women.

Prochaska, F.K., *Women and Philanthropy in Nineteenth-Century England*, Oxford: Clarendon Press, 1980. A detailed account, and one of the first books on this subject. Still important.

Quataert, Jean, *Staging Philanthropy: Patriotic Women and the National Imagination in Dynastic Germany, 1813–1916*, Ann Arbor: The University of Michigan Press, 2001. A new approach to the study of philanthropy.

Other types of associations that women joined are discussed in the following works:
Midgley, Claire, *Women Against Slavery: The British Campaigns, 1780–1870*, London: Routledge, 1992. The most thorough treatment of the abolition movement in Britain.

Shiman, Lilian Lewis, *Women and Leadership in Nineteenth-Century England*, New York: St. Martin's Press, 1992. A treatment of English female social reformers that includes a discussion of the temperance movement.

Chapter 9

Allen, Ann Taylor, *Feminism and Motherhood in Germany, 1800–1914*, New Brunswick, NJ: Rutgers University Press, 1991.

Gordon, Felicia and Máire Cross, eds. *Early French Feminisms, 1830–1940: A Passion for Liberty*, Cheltenham, UK: Edward Elgar, 1996. Particularly useful for its inclusion of the writings of Flora Tristan, Jeanne Deroin, Pauline Roland, Madeleine Pelletier, and Hélène Brion.

Hause, Steven, with Anne Kenney, *Women's Suffrage and Social Politics in Third Republic France*, Princeton: Princeton University Press. Overview and analysis of suffrage and French feminism.

Kent, Susan Kingsley, *Sex and Suffrage in Britain, 1860–1914*, Princeton: Princeton University Press, 1987. Maintains that the feminist movement for suffrage included women's movements that were seeking to end the double standard of sexuality.

Moses, Claire Goldberg, *French Feminism in the Nineteenth Century*, Albany: State University of New York Press, 1984. Especially good on the Saint-Simonian women.

Moses, Claire Goldberg and Leslie Wahl Rabine, *Feminism, Socialism, and French Romanticism*. Bloomington, IN: Indiana University Press, 1993. A helpful analysis of women in the Saint-Simonian movement accompanied by primary texts.

Offen, Karen, *European Feminisms, 1700–1950: A Political History*, Stanford, CA: Stanford University Press, 2000. The fundamental, encyclopedic, account of feminism in Europe, especially good inclusion of feminism in the smaller countries.

Sowerwine, Charles, *Sisters or Citizens? Women and Socialism in France Since 1876*, Cambridge: Cambridge University Press, 1982. Demonstrates the conflicts between feminism and socialism.

Stites, Richard, *The Women's Liberation Movement in Russia: Feminism, Nihilism and Bolshevism*, Princeton: Princeton University Press, 1978. A pioneering and still useful account of the nineteenth-century Russian women's movement.

Taylor, Barbara, *Eve and the New Jerusalem: Socialism and Feminism in the Nineteenth Century*, New York: Pantheon Books, 1983. Still the leading discussion of women in the Owenite movement.

Thompson, Dorothy, *Outsiders: Class, Gender and Nation*, London: Verso, 1993. A discussion of women in the Chartist movement.

Index

Deroin, Jeanne, 132, 163, 164
deserving poor, 140, 141
Dickens, Charles, 80, 153
Die Hausfrau (The Housewife) (Davidi), 73
diet, 37; improvement in, 26, 29
Dietrich, Amalie, 115
difference, sexual, 2
dignity, women's, 105
Dionigi, Marianna Candidi, 121
"dirty savages," 141
disease, venereal, 28
Disraeli, Benjamin, 164
Dittmar, Louise, 163
divorce, 56–7; law of, 13; legalization
    of, 11–12
Divorce Act, 56
divorce law, 21
Dixie, Lady Florence, 79–80, 124
doctors, 82; increasing prominence of, 35; use
    of in childbearing, 52; women, 98
Doll's House, A (Ibsen), 174
domestic chores, 62
domestic missionaries, 141–2
domestic service, 46, 54–5, 65–6; training for,
    144, 145
domesticity, 45, 130; ideology of, 2–4, 74, 138;
    language of, 153, 156, 157; tradition of, 82
dominance, male, 22
double standard, 35, 171
Dowie, Ménie Muriel, 125
dowry, 10, 55
dress reform, 148
Drug Zhenshchin (Women's Friend), 80
Dubay, Auguste, 36
Dumas, Alexandre, 26
Durand, Marguerite, 79, 169
Duruy, Victor, 93
dvor, 59

Eberhardt, Isabelle, 125, 126
economic crisis of 1794, 18
economic liabilities, children as, 33
economic necessity, 107
economic units, 50
economies, changing structure of, 84
education: acquiring an, 84; broadening, 120;
    compulsory primary, 1, 72; female, 9, 130;
    focus on religion, 89; formal, secular, 84;
    girl's unregulated status of, 90; higher, 166,
    178; in the home, 88–90; informal, 89;
    physical, 15; and political instability, 94–5;
    right to, 14, 174; secondary, 178; uneven, 91
Education Act (1870), 95
educational reform, 88
Edwards, Amelia, 123
Ehrmann, Marianne, 20

elderly women, 55
electric lighting, 71
Eliot, George, 110
Ellis, Edith, 171
Ellis, Havelock, 40, 171
emancipation, 63, 93, 146; and bicycle riding,
    136; for unmarried adult women, 165
embroidery, 64
emigration societies, 129
émigrés, 132
Émile, or On Education (Rousseau), 8,
    11, 86–8
employment: search for, 126;
    of women, 166–7
employment agencies, 81
employment, gainful, 120
empowerment, sense of, 137
Encyclopédie, 85
Endowed Schools Act, 92
Enfantin, Père, 133
Enfantin, Prosper, 160
Engels, Friedrich, 175
English Evangelical movement, 8, 142
English Society of Female Artists, 109
Englishwoman's Journal, The, 165
Enlightenment: concept of individual rights,
    155; culture of, 6; ideologies of, 13; lesson of,
    84, 88; and religion, 5; thought, 149; and
    women's education, 85, 86
entrance examinations for universities, 97
equal opportunity, in education and work,
    155, 162
equal pay, 170
equal rights, 155
equal voting rights, 169
equality: of all the people, 17; in citizenship,
    164; in education, 160; in employment, 160;
    in marriage, 160, 164, 170; within
    relationships, 162
equality with men, women's right of, 14
Esquiros, Adèle, 163
ethnic identity, in new locations, 127
European Feminisms, 155
Evans, Marian, 110
exercise, physical, 134
exhibitions, 117
exiles, political, 120, 132–3
exploitation, sexual, 11
extended families, 44

Fabian socialists, 147, 152
Factory Act (1895), 171
Factory and Workshops Acts
    (1874 and 1878), 71
factory inspectors, 72, 81
fallen women, rescue of, 146